THE HIDDEN INNS OF THE
WEST COUNTRY
INCLUDING CORNWALL, DEVON, SOMERSET AND DORSET

By Peter Long

Regional Hidden Places

Cambs & Lincolnshire
Chilterns
Cornwall
Derbyshire
Devon
Dorset, Hants & Isle of Wight
East Anglia
Gloucs, Wiltshire & Somerset
Heart of England
Hereford, Worcs & Shropshire
Highlands & Islands
Kent
Lake District & Cumbria
Lancashire & Cheshire
Lincolnshire & Nottinghamshire
Northumberland & Durham
Sussex
Thames Valley
Yorkshire

National Hidden Places

England
Ireland
Scotland
Wales

Hidden Inns

East Anglia
Heart of England
Lancashire & Cheshire
North of England
South
South East
South and Central Scotland
Wales
Welsh Borders
West Country
Yorkshire
Wales

Country Living Rural Guides

East Anglia
Heart of England
Ireland
North East of England
North West of England
Scotland
South
South East
Wales
West Country

Published by: Travel Publishing Ltd, 7a Apollo House, Calleva Park, Aldermaston, Berks, RG7 8TN

ISBN 1·902·00787·5

© Travel Publishing Ltd

First published 2000, second edition 2003,

Printing by: Ashford Colour Press, Gosport

Maps by: © Maps in Minutes ™ (2003)
© Crown Copyright, Ordnance Survey 2003

Editor: Peter Long

Cover Design: Lines & Words, Aldermaston

Cover Photograph: The George Inn, Chardstock, Axminster, Devon

Text Photographs: © www.britainonview.com

FOREWORD

The *Hidden Inns* series originates from the enthusiastic suggestions of readers of the popular *Hidden Places* guides. They want to be directed to traditional inns "off the beaten track" with atmosphere and character which are so much a part of our British heritage. But they also want information on the many places of interest and activities to be found in the vicinity of the inn.

The inns or pubs reviewed in the *Hidden Inns* may have been coaching inns but have invariably been a part of the history of the village or town in which they are located. All the inns included in this guide serve food and drink and some offer the visitor overnight accommodation. A full page is devoted to each inn which contains a coloured photograph, full name, address and telephone number, directions on how to get there, a full description of the inn and its facilities and a wide range of useful information such as opening hours, food served, accommodation provided, credit cards taken and details of entertainment. *Hidden Inns* guides however are not simply pub guides. They provide the reader with helpful information on the many places of interest to visit and activities to pursue in the area in which the inn is based. This ensures that your visit to the area will not only allow you to enjoy the atmosphere of the inn but also to take in the beautiful countryside which surrounds it.

The *Hidden Inns* guides have been expertly designed for ease of use and this guide is the first to be printed in full colour. *The Hidden Inns of the West Country* is divided into four chapters covering Cornwall, Devon, Somerset and Dorset, each of which is laid out in the same way. To identify your preferred geographical region refer to the contents page overleaf. To find a pub or inn and details of facilities they offer simply use the index to the rear of the guide or locator map at the beginning of each chapter which refers you, via a page number reference, to a full page dedicated to the specific establishment. To find a place of interest, again use the index to the rear of the book or list found at the beginning of each chapter which will guide you to a descriptive summary of the area that includes details of each place of interest.

We do hope that you will get plenty of enjoyment from visiting the inns, pubs and places of interest contained in this guide. We are always interested in what our readers think of the inns or places covered (or not covered) in our guides so please do not hesitate to write to us. This is a vital way of helping us ensure that we maintain a high standard of entry and that we are providing the right sort of information for our readers. Finally if you are planning to visit any other corner of the British Isles we would like to refer you to the list of Travel Publishing guides to be found at the rear of the book.

Travel Publishing

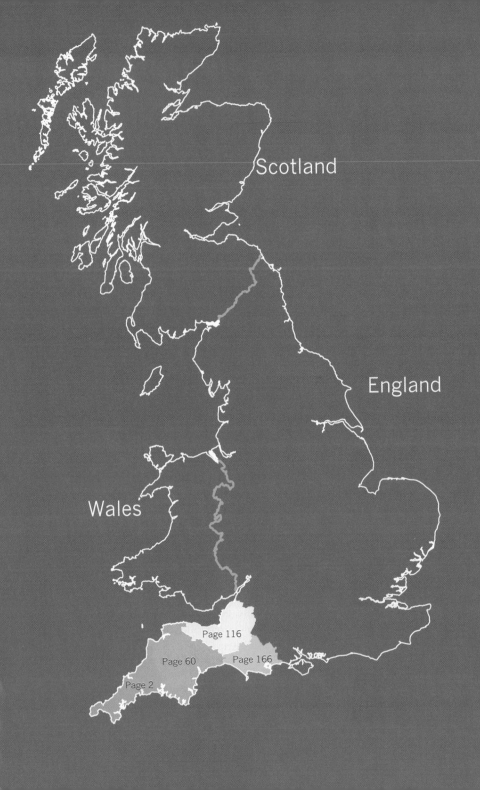

Scotland

England

Wales

CONTENTS

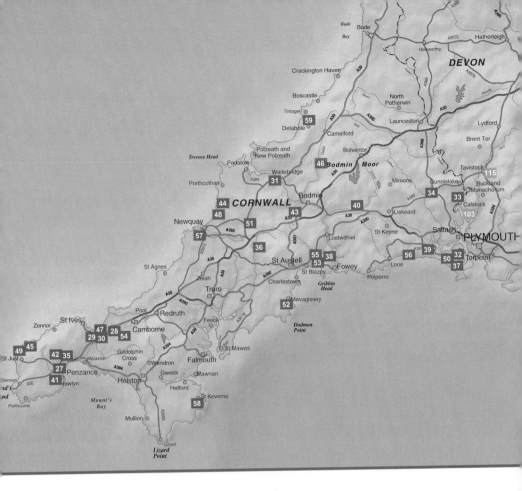

Please note all cross references refer to page numbers

CORNWALL

Land's End, where Cornwall's granite meets the Atlantic Ocean in a dramatic series of steep cliffs, is one of the most famous places in the whole country. On a journey of discovery through the West Country to this most south-westerly point of mainland Britain, visitors will pass many places of equal beauty and charm. This area, known as Penwith, has been settled for over 4,000 years. All over the region there are numerous prehistoric relics including the ancient tomb of Zennor Quoit and Carn Euny Iron Age village.

Throughout history the western region of Cornwall has been mined – for tin, copper and, latterly, china clay. The marks left by this industry are everywhere. Around St Just, close to

PLACES OF INTEREST

Penzance, one of the last tin mines to close, Geevor Mine, has been preserved as a heritage centre while nearby, an old mine steam engine, perched high on the cliff top, still produces power. Further east lie the towns of Redruth and Camborne, which were once at the centre of the mining industry. In the 1850s the mines around Camborne produced two thirds of the world's copper. Not surprisingly, the industry has left its mark in the many ruined mines in the surrounding area. Camborne is also the home of the Royal School of Mines and its Geological Museum. The land around St Austell is somewhat different and, at one time, it was dubbed the Cornish Alps due to the spoil heaps from the china clay industry. Still an important industry today, the surrounding environment has been softened by landscaping. At nearby St Blazey, one china clay pit has been converted into the world-famous Eden Project – massive biodomes (conservatories) that aim to promote the vital relationship between plants, people and resources.

Port Isaac

Elsewhere, the old ports and harbours, which exported the minerals and where the county's great catches of pilchards were once landed, are now sailing and yachting centres.

Padstow is also gaining a reputation as a gourmet retreat while Newquay has become a Mecca for surfers. Falmouth, which lies on the Fal estuary, has the third largest natural harbour in the world. Its strategic importance has been known for centuries and guarding the entrance are two great castles built by Henry VIII. To the south of Falmouth, which is now becoming a fashionable yachting centre, lies the unique Lizard Peninsula, and to the east is the unspoilt countryside of Roseland. In the 18th and 19th centuries Cornwall's mild climate encouraged the creation of numerous gardens stocked with exotic trees and shrubs from newly explored lands. One of the most impres-

Trevarno Manor, Helston

sive is the Lost Gardens of Heligan, which were lost under weeds and ivy for over 70 years before being restored to their former glory. Cornwall is separated from the rest of mainland Britain by the River Tamar, which rises just behind the coast to the northeast of Bude; it was Athelstan, in 928, who first used this natural boundary to define his Celtic kingdom and it is still the county border between Cornwall and Devon. This eastern region of Cornwall has also, like much of the rest of the county, managed to maintain its Celtic heritage and the most common reminders are in the place names – those beginning with Tre, Pol and Pen – but there are also many ancient monuments to discover. Along with providing a boundary, the River Tamar, which for much of its length is now an Area of Outstanding Natural Beauty, was also home to river ports that transported minerals ores and other goods down to the seaports and beyond.

The Tamar Valley also hides one of the best-preserved late medieval estates in the country, Cotehele House, that was the principal home of the earls of Edgcumbe prior to their move to Mount Edgcumbe, another impressive estate, on the south coast. Further upriver lies Gunnislake, a gateway into the county that, as the major crossing point of the river right up until the 1960s, was much fought over down the ages but particularly during the Civil War.

Along the south coast, to the west of Saltash, whose two magnificent bridges now carry both the major road and rail links into the county, there are numerous picturesque fishing towns and villages, such as Looe, Fowey and Polperro, which once prospered on the back of first the pilchard fishing industry and then the mining and china clay industries. By contrast the north coast is much harsher and harbours are few and far between as the Atlantic

Ocean continues to pound the rugged coastline. However, here there is some respite and, particularly, there is Bude that, as the birthplace of British surfing, is not only the preserve of wetsuited surfers but also a popular holiday destination.

At the centre of eastern Cornwall lies the mysterious Bodmin Moor that was the inspiration for Daphne du Maurier's famous novel, *Jamaica Inn*. An isolated expanse of bleak moorland and a place frequented by smugglers, not only are there a wealth of prehistoric monuments to be found here but also several natural features that have given rise to many legends and none more so than lonely Dozmary Pool that is believed to hold the Lady of the Lake of the Arthurian legends. Stories of Arthur continue at Tintagel, a small coastal village whose romantic castle ruins, situated on a craggy headland, are thought to be the birthplace of the legendary king.

Golitha Falls, Bodmin Moor

Bodmin

Situated midway between Cornwall's two coasts and at the junction of two ancient trade routes, Bodmin has always been an important town used, particularly, by traders who preferred the overland journey to the sea voyage around Land's End. The town's impressive church is dedicated to the St Petroc, an early visitor, and in the churchyard can be found one of the many holy wells in Bodmin – **St Goran's Well** – which dates from the 6th century. The Crown Jewels and the Domesday Book were hidden at **Bodmin Jail** during World War I and this former county prison, dating from 1776, is an interesting place to visit. A short distance from the town centre lies **Bodmin Beacon Local Nature Reserve**. From the beacon summit, on which stands the 114-foot-high **Gilbert Memorial**, there are splendid views over the town and moor. To the south of the town lies one of the most fascinating late 19th century houses in England, the National Trust's spectacular **Lanhydrock House,** surrounded by wonderful formal gardens, woodland and parkland.

Jamaica Inn

Bolventor

Situated at the heart of Bodmin Moor, this scenic village is the location of *Jamaica Inn*, the coaching inn immortalised by Daphne du Maurier in her famous novel of the same name. During the 18th and 19th centuries this isolated hostelry, on the main route across the bleak moorland, provided an ideal meeting place for smugglers and other outlaws as well as legitimate travellers journeying between Cornwall and the rest of England. Little changed down the years, **Jamaica Inn** still welcomes tourists and visitors seeking refreshment and accommodation as they have done for centuries.

Bodmin Moor, the bleak expanse of moorland surrounding Bolventor, is the smallest of the three great West Country moors and an Area of Outstanding Natural Beauty. At 1377 feet, **Brown Willy** is the highest point on the Moor, and to the northwest **Rough Tor** (pronounced 'row tor' to rhyme with 'now tor') is the moor's second highest point.

Boscastle

This ancient and picturesque fishing village stands at the head of a remarkable S-shaped inlet that shelters it from the Atlantic Ocean. The inner jetty was built by the renowned Elizabethan, Sir Richard Grenville, when the village was prospering as a fishing, grain and slate port, while the outer jetty, or breakwater, dates from the 19th century when Boscastle had grown into a busy commercial port handling coal, timber, slate and china clay. Next to the slipway where the River Valency meets the sea is Boscastle's famous **Museum of Witchcraft**, where visitors will learn all about witches, their lives, their charms and their curses.

Bude

Bude is a traditional seaside resort with sweeping expanses of sand, rock pools and Atlantic breakers that make it a popular surfing centre. The **Bude Canal,** an ambitious project that aimed to connect the Atlantic with the English Channel via the River Tamar but was never completed, is today a popular leisure resource. Close to the entrance to the canal stands **Bude Castle**, a small, plain fortification

Cotehele Quay

designed by the local 19th century physician, scientist and inventor, Sir Goldsworthy Gurney. It was built on sand and rests on a concrete raft developed by Gurney. The history of the town and its canal can be explored in the **Bude-Stratton Museum**, and in **Bude Military Museum** visitors can learn all about the Duke of Cornwall's Light Infantry from its formation in 1702 to its amalgamation with the Somersets in 1959. A new landmark is the **Bude Light 2000**, the first large-scale public sculpture to combine coloured concrete with fibre optic lighting. One of the high spots in the Bude calendar is the annual jazz festival.

Calstock

Well known for its splendid views of the Tamar valley, the village was an important river port in the 19th century, when vast quantities of tin, granite and copper ore were brought here for loading on to barges to be transported down the Tamar to the coast. In the countryside surrounding Calstock traces of old mine workings, along with the spoil heaps, can still be seen along with the remains of the village's boat-building industry. The decline of Calstock as a port came with the construction of the huge **Railway Viaduct**, which carries the picturesque Tamar Valley Line southwards to Plymouth. Completed in 1908, this giant 12-arched viaduct, the first in the country to be constructed of concrete blocks, stands 120 feet above the river. Southwest of the village lies one of the best preserved medieval estates in the West Country – **Cotehele House**. The River Tamar runs through the estate and close to an old cider house and mill is **Cotehele Quay**, a significant port in Victorian times with a fascinating museum that highlights the vital role the river played in the economy of the area.

Camborne

Camborne was once the capital of Cornwall's tin and copper mining area, and those industries are remembered in the world famous **School of Mining**. The **Geological Museum** displays rocks and minerals from all over the world. Outside the town's library is a statue to Richard Trevithick, a talented amateur wrestler known as the Cornish Giant, who developed the high pressure steam engine, the screw propeller and an early locomotive that predated Stephenson's Rocket by 12 years.

Camelford

This historic little market town on the banks of the River Camel prospered on the woollen trade. The **North Cornwall Museum and Gallery**, housed in a converted coach house, displays aspects of life in this area throughout the 20th century as well as the reconstruction of a 19th century moorland cottage. Just to the north of the town on the Boscastle road is the **British Cycling Museum**, while close by, on the riverbank at **Slaughterbridge**, lies a 6th century slab that is said to mark the place where King Arthur fell at the Battle of Camlann in AD 539. The **Arthurian Centre** houses the Land of Arthur Exhibition.

Charlestown

This small fishing village provides a permanent berth for historic square-rigged boats and has been used as the

Slaughterbridge

location for television series such as *Poldark* and *The Onedin Line*. Close to the docks is the **Charlestown Shipwreck, Rescue and Heritage Centre**. This offers an insight into the town's history, local shipwrecks and the various devices that have been developed over the years for rescuing and recovering those in peril at sea.

Crackington Haven

One of the most dramatic places along this remarkable stretch of coastline, this tiny port is overlooked by towering 400-foot cliffs, which make it Cornwall's highest coastal point. A path leads to a remote beach, curiously named **The Strangles**, where at low tide, large patches of sand are revealed among the vicious looking rocks. During one year alone in the 1820s, some 20 ships were said to have come to grief here.

Delabole

Home to the most famous slate quarry in Cornwall, Delabole, is, almost literally, built of slate. It has been used here for houses, walls, steps and the church. The huge crater of **Delabole Slate Quarry** is over half a mile wide and 500 feet deep – making it the largest man-made hole in the country. The quarry is still worked and there are occasional slate splitting demonstrations. To the southwest of the village lies the first wind farm in Britain, **Delabole Wind Farm**, which produces enough power each year to satisfy over half the annual demands of both Delabole and Camelford. The tall turbines provide an unusual landmark. At the heart of the farm is the **Gaia Energy Centre**, with exhibits explaining the past, present and future of renewable energy.

Pendennis Castle

Falmouth

A spectacular deep-water anchorage that is the world's third largest natural harbour, Falmouth lies in Britain's Western Approaches and guards the entrance into Carrick Roads. Standing on a 200ft promontory overlooking the entrance to the Roads, **Pendennis Castle** is one of Cornwall's great fortresses.

Falmouth's nautical past is revealed at the splendid new **National Maritime Museum Cornwall**, whose exhibits include 120 historic boats.

Feock

To the south of this very pretty village lies **Restronguet Point** and the 17th century Pandora Inn, named after the ship sent out to capture the mutineers from the *Bounty*. From Tolverne, just north of Feock, Allied troops left for the Normandy coast during the D-day landings, and on the shingle beach the remains of the concrete honeycombed mattresses can still be seen. While in the area, General Eisenhower stayed at **Smugglers Cottage** and today this simple house holds a large collection of memorabilia from that era. Close by lies the estate of **Trelissick**, a privately owned 18th century house, surrounded by marvellous gardens and parkland with wonderful views over Carrick Roads.

Fowey

Bodinnick

Guarding the entrance to the river from which it takes is name, Fowey (pronounced Foy) is a lovely old seafaring town with steep, narrow streets and alleyways leading down to one of the most beautiful natural harbours along the south coast. The town's **Museum** is an excellent place to discover Fowey's colourful past, from the days of piracy through to the china clay exports of the 19th century. Fowey has two literary connections: with Daphne du Maurier, who lived at Gribbin Head, and with Sir Arthur Quiller-Couch (or 'Q'), who lived for over 50 years at **The Haven**, on the Esplanade, and modelled his fictional 'Troy Town' on Fowey. Facing Fowey lies the pretty hamlet of **Bodinnick**, which was home to Daphne du Maurier before her marriage and where she wrote her first novel *The Loving Spirit*.

Godolphin Cross

To the northwest of the village lies **Godolphin House**, an exceptional part Tudor, part Stuart house that still retains its original Elizabethan stables. The name of the Godolphin family is best known through the 2nd Earl, who imported the famous Godolphin Arabian, one of three stallions from which all British thoroughbreds are descended. Close by, two headlands enclose the mile long crescent of **Praa Sands**, one of the finest family beaches in Cornwall.

Gunnislake

Often referred to as the first village in Cornwall, it was here in the 1520s that Sir Piers Edgcumbe built the **New Bridge** over the River Tamar that continues to serve as one of the major gateways into the county. During the 18th and 19th centuries the village came alive with mining, and some of the mine buildings were immortalised by Turner in his great painting, *Crossing the Brook*, which also captures Gunnislake's famous bridge.

Gweek

Close to this once important commercial port is the **National Seal Sanctuary**, the country's leading marine rescue centre established over 40 years ago. The sanctuary cares for sick, injured and orphaned seals, and visitors to the sanctuary can witness the joyful antics of the seals at feeding time and explore the **Woodland Nature Quest** around an ancient coppiced wood.

Helford

A picture-postcard village standing on the secluded tree-lined southern banks of the Helford estuary, Helford has one of the most attractive settings in the whole of the county. Once the haunt of smugglers who took advantage of the estuary's many isolated creeks and inlets, it is now a popular sailing centre. During the summer, it is linked to **Helford Passage**, on the northern bank, by a ferry that has been in existence since the Middle Ages. From the village the five-mile-long **Helford River Walk** takes in several isolated hamlets and a 200-year-

old fig tree in the churchyard at **Manaccan** before returning to the tea rooms and pubs of Helford.

Helston

Dating back to Roman times, when it was developed as a port, Helston is the westernmost of Cornwall's five medieval stannary towns, and its long history has left it with a legacy of interesting buildings. **The Blue Anchor Inn** was a hostel for monks in the 15th century, while the 16th century **Angel House** was the former town house of the Godolphin family. Housed in one of the town's old market halls, close to the classical 19th century Guildhall, is the **Helston Folk Museum**, which covers many aspects of the town's and the local area's history.

The famous Festival of the Furry, or **Flora Dance**, a colourful festival of music and dance, brings people in droves each May. To the east of the town lies another interesting and award-winning family attraction, **Flambards**, whose centrepiece is a faithful recreation of a Victorian street. Close by is the Royal Navy's land and sea rescue headquarters at **Culdrose**, one of the largest and busiest helicopter bases in Europe.

Helford Jetty

Land's End

Mainland Britain's most westerly point and one of the country's most famous landmarks. The scenic grandeur of this ultimate destination has been complemented down the years with an ever-

Land's End

expanding complex of man-made attractions, including exhibitions on the life-saving exploits of the RNLI, Royal Navy and RAF; a recreation of farming life 200 years ago; and Return to the Last Labyrinth, a multi-sensory spectacular that blends true tales, myths and legends, all brought vividly to life by state-of-the-art images, sounds and special effects.

Launceston

Situated on the eastern edge of Bodmin Moor close to the county border with Devon, Launceston (pronounced locally Lawn-son) was a particular favourite of Sir John Betjeman, who called it 'the most interesting inland town in Cornwall'. Shortly after the Norman Conquest, William I's half-brother, Robert of Mortain, built the massive **Launceston Castle** overlooking the River Kensey. Elsewhere in the town, the streets around the castle are filled with handsome buildings including the impressive

Lawrence House that was built in 1753 for a wealthy local lawyer and now contains the town museum. To the west of the town and running through the beautiful Kensey Valley, the **Launceston Steam Railway** takes visitors on a nostalgic and scenic journey back in time.

Liskeard

Situated between the valleys of the East Looe and Seaton rivers, this picturesque and lively market town was one of Cornwall's five medieval stannary (tin trading) towns – the others being Bodmin, Lostwithiel, Truro and Helston. Liskeard had been a centre for the mining industry for centuries, and after the construction of a canal linking the town with Looe, vast quantities of copper ore and granite joined the cargoes of tin. In the 1850s, the canal was replaced by the Looe Valley branch of the Great Western Railway, and a scenic stretch of this line is still open today. Liskeard boasts several handsome public buildings that act as a reminder of its past importance and prosperity.

The Lizard

The most southerly village in mainland Britain, The Lizard is a place of craft shops, cafés and art galleries and lends its name to the **Lizard Peninsula**, an Area of Outstanding Natural Beauty. The Lizard is also known for its unique Serpentine rock, a green mineral that became fashionable in the 19th century after Queen Victoria visited Cornwall and ordered many items made from the stone for her house, Osborne, on the Isle of Wight. Nearby lies the famous beauty spot, **Kynance Cove**, whose marvellous sandy beach and dramatic offshore rock formations have been a favourite destination ever since Prince Albert paid a visit with his children in 1846.

Lighthouse on the Lizard

Looe

The tidal harbour at Looe, created by the two rivers the East Looe and West Looe, made this an important fishing and seafaring port from the Middle Ages through to the 19th century. Looe is still Cornwall's second most important fishing port, with fish auctions taking place at East Looe's busy quayside market on the famous **Banjo Pier**. The Looe Valley Line railway replaced the Liskeard to Looe canal and today the same journey can be made by following the **Looe Valley Line Footpath**. For an all round view of the area's flora and fauna, the **South East Cornwall Discovery Centre**, in West Looe, introduces visitors to the wealth of wildlife, plant life and scenery in the southeastern region of the county. Fish and other creatures of the deep can be seen at the **Aquarium**, while **Looe Island**, just off the coast, is a bird sanctuary.

Lostwithiel

Nestling in the valley of the River Fowey and surrounded by wooded hills, Lostwithiel's name – which means 'lost in the hills' – perfectly describes its location. It was once the capital of Cornwall, and as one of the stannary towns, tin and other raw materials

Restormel Castle

were brought here for assaying and onward transportation until the mining activity cause the quay to silt up and the port moved further down river. Throughout the town there are reminders to Lostwithiel's once important status, including the remains of the 13th century **Great Hall**, and the early 18th century **Guildhall**. Lostwithiel's strategic position as a riverside port and crossing place led to the construction of **Restormel Castle**, built in the early 12th century by Edmund, Earl of Cornwall; this magnificent keep survives in remarkably good condition.

Marazion

Cornwall's oldest charter town (dating from 1257), Marazion was for many centuries the most important settlement around Mount's Bay. The legacy of this harbour town is its fine old inns and residential houses overlooking the sandy beach. The town is now a windsurfing and sailing centre, while to the north-west is **Marazion Marsh**, an RSPB reserve with breeding colonies of grey herons and visiting waders and wildfowl. Offshore, **St Michael's Mount** rises dramatically out of the waters of Mount's Bay, connected to Marazion by a cobbled causeway that is exposed at low tide. In the 11th century, Edward the Confessor founded a priory on the mount, and its remains are incorporated into the marvellous **St Michael's Mount Castle** owned by the St Aubyn family from 1660 until the 1950s, when it was donated to the National Trust.

Mawnan

The tower of the 15th century church at Mawnan has been a local landmark for sailors for centuries. An excellent place from which to take in the sweeping coastline, the tower was also used as a lookout post during times of war. Further up Helford Passage is the tiny fishing hamlet of **Durgan** along with the **Trebah Garden**, which has often been dubbed 'the garden of dreams'.

Mevagissey

The largest fishing village in St Austell Bay, Mevagissey was an important centre of the pilchard industry and everyone who lived here was linked in some way with either the fishing boats or processing the catch. The **Mevagissey Folk Museum** has a broad collection of artefacts that includes not only the pilchard industry but agricultural machinery, early photographs of village life and the story of Pears soap – originally created by Cornishman, Andrew Pears, in the 18th century. Elsewhere around the harbour, visitors can see the fascinating displays and models at the **World of Model Railway Exhibition**, and the old lifeboat building is now an aquarium.

To the northwest of Mevagissey lie the famous **Lost Gardens of Heligan**, one of the country's most interesting gardens. Originally laid out in 1780, the gardens lay undisturbed, or 'lost', for 70 years before being rediscovered in 1990. One of the greatest garden restoration programmes then followed, and today this beautiful and intriguing place is once again attracting people from all over the world.

Minions

Boasting the highest pub in Cornwall, this moorland village was a thriving mining centre during the 19th and early 20th centuries with miners and quarrymen extracting granite, copper and lead from the surrounding area. One of the now disused mine engine houses has become the **Minions Heritage Centre**.

Close to the village stands the impressive **Hurlers Stone Circle**, a Bronze Age temple comprising three circles, and the **Cheesewring**, a natural pile of granite slabs whose appearance is reminiscent of a cheese press, also lies close to the village. **Trethevy Quoit** is an impressive enclosed chamber tomb that originally formed the core of a vast earthwork mound. The largest such structure in Cornwall, this quoit is believed to be over 5,000 years old. To the northeast lies **Upton Cross**, the place where the famous **Cornish Yarg Cheese** is made. Downstream from the Stone the River Fowey descends through dense broadleaved woodland in a delightful series of cascades known as **Golitha Falls**.

Mullion

An ideal base from which to explore a remarkable part of Cornwall. A mile to

Mullion Cove

the east lies the pretty, weather-worn harbour of **Mullion Cove** and, just up the coast is the popular sandy beach of **Poldhu Cove**. It was from the clifftops above the beach that, in 1901, the radio pioneer, Guglielmo Marconi, transmitted the first wireless message across the

The Pilchard Works

Atlantic and a granite column commemorates the event although the historic buildings were dismantled in 1937.

Just a couple of miles inland, on the windswept heathland of **Goonhilly Downs**, is a monument to the very latest in telecommunications – the **Earth Satellite Station**.

Newlyn

The largest fish landing port in England and Wales, this town has a long association with fishing, and is still the base for around 200 vessels. The **Pilchard Works Heritage Museum** offers a unique insight into the fascinating history of the industry in Cornwall. It was not fish but the exceptionally clear natural light that drew Stanhope Forbes to Newlyn in the 1880s. He was soon joined by other artists, keen to experience the joys of painting outside. The **Newlyn School** of art was founded with the help of other artists such as Lamorna Birsh, Alfred

Munnings and Norman Garstin, and, today, it is art that brings most visitors to the town.

A mile down the coast lies **Mousehole** (pronounced 'Mowzel') which was described by Dylan Thomas, who honeymooned here in 1937, as "the loveliest village in England".

Newquay

Formerly a centre of the fishing industry and a major port for the export of minerals and china clay, Newquay is today a popular seaside resort, famed throughout the world for its surfing and its superb beaches. Among its attractions are a renowned aquarium and zoo. Inland from Newquay lie the imposing engine house and chimney stack of **East Wheal Rose** mine, Cornwall's richest lead mine that was the scene, in 1846, of the county's worst mining disaster. Also nearby is the delightful small Elizabethan manor house, **Trerice**, now owned by the National Trust. As well as being a real architectural gem, it is home to a **Mower Museum** which traces the history of lawn mowing machines.

North Petherwin

Located above the River Ottery, this village is home to the **Tamar Otter Park**, a branch of the famous Otter Trust, dedicated to breeding young otters for release back into the wild to prevent the species from becoming extinct in lowland England. Visitors can watch the otters playing in large natural enclosures, see them in their breeding dens, or holts, and watch the orphans in the rehabilitation centre.

Padstow

The silting up of the River Camel in the 19th century put paid to Padstow continuing as a major port, but the harbour still teems with people and the influence of the sea is never far away. The **Harbour** remains the town's focal point and here too can be found many of Padstow's older buildings including **Raleigh Cottage**, where Sir Walter Raleigh lived while he was Warden of Cornwall, and the tiny **Harbour Cottage**. The harbour is also home to the **Shipwreck Museum** filled with artefacts recovered from ships that foundered off the north coast of Cornwall. On the northern outskirts of the town and built on the site of St Petroc's monastery lies **Prideaux Place**, a magnificent Elizabethan mansion surrounded by glorious gardens and parkland laid out in Capability Brown style in the 18th century.

Penzance

For centuries a remote market town that made its living from fishing, mining and smuggling, Penzance today is popular with holidaymakers and is the ferry port for the Isles of Scilly. A major port in the 19th century for the export of tin, the fortunes of Penzance were transformed by the railway's arrival. Not only could the direct despatch of early flowers, vegetables and locally caught fish to the rest of Britain be undertaken but the influx of holidaymakers boosted the town's fledgling tourist industry. Still a

Padstow Harbour

busy town and harbour, Penzance is home to Cornwall's only promenade, which stretches south-westwards to Newlyn. On the promenade the wonderful open-air sea water pool, the **Jubilee Swimming Pool**, retains its original art deco styling. Most of the town's more interesting buildings can be found on Chapel Street, which leads down from the domed **Market House** (built in 1836) to the quay. Outside Market House is a statue to Penzance's most famous son, Sir Humphry Davy, the scientist best remembered for inventing the miners' safety lamp. From **The Union Hotel**, whose Georgian façade hides an impressive Elizabethan interior, the first announcement in mainland England of the victory of Trafalgar and the death of Lord Nelson was made. Penzance has not forgotten its long-standing links with the sea. At the **Maritime Museum** there is a fascinating collection of artefacts that illustrate the ferocity of the waters along this stretch of coast while down at the harbour, at the **Trinity House Lighthouse Centre**, the story of lighthouse keeping is told. Elsewhere in Penzance, local history and the work of the Newlyn School of artists can be seen at the **Penlee House Art Gallery and Museum**. The county's long association with the mining industry is highlighted at the **Cornwall Geological Museum**.

Polperro Harbour

Polperro

Polperro is many people's idea of a typical Cornish fishing village as its steep, narrow streets and alleyways are piled high with fisherman's cottages built around a narrow tidal inlet. For centuries dependent on pilchard fishing for its survival, Polperro also has a long association with smuggling, and at the **Museum of Smuggling** artefacts and memorabilia illustrate the tales of the characters who dodged the government taxes.

Polzeath and New Polzeath

Surfers and holidaymakers flock to these two small resorts as the broad west-facing beach is not only ideal for surf but also the fine sands, caves and tidal rock pools make it a fascinating place for children. To the north of the villages is a beautiful coastal path that takes in the cliffs and farmland of **Pentire Point** and **Rumps Point**, where stands **Rumps Cliff Castle**, an Iron Age fortification with traces of four defensive ramparts. To the southwest of Polzeath lies the delightful **Church of St Enodoc**, a Norman building that, on several occasions, has been submerged by windblown sand. The beautiful churchyard contains many graves of shipwrecked mariners but what draws many people to this quiet place is the grave of Sir John Betjeman, who is buried here along with his parents.

Pool

Now consumed into the Camborne and Redruth conurbation, this village was very much at the heart of Cornwall's mining industry. The **Cornish Mines and Engines**, owned by the National Trust, shows the two huge engines that were used to pump water from the mines. At the **Industrial Discovery Centre**, the story of the county's dramatic heritage is told. Before the days of steam, heavy work was carried out by horses and the **Shire Horse Farm and Carriage Museum**, at nearby Treskillard, pays a living tribute to these gentle giants. As well as seeing the magnificent

shires at work and rest, visitors can look round an impressive display of private and commercial wagons and the largest collection of horse-drawn buses in the United Kingdom.

Porthcothan

This tiny village overlooks a sheltered cove with a sandy beach, part of a stretch of coastline owned by the National Trust. To the south lie the **Bedruthan Steps** (not National Trust), a curious beach rock formation that is best viewed from the grassy clifftops. To the north, the **South West Coast Path** leads walkers around **Constantine Bay** and past a succession of sandy beaches which are ideal for surfing, but the strong currents along this stretch make swimming hazardous. Beyond Constantine Bay lies the remote headland of **Trevose Head** from where there are wonderful views down the coast, taking in bay after bay. At the tip of the headland stands

Minack Theatre

Trevose Lighthouse, which has a beam that can be seen up to 27 miles away.

Porthcurno

It was from this dramatic cove, in 1870, that the first telegraph cable was laid linking Britain with the rest of the world. The **Porthcurno Wartime Telegraph Museum**, housed in a secret underground wartime communications centre, explains the technology that has been developed from Victorian times to the present. This interesting village is also home to the **Minack Theatre**, an open-air amphitheatre cut into the cliff.

Redruth

This market town owes its past prosperity to its location – at the heart of Cornwall's mining industry. It was the home of the Scottish inventor William Murdock, who is famous for such innovations as coal-gas lighting and vacuum powered tubes. His home was the first private house to have gas lighting, in 1792.

St Agnes

Once known as the source of the finest tin in Cornwall, this old village still retains many of its original miners' cottages and grander mine owners' houses. Of particular interest is the steeply terraced row of 18th century cottages known as **Stippy-Stappy**. Surrounding the village are the ruins of old mine workings, notably **Wheal Coates**. Now in the hands of the

National Trust, this mine operated between 1860 and 1890 and the derelict **Engine House** is one of the more exceptional landmarks along this stretch of coast. For industry of a very different kind, the **Cider Farm** just south of nearby **Penhallow** offers a tour of the orchards, and the **Cider Museum** tells the history of cider making through displays of old equipment and artefacts.

St Austell

This old market town, which had for centuries been at the centre of the tin and copper mining industries, was transformed in 1748, when William Cookworthy, a chemist from Plymouth, discovered large deposits of kaolin, or china clay, here. Over the years, the waste material from the clay pits to the north and west of the town has been piled up into conical spoil heaps that led to these bare, bleached uplands being nicknamed the **Cornish Alps**. More recently the heaps and disused pits have been landscaped with acid loving plants, such as rhododendrons, and they now have gently undulating footpaths and nature trails. The town is also the home of another important local business – the St Austell Brewery. The 150-year history of the company and an insight into the brewing process can be found at the informative **St Austell Brewery Visitor Centre**.

North of the town, in the heart of the Cornish Alps, lies Wheal Martyn, an old clay works that is now home to the **Wheal Martyn China Clay Museum**.

St Blazey

To the west of the village in the heart of the china clay area, lies the **Eden Project**, a world-famous attraction that aims to "promote the understanding and responsible management of the vital relationship between plants, people and resources." Massive biomes (the largest conservatories in the world) and extensive external display grounds have been constructed and planted in the bottom of a giant disused clay pit. Plants, tress and shrubs from around the world have been carefully chosen and planted in a range of climatic settings and visitors can walk from steamy rainforests to the warmth of a Mediterranean landscape.

Barbara Hepworth Sculpture Garden

St Ives

With five sandy beaches, a maze of narrow streets and a picturesque harbour, this lovely old fishing town manages to retain its charm despite being deluged by tourists from late spring until early autumn. One of the most important pilchard fishing centres in Cornwall until the early 20th century, St Ives holds a record dating back to 1868 for the greatest number of fish caught in a single seine net. Housed in a building that once belonged to a mine, **St Ives Museum** displays a range of artefacts chronicling the natural, industrial and maritime history of the area. The decline of the fishing and mining industries in the late 19th century saw St Ives develop as an artists' colony. The special quality

of the light drew painters such as Turner, Whistler, Sickert, McNeill, Munnings and Hepworth to the town. Art still dominates, and in the **Tate Gallery** the work of modern painters and sculptors is permanently on display. Also not to be missed is the **Barbara Hepworth Sculpture Garden and Museum** at Trewyn Studio, where she both lived and worked until her tragic death in a fire in 1975. The St Ives Society of Artists has its home in the former Mariners Church.

St Just

To the northwest of the town, the westernmost in mainland Britain, lies **Botallack**, where the remains of Three Crowns Mine stand on the picturesque clifftop. Here, tunnels were cut over half

St Keverne

Something of a focal point on this part of the Lizard Peninsula, the pleasant village of St Keverne is rare in Cornwall in that it has a handsome village square. Its elevated position has led to its church spire being used as a landmark for shipping attempting to negotiate the treacherous rocks, **The Manacles**, which lie offshore. In the churchyard, there are some 400 graves of those who have fallen victim of the dangerous reef.

St Keyne

Named after one of the daughters of a Welsh king who settled here during the 5th century, St Keyne is home to the famous holy well – **St Keyne's Well** – that lies a mile from the village. Newly married couples came here to drink, as the first to taste the waters was said to be the one to wear the trousers in the marriage. Another attraction in St Keyne is **Paul Corin's Magnificent Music Machines**, a wonderful collection of mechanical instruments housed in old mill buildings where Paul was the last miller. Just to the south of St Keyne, in the valley of the East Looe river, is a **Stone Circle** of eight standing quartz stones, said to be older than Stonehenge.

St Mawes

This popular sailing centre in the shelter

Botallack

a mile out to sea, under the seabed, to extract rich copper lode. To the north-east lies **Pendeen**, where tin has been mined since prehistoric times. The last of 20 or so mines in this area, **Geevor Tin Mine and Heritage Centre**, closed as a working mine as recently as 1990; the mine is now preserved and offers visitors the chance to experience the conditions of miners underground. Close by, housed in a tiny building perched high on the cliff, is the National Trust-owned **Levant Steam Engine**, once again producing power.

St Mawes Castle

of Carrick Roads is dominated by its artillery fort, **St Mawes Castle**. Built in the 1540s as part of Henry VIII's coastal defences, it is a fine example of Tudor military architecture, and its trefoil design ensured that, whatever the direction of an attack, the castle could defend itself (though it never had to). Ferries take passengers across the river to Falmouth and, during the summer, a boat takes the trip takes a trip down the river to the remote and unspoilt area of Roseland around **St Anthony**.

Saltash

A medieval port on the River Tamar, Saltash was once the base for the largest river steamer fleet in the southwest. Today, it remains the gateway to Cornwall for many holidaymakers who cross the river into Cornwall via one of the town's mighty bridges. Designed by Isambard Kingdom Brunel in 1859, the iron-built **Royal Albert Bridge** carries the railway while, alongside, is the much

more slender **Tamar Bridge**, a suspension road bridge that was opened in 1961 to replace a ferry service that had operated since the 13th century.

Tintagel

The romantic remains of **Tintagel Castle**, set on a wild and wind-swept headland that juts out into the Atlantic, are many people's image of Cornwall. Throughout the year, many come to clamber up the wooden stairway to **The Island** to see the castle that is thought to be the birth-place of King Arthur. The cave at the foot of the island is known as Merlin's Cave and is said to be haunted. The cliffs are at the heart of a Site of Special Scientific Interest, providing breeding grounds for sea birds, lizards and butter-flies. The village, of course, owes much of its popularity to its Arthurian connec-tions and one of its other interesting attractions along this theme is **King Arthur's Great Hall**. In the High Street is the weather-beaten **Old Post Office** – a 14th century small manor house that first became a post office in the 19th century and has been preserved in the care of the National Trust.

Truro

This elegant small town at the head of a branch of the River Fal is the administrative and ecclesiastical centre of Cornwall. A fashionable place to rival Bath in the 18th century, it retains an attractive feature of Georgian streets and houses. The arrival of the railway in 1859 confirmed Truro's status as a regional capital and in 1877 it became a city in its own right when the

Truro Cathedral

diocese of Exeter was divided and Cornwall was granted its own bishop. The foundation stone of **Truro Cathedral** was laid by the future Edward VII in 1880. This splendid Early English style building, with its celebrated Victorian stained glass window, was finally completed in 1910.

Wadebridge

Linking the north and south coasts of Cornwall and the moorland with the sea, Wadebridge boasts one of the longest bridges in the county. In the 1460s the vicar of St Petroc's was looking to convey his flock of sheep across the river in safety and built the 320-foot long and now 14-arched bridge (originally it had 17 arches) which can still be seen today. It is said that the bridge, dubbed the **Bridge on Wool**, was constructed on bridge piers that were sunk on a foundation of woolsacks. The town's former railway station is now home to the **John Betjeman Centre**, dedicated to the life and work of the much-loved onetime Poet Laureate.

Wendron

Close to this bleak village is one of the many mines that have been worked in this area since the 15th century. Now re-opened as the **Poldark Mine Heritage Complex**, visitors to this interesting attraction can take an underground tour of the tunnels, see the famous 18th century Poldark village and wander around the numerous machinery exhibits, some of which are in working order.

Zelah

This is the location of 18th century Chyverton House and its splendid landscaped grounds. Best known for its rhododendrons (the first were planted in 1890), **Chyverton Garden** also has some notable magnolias and camellias and a fine collection of conifers.

Zennor

For an insight into the history of this delightful old village and the surrounding area, the **Wayside Folk Museum** has numerous exhibits that tell of this region's past tin mining industry. To the southeast of the village lies the Neolithic chamber tomb, **Zennor Quoit**. One of the many ancient monuments in the area, the tomb has a huge capstone that was once supported on five broad uprights.

A couple of miles to the south of Zennor, on a windy hillside, lies **Chysauster Ancient Village**, a Romano-Cornish village which has one of the oldest identifiable streets in the country.

ADMIRAL BENBOW

CHAPEL STREET, PENZANCE, CORNWALL TR18 4AF
TEL: 01736 363448 FAX: 01736 333574

Directions: From junction 31 on the M5 take the A30 past Bodmin to Penzance. The Admiral Benbow can be found in the centre of town just a short distance from the harbour.

Found in the heart of Penzance, the **Admiral Benbow** inn is one of the town's oldest hostelries and the charming 17th-century building is distinguished by the statue of a smuggler lying astride the roof, musket in hand. An attractive whitewashed building that is bedecked with colourful hanging baskets and surrounded by flower-filled tubs during the summer, this is certainly one place that is well worth visiting while exploring this ancient port.

The interior of the inn, which was once the headquarters of the notorious Benbow pirates, boasts a fascinating collection of nautical memorabilia. Many of the artefacts have been recovered from shipwrecks off the Cornish coast. Naval memorabilia and carvings share pride of place with ships figureheads and ships.

Landlady Patricia McGregor has helped maintain the pub's excellent reputation for fine food, drink and ambience. Highly regarded for the excellent condition of the real ales, there is also a well-chosen wine list and both morning coffee and cream teas available. The Great Cabin restaurant is located downstairs, in a replica ship's galley, and serves up hearty fare; tempting and tasty bar meals and snacks are served in the rest of the inn. Naturally fish is a speciality here, along with wonderful home-cooked daily specials.

- 🕐 Mon-Sat 11.00-23.00; Sun 12.00-22.30
- 🍴 Bar meals and snacks, a la carte
- £ All major credit cards
- Ⓟ Car parking close by, children welcome
- ♫ Themed evenings in winter, live music, quiz nights, darts, pool table
- @ e-mail: enqs@theadmiralbenbow.com website: www.theadmiralbenbow.com
- ❓ Penzance Harbour, Trengwainton Gardens (2 miles), Carn Euny Ancient Village (4 miles), St Michael's Mount (4 miles), Lands End (8 miles), beaches, coastal walks, surfing, swimming, horse riding, cycling, fishing, sailing

THE ANGARRACK INN

12 STEAMERS HILL, ANGARRACK, NEAR HAYLE, CORNWALL TR27 5JB
TEL: 01736 752380

Directions: From junction 31 on the M5 take the A30 round Bodmin to Camborne. Stay on the A30 to Hayle, at Loggans Moor roundabout at the entry to Hayle take the second exit. Inn is signposted. Continue along this narrow road to the T junction and turn left. Inn can be seen 200yds on the right.

Found in the heart of the village, **The Angarrack Inn** is an attractive and distinctive traditional village pub. A black and white building with a large courtyard out front, this pub has featured on ITV's *Tales from the Snug*. The L-shaped bar area is immensely atmospheric and cosy. Prints and local scenes of people and places adorn the walls, together with an interesting collection of pots and plates. The interior also features a piano and 'newspaper corner', just the place for a quiet drink while you peruse the dailies. Glass screens and tasteful curtaining separate the bar from the

restaurant. From bar snacks to a la carte, the choice is extensive, with many tempting dishes. To drink, there is a good compliment of at least three real ales, from the St Austell brewery, as well as spirits, ciders and soft drinks, together with a selection of wines from around the world.

The Angarrack Inn is managed by Patricia and Neville Allen, a welcoming couple who work hard to maintain the excellent reputation which the inn enjoys. This stylish and characterful establishment is renowned for splendid homecooked food, all of which is cooked to order. The standard menu is supplemented by daily specials. On Friday nights the specials are of locally caught fish. Children are welcome.

- 🕐 Mon-Sat 11.30-15.00, 18.00-23.00; Sun 12.00-15.00, 19.00-22.30
- 🍴 Bar snacks and meals, a la carte
- 💷 All major credit cards
- 🅿 Patio garden, car parking, children welcome
- 🎵 Darts, themed nights, curry nights
- @ nevilleall@supanet.com
- ❓ Beach 2 miles, Godolphin House 4 miles, St Ives 5 miles, St Michael's Mount 6 miles, walking, horse riding, fishing, sailing, swimming, bird watching, golf

THE BADGER INN

FORE STREET, LELANT, NEAR ST IVES, CORNWALL TR26 3JT
TEL: 01736 752181 FAX: 01736 759398

Directions: A30 at Hayle to the St Ives road; The Badger Inn is in the heart of Lelant village centre

Superbly located for anyone who wants to explore the beauty and mysteries of the far west of Cornwall, **The Badger Inn** is a very attractive and pristine inn. The immaculate frontage is stonebuilt and festooned with hanging baskets – one reason the inn has been winner several times of the county Council's 'Flowers in Bloom' awards. The interior is open-plan yet remaining cosy, with exquisite features and touches everywhere you look, all of which enhance guests' comfort and relaxation. The beautiful conservatory – contains potted trees and offers a view of the

splendid outdoor garden, where there is more seating for fine days. The atmosphere is always warm and friendly.

The accent here is on delicious food, with a broad range of dishes from sandwiches and snacks to carvery dishes, vegetarian choices, roasted joints, and home-made specials making use of the freshest local produce including free-range poultry. As befits an inn located so close to the sea, there is also a wealth of fresh seafood and fish dishes on offer. And make sure to leave room for one of the tempting home-made desserts. And to drink? A comprehensive wine list, a selection of real ales, lagers, spirits, teas, coffees and soft drinks.

Just the place to take a short break, this distinctive inn has six en suite guest bedrooms that are handsomely decorated and very comfortably furnished with every amenity guests could wish.

- ⏰ Mon-Sat 11.30-23.00; Sun 11.30-22.30
- 🍴 Bar meals and restaurant
- 💷 Visa, Mastercard, Switch, Delta, Eurocard
- 🛏 6 en suite bedrooms
- 🅿 Car park, landscaped garden and patio
- 🎵 Live music first Sunday evening every month
- @ enquiries@badgerinnstives.co.uk
  www. badgerinnstives.co.uk
- ❓ Porthkidney Beach and sand dunes, walking, bird watching, fishing, golf, surfing, horse riding, Hayle Estuary, St Ives branch railway, St Ives (3 miles), Penzance (9 miles)

THE BIRD IN HAND

TRELISSICK ROAD, HAYLE, CORNWALL TR27 4HY
TEL: 01736 753974 FAX: 01736 753974

Directions: A30 to Hayle · through town to Paradise Park

Found adjacent to Hayle's popular attraction, Paradise Park, **The Bird in Hand** is a rather grand building that was originally the old coaching house to the park before being converted into an inn in the 1970s. Both inside and out there are many reminders of

the inn's illustrious past, such as its high ceilings and original feeding hoppers and grills adorning the walls. In such interesting surroundings, landlords Lesley and George offer superb hospitality that has gained the inn many regular customers.

- Mon-Sat 12.00-23.00; Sun 12.00-22.30
- Bar meals and a la carte
- All major credit cards
- Car parking, outdoor barbecue in season
- Live music Friday/Saturday
- george@birdinhand-hayle.co.uk, www.birdinhand-hayle.co.uk
- Paradise Park adjacent

The spacious open-plan layout increases the inn's charm and inviting atmosphere. Well known for serving an excellent range of real ales, there are always six on tap. George has a micro-brewery, Wheal Ale Brewery, and his two ales, Millers and Speckled Parrot, can be savoured here. Other beers served include Courage Best and Courage Directors, and there is also a selection of lagers, ciders, wines, spirits and soft drinks.

The food served is home-cooked and home-prepared, offering a range of snacks and bar meals, supplemented by the ever-changing specials board. In fine weather barbecues are held in the attractive and very well maintained beer garden. There is a popular happy hour throughout the year.

BRIDGE ON WOOL

THE PLATT, WADEBRIDGE, CORNWALL PL27 7AQ
TEL: 01208 812750

> **Directions:** Off the A39 follow signs for Wadebridge Town Centre.

The Bridge on Wool takes its name from Wadebridge's 320-foot 14-arched bridge, built in 1468 to span the River Camel at its lowest bridging point. It was built by the Reverend Thomas Lovibond, the vicar of Egloshayle, so that his flock could cross the river in safety. No one knows precisely why this bridge is known as The Bridge on Wool – some say because it was paid for by wealthy wool merchants, others that its foundations were laid on bales of wool, an absorbent material which solidifies when soaked and compressed. This striking feature is just a few steps from its namesake pub, itself a very attractive and gracious building, three storeys tall and both impressive and welcoming. The open-plan bar and lounge have high ceilings and a spacious, relaxed area. Victorian and sports memorabilia adorn the walls,

- All day opening
- Bar snacks
- All major credit cards
- Car parking, beer garden
- Darts, pool, live music Friday and Saturday nights
- stephen.harrison@btopenworld.com
- Newquay 20 mins, Bodmin/Padstow 10 mins.

including a fascinating array of pencilled portraits of famous football stars, sketched by the Bar Manager. To the rear there's a lovely new beer garden. Real ales of SIBA standard are served. These are changed regularly: landlord Steve Harrison has put over 300 different ales through since taking over here in 1996. There's also a good selection of lagers, wines, spirits and soft drinks, teas and coffees are also available. The bar snacks are well worth sampling, as they are freshly prepared and delicious.

CARBEILE INN

TREVOR ROAD, TORPOINT, CORNWALL PL11 2NJ
TEL: 01752 814102

Directions: 1 mile out of Torpoint off the car ferry, turn off to HMS Raleigh, just ¼ mile

Great home-cooked food, real ales, comfortable accommodation and a warm welcome await you at **Carbeile Inn**. Landlady Gail Carroll is justly proud of the reputation the pub has gained for quality and hospitality.

Having recently undergone an extensive refurbishment, the interior of this delightful inn is spacious and light, and combines the best of the old world and the new.

The menu is a comprehensive list of home-cooked and home-prepared dishes. Everything from hearty snacks such as soup, burgers, salads and ploughmans to full meals including steaks, chicken, fish and vegetarian dishes. On Thursday,

Friday and Saturday evening, and all day Sunday, there's an excellent carvery. There are also tempting daily specials – and guests will want to leave room for one of the mouthwatering desserts. The restaurant is also available for private functions. Gail specialises in catering for weddings.

There are always three real ales on tap, together with a good range of lagers, ciders, spirits, malts, an excellent wine list and a choice of soft drinks and hot beverages.

The attractive lawned garden, planted with lovely shrubs and border plants, is just the place to enjoy a quiet drink or meal on fine days.

The excellent accommodation comprises two doubles, two family rooms and a twin, all en suite and with many facilities and amenities.

- 🕐 Mon-Sat 11.00-23.00; Sun 12.00-22.30
- 🍴 Lunchtime and evening menus; daily specials
- 💷 All major credit cards
- 🛏 5 rooms (twins and doubles) en suite B&B
- 🅿 Car parking, beer garden/play area
- 🎵 Games, darts, pool table, live music, quiz nights, discos
- ❓ Antony House (Torpoint), Mount Edgcumbe House, Rame peninsula, Devonport Dockyard, Cornish coastal attractions

THE CARPENTERS ARMS

LOWER METHERELL, NEAR CALLINGTON, CORNWALL PL17 8BJ
TEL: 01579 350242 FAX: 01579 350242

Directions: From Plymouth take the A3064 to Saltash and then the A388 towards Launceston. At Callington turn right on to the A390 and then follow the signposts to Harrowbarrow and Lower Metherell.The Carpenters Arms can be found 1 mile from Cotehele House.

Dating back to the 15th century, **The Carpenters Arms** is a welcoming and picturesque traditional Cornish inn at the hub of this charming Tamar Valley community. Built of the local stone, the inn acquired its name from the carpenters who stayed here while constructing nearby Cotehele House during Tudor times. Many original features remain, including the flagstone floors and old oak beams. The inn is well known locally for its relaxed atmosphere and owners Kim and Richard Lennon take great pride in this wonderful English country inn and make every guest feel more than welcome.

- 🕐 Mon-Sun 12.00-15.00, 18.00-23.00
- 🍴 Lunch time menu 12.00-14.15 Dinner menu 19.00-21.15 Booking advisable
- £ Visa, Access, Mastercard, Switch, Delta, Eurocard, Solo
- P Patio garden, car parking
- ♪ Live music first Sunday evening every month
- ? Cotehele House 1 mile, Kit Hill 2 miles, Morwellham Quay Museum 3 miles, Bodmin Moor 5 miles, Eden Project 30 miles, walking, bird watching, fishing

Although not on the coast, there is a nautical theme here and includes a mass of gleamng brassware, pictures and other memorabilia.

There is a fine selection of real ales, including Cornish beers from Sharps at Wadebridge, as well as wines, spirits and ciders at the bar, and there's a tasty menu of delicious homecooked bar meals and snacks as well as delicious meals served in the restaurant area, which seats 54. Richard, a trained chef, oversees all the cooking, which uses local fish, meat and vegetables whenever possible and also includes a variety of salads and a full junior menu. The Sunday roast lunches are a particularly tempting treat. In good weather the attractive patio-style beer garden comes into its own.

THE COACHMAKERS ARMS

NEWPORT SQUARE, CALLINGTON, CORNWALL PL17 7AS

TEL: 01579 382567 FAX: 01579 384679

> **Directions:** From Plymouth take the A3064 to Saltash and then the A388 towards Launceton to reach Callington. The Coachmakers Arms is just past the town centre off Launceston Road

The Coachmakers Arms in Callington is a handsome and welcoming pub. The long, two-storey whitewashed building is impressive, with its exterior adorned with hanging baskets. Inside, there are lots of cosy areas, centered around tables of all shapes and sizes. Prints and photographs depict local scenes, while horse brasses hang from the low beamed ceilings and the walls are festooned with copper ornaments, various interesting time pieces and navel shield from notable HM ships.

Food is served here seven days a week and the menu features an extensive range of fish, poultry and meat dishes, as well as a daily specials board with further options. One house speciality is steak (Tuesday is steak night) and there are also tempting salads, ploughman's plates, and a selection of burgers. Homemade specials include mouth-watering pies and curries. Children are happily catered for. To drink, there is a good range of real ales, ciders, wines, spirits and hot and cold drinks.

The accommodation here comprises a double, twin and family room. One room has exclusive use of an upper-level patio.

Landlord Les Elliott has been at The Coachmakers Arms since 1998. A Plymouth man by birth, he has a wealth of experience in the pub trade and this shows in his hospitality and attention to service and detail. For a truly relaxing and enjoyable drink, meal or stay, this hidden inn is well worth seeking out.

- 🕐 Mon-Sun 12.00-14.00, 19.00-21.30
- 🍴 Bar meals and snacks. A la carte. Sunday roasts
- £ Visa, Mastercard, Switch, Delta, Eurocard, Solo, Amex, Diners
- 🛏 4 rooms en suite
- Ⓟ Car parking, children welcome
- 🎵 Quiz night (Weds), steak night (Tues)
- ❓ Morwellham Quay Museum 2 miles, Bodmin Moor 4 miles, Kit Hill 2 miles, Plymouth Hoe xx miles, Launceston xx miles, walking, bird watching, fishing

GULVAL, NEAR PENZANCE, CORNWALL TR18 3BB
TEL: 01736 362072

Directions: A30 to heliport Penzance. Slip road opposite, bear left at church

Standing just opposite the ancient village church in Gulval, **The Coldstreamer Inn** is a comfortable and friendly inn that makes a perfect place to enjoy a quiet drink or meal while exploring this part of southwest Cornwall.

Large and spacious, the exterior presents a friendly face to the world, with its mix of stone and brickwork and Tudor-style gables. Inside, the inn is stylishly furnished and decorated throughout, with an eye towards comfort and quality.

The attractive open-plan bar area has a wealth of attractive features that add to the cosy and welcoming ambience. Real ales are on tap, together with a good selection of lagers, ciders, wines, spirits, soft drinks, teas and coffees.

The spacious restaurant is relaxed and gracious, offering a range of delicious meals including the freshest locally caught seafood and tempting meat, fowl and vegetarian meals. Bookings are advisable for this justly popular place.

Heather and Malcolm are your hosts; they have been here at the inn since 1996 and have in that time earned a solid reputation for quality, service and hospitality. The Coldstreamer Inn proviedes its customers, both old and new, with good company in charming surroundings.

- Mon-Sat 11.30-14.30, 18.30-23.00; Sun 12.00-15.00, summer 18.00-23.00
- Lunchtime bar snacks; evening a la carte
- All major credit cards
- Car parking
- Quiz nights Wednesdays
- malcolm.c.craigie@lineone.net

THE COMMERCIAL INN

TRELAVOUR SQUARE, ST DENNIS, NEAR ST AUSTELL,
CORNWALL PL26 8AX
TEL: 01726 822451

Directions: Take the A3058 St Austell to Newquay road and turn right at the B3279 to St Dennis.

Landlord and -lady Ken and Pat welcome all visitors to **The Commercial Inn** with real hospitality. This friendly inn is located in the town centre square, a true hub of the community. Inside all is warm and cosy, with an open-plan area and handsome features such as the exposed beams and stonework and panelled wall dividers. In fine weather, the lovely beer garden is a wonderful place to enjoy a drink or meal.

There are always at least two real ales on tap, together with a good compliment of lagers, ciders, teas and coffees. Pat and

Ken have been here since 2000, and have built up an enviable reputation for quality and service.

The tempting home cooked snacks and meals are prepared by Pat – booking is advised for her excellent Sunday lunches. The intimate restaurant area is separate from the main bar; here the atmosphere is just as relaxed and the décor and furnishings very tasteful and comfortable.

B&B accommodation is available upstairs in one of five en suite rooms (twins and doubles). Pat and Ken take justifiable pride in maintaining excellent standards of care and hospitality. This hidden inn is well worth seeking out.

- Mon-Thurs 11.00-15.00; Fri-Sun 11.00-23.00 (summer)
- Lunchtime and evening menus; daily specials
- 5 rooms (twins and doubles) en suite B&B
- Car parking, beer garden
- Games room, darts, skittles, quiz nights
- St Austell, Newquay, walking

THE DEVON & CORNWALL

1 WEST STREET, MILLBROOK, TORPOINT, CORNWALL PL10 1AA
TEL: 01752 822320

> **Directions:** From Plymouth take the Torpoint ferry to Torpoint village

The Devon & Cornwall, or the 'D & C', as it is affectionately known locally, got its name because it straddles the stream that was once the original dividing line between these two counties.

Built in the 17th century as a coaching inn, this impressive and friendly pub offers good food and drink and comfortable accommodation. Located in the centre of the village of Millbrook, the interior is cosy and welcoming, with original features and a warm and relaxed ambience.

There is a wide range of bar snacks (sandwiches, pasties, pizzas and burgers) and full meals (including vegetarian choices) on the menu, as well as Sunday roasts, all home-cooked and home-prepared. Blackboard specials include seafood and traditional favourites such as

steak and ale pudding. There are also children's meals available. To accompany your meal there's a good choice of real ales and ciders, lagers, wines, spirits, soft drinks, teas and coffees.

The accommodation comprises six en suite rooms, all newly refurbished and offering a high standard of comfort and quality.

The excellent food and drink, complemented by the warm and friendly atmosphere, make this fine inn well worth seeking out.

- 🕐 Mon-Sat 10.30-23.00; Sun 12.00-22.30
- 🍴 Lunchtime and evening menus; daily specials; Sunday roasts
- 💷 All major credit cards
- 🛏 6 rooms (twins and doubles) en suite
- 🅿 Car parking, beer garden
- 🎵 Darts, live music three times a week

THE FISHERMANS ARMS

FORE STREET, GOLANT, NEAR FOWEY, CORNWALL PL23 1LN
TEL: 01726 832453

Directions: A390 Liskeard to Lostwithiel, then the B3269 Fowey Road. Turn off for Golant village.

Situated right on the water's edge of this attractive fishing village, with an array of local boats lining the shore, **The Fishermans Arms** is a pristine whitewashed inn built in 1800. There's a lovely garden to the front, where and in fine weather a marquee is erected.

The interior is just as charming, with a real old-world feel. Prints and brass and copper ornaments adorn the walls. Everything's cosy and comfortable – just the place to enjoy a quiet drink or delicious meal. Real ale is available at this excellent pub, which prides itself on a range of fine real ales from local breweries and further afield. There is also a good selection of wines, spirits, lagers and ciders, as well as soft drinks, teas, coffees and hot chocolate. The home-cooked bar snacks at lunch (served 12.00-14.00) and the evening meals (served 18.30-21.00) are a treat well worth sampling.

Run by Stephen and Susan Perry, who are both Cornwall born and bred, the atmosphere throughout this delightful inn is relaxed and welcoming. Accommodation is on hand in a lovely double room en suite offering marvellous river views. For a taste of genuine Cornish hospitality, look no further.

- Winter: Mon-Fri 12.00-15.00, 18.00-23.00; Sat-Sun - all day. Summer: all day every day
- Full menu available
- All major credit and debit cards
- 1 double room, en suite
- Garden, car parking
- Live music, quiz nights
- Eden Project 6 miles, Fowey 2 miles, fishing, golf, walking

HALFWAY HOUSE

POLBATHIC, TORPOINT, CORNWALL PL11 3EY
TEL: 01503 230202

> **Directions:** Midway on Torpoint-to-Liskeard road

The Halfway House in Polbathic is a large and welcoming inn with a long and distinguished history of offering great food, drink and accommodation. Licencees Andy and Alex Hobden are

- 🕐 Mon-Sat 12.00-3.00, 17.00-23.00; Sun 12.00-14.00, 19.00-22.30
- 🍴 Food served daily
- 💷 All major credit cards
- 🛏 4 rooms
- 🅿 Car parking, beer garden
- 🎵 Games, darts, pool table
- ❓ Plymouth, St Germains, Liskeard

enthusiastic hosts who offer every guest a warm welcome and genuine hospitality.

A range of everything from sandwiches and snacks to full meals such as steaks, fish dishes, vegetarian choices is available every day. Meals can be taken in either of the two cosy bars, in the intimate restaurant or, on fine days, in the beer garden. To drink, there are real ales, lagers, ciders, wines and spirits along with soft drinks, teas and coffees.

For those wishing to prolong their stay in this lovely part of the world, there is bed and breakfast accommodation available.

THE HALFWAY HOUSE INN

TWOWATERSFOOT, NEAR LISKEARD, CORNWALL PL14 6HR
TEL: 01208 821242 FAX: 01208 821115

Directions: From junction 31 on the M5 take the A38 to Liskeard and continue for approximately 7 miles. The Halfway House Inn lies on this road, midway between Liskeard and Bodmin.

Here in the tranquil hamlet of Twowatersfeet, which takes its name from the meeting of two rivers – the Fowey and the Neot – **The Halfway House Inn** is so-called because it lies halfway between Bodmin and Liskeard. A former coaching house that was built in the

1850s, this inn lies in an outstanding location, on the edge of Bodmin Moor. To the rear and to the side it boasts its own splendid gardens. An extensive refurbishment was undertaken in 1999, and the results are charming and elegant.

The inn has a relaxed atmosphere and

is well known for serving excellent real ales and a fine choice of wines, but what makes the inn so popular is the marvellous menus. Owner Steven Couzens is a trained chef with international experience, and it shows: the menus offer a variety of home-made meat, poultry, fish and vegetarian dishes. There's also a range of daily specials. The emphasis is on presenting dishes that use top-quality fresh local produce.

Together with his son and daughter, Steven offers all his guests warm hospitality and excellent service. This spacious inn is a welcoming and comfortable place to enjoy a quiet drink or superb meal. Renowned and highly regarded locally, booking is essential at weekends.

- 🕐 Mon-Sat 11.00-15.00, 18.00-23.00; Sun 12.00-15.00, 19.00-22.30
- 🍴 Bar meals and snacks, a la carte
- 💷 All major credit cards
- 🅿 Car parking, beer garden, children welcome, functions catered for
- 🎵 Darts, pool table, quiz nights
- @ www.thehalfwayhouse.com
- ❓ Bodmin Moor (2 miles), Dobwalls Family Adventure Park (2 miles), King Doniert's Stone (4 miles), coast (9 miles), walking, cycling, horse riding, fishing, birdwatching

THE KINGS ARMS

PAUL, NEAR PENZANCE, CORNWALL TR19 6TZ
TEL: 01736 731224 FAX: 01736 732327

Directions: From junction 31 on the M5 take the A30 round Bodmin to Penzance. From the town take the B3315 and, after passing through Newlyn,go up the hill for 1 mile and the pub is signed on the road to Mousehole on the left.

Found in the heart of the small village of Paul, **The Kings Arms** is an attractive inn that was once workmen's cottages built to house those involved in constructing the adjacent St Pol-de-Leon Church. With benches and tables outside and the front of the building bedecked in colourful hanging baskets, the courtyard in front of the inn is a particularly pleasant place to sit during the summer. Inside, the inn is equally delightful and, while the bar area has been refurbished, it has not lost any of its character or charm. The flagstone floors

have remained, along with the painted coat of arms that decorates one wall. A warm and inviting inn, landlords Anthony and Penny Harvey have been here only since 1999, but they have lived in the area for many years. Anthony was born and bred in Paul and, before coming to The Kings Arms, was for 42 years a local dairy farmer. The couple's knowledge of the local area and its people is extensive.

The range of real ales, including local brews, and all the usual drinks ensures that everyone who visits the inn can enjoy their favourite tipple, while the delicious and varied menu of tasty, homecooked dishes includes a good variety of daily specials. The inn is renowned for superb steaks that are a treat not to be missed. Add to this the excellent accommodation and the warm welcome that children receive.

- 🕐 Winter · Mon-Sat 11.00-15.00, 18.00-23.00; Sun 12.00-15.00, 18.00-23.00. Summer · Mon-Sat 11.00-23.00; Sun 12.00-22.30
- 🍴 Bar meals and snacks
- 💷 Visa, Access, Mastercard, Switch, Delta, Solo.
- 🛏 3 doubles
- 🅿 Patio garden, off-road parking, children welcome, dogs on leads welcome
- 🎵 Occasional live music; quiz nights in winter
- ❓ Coast ½ mile, Mousehole ½ mile, Newlyn 1 mile, Penzance 2 miles, Land's End 8 miles, walking, fishing, sailing, bird watching

KING WILLIAM IV

CHURCH ROAD, MADRON, NEAR PENZANCE, CORNWALL TR20 8SS
TEL: 01736 363022

Directions: Penzance to Heamoor and Madron Road, 2 miles out of Penzance

Standing in the village centre, the **King William IV** is a traditional and venerable old inn run by Alma and Denis Preece. Picturesque inside and out, the interior of this delightful inn boasts heavy ceiling beams decorated with gleaming horse brasses, some interesting memorabilia and lots and prints and photographs of local scenes adorning the walls, and a splendid feature fireplace to add to the cosy feel.

The open-plan bar on two levels serves an excellent selection of real ales, ciders, beers, wines, spirits, soft drinks, teas and coffees. All the food is homemade by

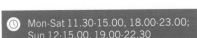

Mon-Sat 11.30-15.00, 18.00-23.00;
Sun 12-15.00, 19.00-22.30

Bar meals and snacks, a la carte

All major credit cards

Beer garden, car parking

Pool, darts, local leagues, weekend entertainment

denispreece@lineone.net

Trengwainton Garden ½ mile, Penzance 2 miles, Men-an-Tol 1 mile.

Alma, who cooks everything to order. From snacks and sandwiches to the specials board and a la carte lunch and dinner menu choices, everything is worth sampling, and made with the freshest local ingredients according to season and availability.

Fish pies are one of Alma's specialities. She and husband Denis are a local couple who have both had many years' experience in hospitality. They are happy to share their knowledge of local sights and attractions, and they and their friendly, conscientious staff make every guest feel welcome.

As well as catering for children, this is one inn where dogs too are welcome, so all can enjoy a lovely day out savouring the delights of this lovely village inn.

LANIVET INN

TRURO ROAD, LANIVET, BODMIN, CORNWALL PL30 5ET
TEL: 01208 831212

Directions: A389 from Bodmin; off A30, after ¾ mile at Innisdowns Roundabout. (2 miles west of Bodmin).

Dee Masters and Trevor Hancock offers all their guests a warm welcome at the superior **Lanivet Inn**. Dating back some 250 years, this distinguished inn is cosy and comfortable, with a relaxed ambience. The handsome stonebuilt exterior, festooned with hanging baskets, presents a welcoming face to the

world. The interior is very comfortable and attractively decorated and furnished. Together with their capable, friendly staff, Dee and Trevor provide genuine hospitality for locals and visitors alike. This charming inn offers a good range of real ales, including those from the local

brewery at St Austell, together with a variety of lagers, ciders, wines, spirits and soft drinks, teas and coffees.

The menu at this fine establishment includes snacks and light meals such as sandwiches, burgers, jacket potatoes and other firm favourites. Main meals comprise such delicious options as homemade steak and kidney pie, seafood platter, a variety of steaks and homemade chicken curry. There are also changing daily specials. The Sunday roasts are justly popular. All food is home-cooked and home-prepared, using fresh local ingredients and expertly presented. It's a good idea to leave room for the tempting puddings. This delightful inn is well worth a visit, both for the excellent food and drink and for the atmosphere.

- Mon-Fri 11.00-15.00, 17.00-23.00; Sat 11.00-23.00; Sun 12.00-15.00, 18.00-22.30
- Lunchtime and evening menus; daily specials
- All major credit cards
- Car parking, orchard/garden
- Games, darts, pool table, live entertainment Saturdays and at some other times, quiz nights
- 'Saints' Way' (geographic centre of Cornwall), Eden Project

THE MERRYMOOR INN

MAWGAN PORTH, NEWQUAY, CORNWALL TR8 4BA
TEL: 01637 860258 FAX: 01637 860258

> **Directions:** Take the M5 south onto the A30, then the A392 to Newquay. B3276 coast road to Mawgan Porth

Built in the 1930s, **The Merrymoor Inn** is set in an extensive area of lovely grounds covering about an acre. With gardens at the front and just 100 yards from the beach, this family-run inn offers picturesque panoramas all round.

Lynne and Dudley Bennett, who have run this fine inn for some 35 years, have made recent improvements such as adding a lovely beer garden, and increased family areas. Good food, beer and comfortable accommodation are the bywords here.

The interior boasts an attractive main bar and family room. Panoramic views from the elevated windows overlook the stunning beach of Mawgan Porth.

Home-cooked meals are supervised by Lynne. There's a tempting carvery on Sundays and every night in July and August. Bar snacks and meals are available at lunchtime and evenings. From sandwiches to a la carte, all dishes are expertly prepared and delicious.

To accompany your meal there is a good selection of real ales, ciders, lagers, spirits and soft drinks, together with a very good wine list.

The comfortable accommodation provided comprises seven en-suite, handsomely furnished and decorated guest bedrooms, most featuring superb views of the bay. This cosy, welcoming inn makes for the perfect base from which to explore the many scenic and historic delights of the region.

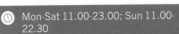

- 🕐 Mon-Sat 11.00-23.00; Sun 11.00-22.30
- 🍴 Lunchtime and evening menus; daily specials
- 💷 All major credit cards
- 🛏 7 rooms en suite B&B
- 🅿 Car parking, extensive grounds
- 🎵 Quiz nights (winter)
- @ info@merrymoorinn.com www.merrymoorinn.com
- ❓ Beaches, coastal walks, Newquay, St Columb, The Eden Project, Heligan Gardens, Falmouth, Bedruthan Steps

THE NORTH INN

THE SQUARE, PENDEEN, NEAR PENZANCE, CORNWALL TR19 7DN
TEL: 01736 788417   FAX: 01736 787504

> **Directions:** From junction 31 on the M5 take the A30 round Bodmin to Penzance. Take the A3071 towards St Just and, approximately 1 mile after Newbridge, turn right and follow the road to the junction with the B3306. Turn left and The North Inn lies along this road.

Dating back to the early 18th century, **The North Inn** is a splendid, creeper covered building in the centre of this attractive and peaceful village. This was once a busy tin-mining village, with miners coming from places such as St Just to work. This is how the inn got its name – Pendeen was known as the *north country*. The inn is still busy today, and although there are no mines left open in the area, visitors tend to arrive here whilst exploring the delights of the beautiful Cornish coast and to visit the Geevor Mine Heritage Centre.

Landlord John Coak and his brother Andrew are both local men and have been here since November 1998. As well as the excellent choice of Cornish real ales on tap, and all the usual beers, lagers and spirits, the inn is highly regarded for the high standard of its cuisine. The lunchtime menu is a tasty mix of freshly cut sandwiches and baguettes and other tempting snacks, while the evening menu features, among other dishes, the house speciality – curries. There are always several from which to choose and the inn's special curry nights (with even more choice) are always a popular event. Add to this the excellent accommodation at the inn, in an adjoining cottage and the adjacent campsite, and The North Inn is near perfect.

- Ⓒ Mon-Sat 11.00-23.00; Sun 12.00-22.30
- 🍴 Bar meals and snacks, a la carte, themed nights
- 💷 Visa, Electron, Switch, Solo
- 🛏 2 double rooms, 1 family room, all en suite, self-catering cottage, campsite
- Ⓟ Beer garden, car parking
- @ ernestjohncok@aol.com
- ❓ Pendeen Lighthouse, beach 1 mile, Levant Steam Engine 1 mile, Eden project 35 miles, Geevor Mine ½ mile, walking, cycling, horse riding, fishing, sailing, bird watching

THE OLD INN

CHURCHTOWN, ST BREWARD, BODMIN MOOR, CORNWALL PL30 4PP
TEL: 01208 850711 FAX: 01208 851671

Directions: From junction 31 on the M5, take the A30 towards Bodmin. After passing Launceston, continue for a further 16 miles and, just after Temple, turn right and follow the signs to St Breward. The Old Inn lies on the far side of the village.

Finalist in the 'Bar Food of the Year' competition sponsored by the Pub Food Awards 2002, and in the Times Newspaper Pub of the Year 2000, and awarded the Platinum award for excellence by the West Country Hotel & Restaurant Guide 2000, **The Old Inn** in St Breward is a charming inn dating back to the 11th century. Built to house workers constructing the village church, this fine inn has real character and atmosphere. It became an inn in the 1500s and was once the haunt of smugglers. The interior boasts traditional features such as exposed stone walls, low beamed ceilings and roaring log fires. Here, in cosy surroundings, guests can

enjoy a good choice of real ales, ciders, lagers, spirits and soft drinks. There's also a very good wine list.

In the bar or conservatory dining area guests can savour an extensive menu of dishes such as fresh fish and seafood from Port Isaac. All meals, from sandwiches to a la carte, are home-cooked and delicious. The menu is complemented by at least 15 daily specials, so there's plenty of choice to suit every palate. Owner Darren Wills, here since 1999, is a local man and head chef, and it is his imagination that has created the marvellous menu. He and his co-owner Simon Hetherington have earned the inn an enviable reputation for quality and service. Outside, there's a delightful beer garden and children's pets corner complete with resident guinea pigs and rabbits.

- 🕐 Mon-Sat 11.00-23.00; Sun 12.00-22.30
- 🍽 Bar meals and snacks, a la carte
- 💷 All major credit cards
- 🅿 Car parking, beer garden
- 🎵 Occasional live music, quiz nights (off-season)
- @ darren@theoldmill.fsnet.co.uk, www.theoldinnandrestaurant.co.uk
- ❓ Pencarrow House (5 miles), Bodmin (7 miles), Tintagel (7 miles), coast (8 miles), walking, cycling, horse riding, fishing, birdwatching

THE OLD QUAY HOUSE

GRIGGS QUAY, HAYLE, CORNWALL TR27 6JG
TEL: 01736 753988

Directions: Just off the A30 Hayle to St Ives road

As its name tells us, **The Old Quay House Inn** stands on its own quay at the head of the Hayle Estuary. Ideally located on the narrow neck of the Land's End peninsula, this fine inn is believed to have once played its part as a toll house for those crossing the causeway built across the treacherous tidal sands in 1826. This traditional inn is constructed of Cornish materials such as granite and slate. Charming and cosy, it is that rare mix of traditional and modern. The spacious lounge bar features exposed beams and timbers, with plenty of cosy corners and a warm, welcoming atmosphere; the mezzanine area, just as comfortable and attractive, provides another lounge bar and family area, and makes for an attractive dining venue. The extensive gardens are just the place

to relax and enjoy a quiet drink or pleasant meal in fine weather, with glorious views of the estuary and its bird life..

The food enjoys an enviable and well-deserved reputation for taste and quality. From sandwiches to delicious a la carte meals, the menu offers a range of grills, chicken, fish, vegetarian dishes and much, much more, including a wonderful self selection salad bar. To accompany your bar snack or meal there's a good selection of real ales, wines, lagers, spirits, soft drinks, teas and coffees.

The charming motel-style accommodation comprises six guest en suite bedrooms, offering a high standard of quality and comfort. Special breaks are on offer during off-peak months, and there is all year golf playable at the four links courses in the area.

- Mon-Sat 11.00-23.00; Sun 12.00-14.30, 20.00-22.30
- Bar snacks to a la carte
- All major credit cards
- 6 bedrooms
- Car parking
- Walking, Hayle Bird Sanctuary, golf, St Ives, Isles of Scilly, Penzance, coastal railway

THE PHOENIX

WATERGATE BAY, NR NEWQUAY, CORNWALL TR8 4AB
TEL: 01637 860353

Directions: From Newquay take the B3276. The pub is 50 yards from the beach.

The Phoenix at Watergate Bay offers the finest hospitality and great food and drink, all amid lovely surroundings. Set in a small, unspoilt village and just 50 yards from the beach, the upper level of the pub features massive windows to make the most of the spectacular views of the quiet cove and seafront. Chef proprietor Mike Sanders runs the pub with flair and attention to detail, making sure all his customers have an enjoyable, relaxing time of it. Great locally caught seafood – including a

choice of five fish dishes daily – is of course a main feature of the fine menu, which also offers a range of grills, steaks, chicken, pork and vegetarian dishes. Tempting bar snacks are also available at lunchtime.

The drinks selection includes excellent real ales together with a variety of lagers, ciders, stout, wines, spirits, soft drinks, teas and coffees.

Well worth seeking out, this charming inn has long been welcoming seafarers and land-lubbers alike to its doors. The interior is cosy and very comfortable, with traditional features and walls adorned with interesting memorabilia. The atmosphere throughout always friendly and relaxed.

- 🕐 11.00-11.00 every day
- 🍴 Lunchtime and evening menus; daily specials
- 💷 All major credit cards
- 🅿 Car parking, beer garden
- @ e.mail: mike@thephoenixpub.co.uk, website: www.thephoenix-pub.co.uk
- ❓ Coastal walks, surfing, bathing, Redruth, The Mineral Tramway trail, diving, fishing

THE QUEENS ARMS

BOTALLACK, NEAR PENZANCE, CORNWALL TR19 7QG
TEL: 01736 788318

> **Directions:** From Penzance take the A3071 to St Just and from there, take the B3306 towards St Ives. Botallack can be found after approximately 1 mile.

The Queens Arms is a Grade II listed building dating back to the mid-18th century. Originally a private residence built by a member of the Bolitho family, becoming a pub in 1856, some 100 years after it was built, and known then as the New House. Its name was changed in 1897, and though briefly known as The Kings Arms during the reign of Edward VII, it reverted back to The Queens Arms shortly thereafter. The ornate ceiling over the stairs is over 150 years old, and it was this that helped gain the pub its Grade II status. It remains a homely and welcoming place, with low beamed ceilings and exposed stonework. The large open fireplace makes for a very cosy sight in colder

weather. Behind the L-shaped bar guests will find Peter Beech and Sharon Smith, who run this pub to a high standard of service and hospitality. The atmosphere is relaxed, and all the food is chef-prepared and cooked to order. There is a wonderful range of dishes on offer including venison, duck, pheasant and, more unusually, ostrich and kangaroo. Among the many seafood meals are those made with swordfish, lobster, megrim, John Dory and crab.

Real ales, cask-marque ciders, lagers, spirits and a carefully selected wine list, as well as hot and cold beverages.

For great food and drink in a friendly and relaxing atmosphere, look no further.

Self-catering accommodation is also available in 'The Queens Lodge', which sleeps two.

- Winter · Mon-Fri 18.00-23.00; Sat-Sun 11.00-23.00; Summer – Mon-Sun 11.00-23.00
- Lunchtime and evening menus; daily specials
- All major credit cards
- Self-catering
- Car parking
- Music, quiz nights
- petermbeech@btopenworld.com, www.queensarms.info
- Golf, coastal walks, swimming

RING O' BELLS

Cornwall

ANTONY, NR TORPOINT, CORNWALL PL11 3AB
TEL: 01752 812572

Directions: On main A387 from the Torpoint Ferry

The **Ring O'Bells** in Antony is owned and run by Matthew, who used to be in the Royal Navy, and his American wife Liz, who hails from North Carolina. Aided by their son, who is head chef, they have created the only US-themed pub in Cornwall. The accent at this delightful inn is on genuine American-style foods. Everything from barbecued chicken wings to filled-to-bursting sandwiches, hearty burgers and platters of steak, chicken, pork chops or vegetarian lasagna is available here, to eat in or to take away. All dishes are homemade and expertly prepared, with hearty portions and served with flair. The desserts include tempting fare such

as pecan pie and a range of delicious choices well worth leaving room for.

The décor throughout the pub continues the American theme, with the restaurant kitted out in Western style along with appropriate accompanying music and, occasionally, live bands. The atmosphere is welcoming and convivial throughout this excellent pub, which began life as a coaching inn back in the 17th century.

In the bar, customers can enjoy a traditional English pint, with a range of real ales, domestic and imported lagers, wines, spirits and soft drinks on offer.

The service and hospitality are second to none, as Matthew, Liz and their friendly, helpful staff make every guest feel welcome.

Bookings are advised at this justly popular place, especially at weekends.

🕐 Summer: Mon-Fri 12.00-23.00
Winter: Mon-Fri 12.00-15.00, 18.00-23.00
Sat-Sun all day, every day.

🍴 Lunchtime and evening menus; daily specials

£ All major credit cards

🅿 Car parking, beer garden

🎵 Occasional live music

❓ Torpoint, Plymouth. River Tamar, River Lynher, Antony House, Kingsand, Cawsand, Mount Edgcombe, coastal walks.

RING O' BELLS

3 BANK STREET, ST COLUMB MAJOR, CORNWALL TR9 6AT
TEL: 01637 880259

Directions: Take the A39 south from Wadebridge for about 8 miles.

Here in this delightful town, **Ring O' Bells** is a traditional inn in the best sense of the word. The pub was built in the 1400s under the aegis of Sir John Arundall, who also sponsored the building of St Columb Major's bell tower. The oldest pub in the area, it exudes old world charm, which draws people from near and far to enjoy its unique ambience. Cosy and comfortable, the bars – running in sequence from front to back - feature blackened exposed beamwork and a stonebuilt bar, while the dining area is brightly painted and cheerful. Brasses, banknotes and coins adorn the ceiling beams; low lighting adds to the pleasant atmosphere. The first room welcomes children. This free house and restaurant is run by Christine and Brian Bazeley; they and their friendly, helpful staff offer a high standard of service and quality. From

snacks to a la carte, the food on offer ranged from sandwiches, burgers, grills, fish dishes and vegetarian options, all expertly prepared using the freshest local ingredients to create a range of both traditional and more innovative dishes. The changing daily specials are also well worth sampling. Guests can be assured of finding a good choice of well-kept ales here, along with draught lagers, a good wine list, spirits, ciders, soft drinks, teas and coffees.

- Mon-Sat 12.00-14.00, 17.00-23.00; Sun 19.00-22.30
- Bar snacks to a la carte
- All major credit cards
- Quiz nights
- brianbazeley@hotmail.com

THE RISING SUN INN

PORTMELLON COVE, NEAR MEVAGISSEY, CORNWALL PL26 6PL
TEL: 01726 843235 FAX: 01736 732327

Directions: Through Mevagissey and a futher 1 mile on the coast road.

One of the best-kept secrets in this delightful part of Cornwall, **The Rising Sun Inn** is a gem worth finding. Right on the water's edge, this glorious whitewashed inn was built around 1830 and was owned originally by Lord Gordon, of Gordon's gin fame. Out front there is a very attractive garden, a real sun-trap in fine weather, festooned with flowering plants. Inside all is exposed beamwork and handsome panelling, with a stone decorative chimney and open fire. Underfoot is a highly polished crazy-paved floor; the seating is supremely comfortable.

The accent of the evening menu is firmly on fish and seafood, as befits this coastal setting, with an excellent range of delicious and innovative starters, main courses (where meat and vegetarian dishes complement the selection of fish courses) and mouth-watering sweets.

Nothing is too much trouble for welcoming host Cliff Walker (now there's a name for a Cornwall resident!) and his wife Sheila, who treat every one of their guests as an individual, and provide a high standard of friendly service and hospitality.

The accommodation comprises seven rooms (doubles, twins, family rooms), all en suite, and has earned 3 Diamonds from the English Tourist Board. Attractive and welcoming, they make for an ideal base from which to explore this part of the Cornish coast.

- 🕐 Mon-Sat 12.00-15.00, 18.00-23.00; Sun 12.00-15.00, 18.00-23.00. July-Aug · Mon-Sun 11.00-23.00
- 🍴 Bar meals and a la carte
- £ All major credit cards
- 🛏 7 rooms, en suite
- 🅿 Nearby and off-road parking, garden
- @ www.risingsunportmellon.co.uk
- ❓ Coast, Mevagissey, Eden Project, golf, walking, sunbathing, fishing, bird watching

THE ROYAL INN

66 EAST CLIFFE ROAD, PAR, CORNWALL PL24 2AJ
TEL: 01726 815601 FAX: 01726 816415

> **Directions:**From any direction enter Par and follow signs to Railway Station·Royal Inn immediately opposite.

Newly and fully refurbished to provide a very high standard of comfort and quality, **The Royal Inn,** located opposite to the Par Railway Station in this charming village, is a large and spacious pub, restaurant and hotel run by David Hodgkinson and his

friendly, welcoming staff. The 'Royal' in this fine establishment's name refers to the name given to the topsail of traditional sailing ships.

The open-plan bar has slate floors and a large open fire. The atmosphere is relaxed and welcoming. There are real ales on tap as well as a good range of lagers, ciders, spirits, wines and, of course, soft drinks, teas and coffees.

The separate dining restaurant is located in the conservatory, a sun-lit space enhanced by the pale stonework walls, bleached wood beamwork and attractive French Oak dining tables and chairs.

The imaginative and tempting menu features such delights as Portuguese sardines, salmon, salads, sweet and sour chicken, steaks and vegetarian lasagne. There is also a changing selection of specials. Everything from sandwiches and snacks to a la carte is freshly prepared to order.

The superb accommodation comprises 18 en suite rooms, including twin, double and family rooms.

- 🕐 Mon-Sat inc 11.30am-11.00pm Food available all day
  Sun 12noon-10.30pm Food available all day
- 🍴 Bar snacks and meals, a la carte
- £ All major credit cards
- 🛏 18 rooms en suite
- Ⓟ Car parking
- @ Par4hodge@aol.com
- ❓ Eden Project, Hidden Gardens of Heligan, golf, walking

THE ROYAL STANDARD

50 CHURCH TOWN, GWINEAR, NEAR HAYLE, CORNWALL TR27 5JL
TEL: 01736 850080 FAX: 01736 850080

Directions: A30 from Hayle to Gwinear village centre

The Royal Standard in the charming village of Gwinear is a welcoming stonebuilt traditional pub and restaurant offering the very best in Cornish hospitality. This excellent Free House has an open-plan bar area, which is spacious without losing any of its cosiness and charm.

Decorated and furnished as befits the age and setting of this esteemed inn, it has a relaxed atmosphere.

There is a good range of real ales, ciders, lagers, wines, spirits, soft drinks, teas and coffees on offer. The home-prepared snacks and sandwiches are well worth sampling, Thursday nights are curry night and on Friday and Saturday nights there is an excellent carvery along with Sunday lunchtimes. The separate restaurant is elegant and well-appointed, with a fine menu of traditional and modern favourites, expertly prepared and presented.

A wonderful base from which to explore the Cornish coast, there are five guest bedrooms – one double, one twin and three family rooms – all attractively furnished and decorated.

Owners John and Robert have been here since 2000. Originally from Lancashire, they and their staff offer all guests the highest standard of friendly service and quality.

- Mon-Sat 12.00-15.00, 18.30-23.00; Sun 11.00-23.00
- Bar meals and snacks, a la carte
- All major credit cards
- 5 guest rooms
- Car parking
- Occasional live music, pool, darts, quiz night
- theroyalstandard@aol.com, www.royalstandardgwinear.com
- Beach, walking, bird watching, fishing

THE SHIP INN

1 POLMEAR HILL, PAR, CORNWALL PL24 2AR
TEL: 01726 812540 FAX: 01726 813797

Directions: From junction 31 on the M5 take the A30 to Bodmin and continue to the roundabout at the end of the dual carriageway. Turn left onto the A391 towards St Austell and continue until the junction with the A390 and turn left. At the next roundabout turn right onto the A3082. The Ship Inn is situated adjacent to the beach entrance.

Set almost at the water's edge, **The Ship Inn** is a wonderful place to enjoy a quiet drink or meal or a longer stay. The interior is spacious with stylish fittings, furniture and lighting which tastefully complements the old world atmosphere. Guests can relax with a cream tea in the gardens or with a cool drink in the bar, where good food is served daily. Everything from sandwiches and curries

to full a la carte are available lunchtime and evenings. There are always three real ales on tap, together with a selection of lagers, ciders, wines and spirits.

Run jointly by Pauline and Christopher Giles and Nick and Jane Moore, this gracious pub is well worth seeking out, and using as a base for exploring the area. 'Pop's Cottage' (sleeps four) is a very comfortable, carefully restored cottage tucked away in a private area beside the inn; the well-equipped caravan (sleeps eight), or the two log cabins (one sleeps eight, the other six), fitted and furnished to a high standard of quality and comfort. A laundry room is available and a gas-fired charcoal grill for hire per day for a family barbecue.

- 🕐 Summer: Mon-Sun 11.00-23.00; Winter: Mon-Sun 11.00-15.30, 17.30-23.00

- 🍴 Bar meals and snacks, a la carte

- 💷 All major credit cards

- 🛏 Self-catering cottage, 1 static caravan, 2 log cabins

- 🅿 Car parking, lawned gardens/beer garden, children's play area

- ♫ Regular live music – jazz, folk, brass bands - from the bandstand in summer, quiz nights, themed food nights (Jan-Mar), euchre

- @ gilespauline5@aol.com; www.theshipinnpar.com

- ❓ St Austell Bay and beaches (2 miles), Eden Project (2 miles), St Austell (3 miles), St Catherine's Castle (3 miles), Restormel Castle (6 miles), walking, fishing, sailing, birdwatching

SMUGGLERS INN

SEATON, CORNWALL PL11 3JD
TEL: 01503 250646

Directions: South of the A387 on the coast just east of Looe.

With the seafront nearby and set against a backdrop of rugged bluffs, **Smugglers Inn** in Seaton is a real oasis offering wonderful views to accompany great food and drink. The beach is only 50 yards away, and the pub has a lovely patio garden with heaters for the cooler evenings. Gary Stephen bought this charming pub in May 2002, bringing a wealth of experience in the trade to the Smugglers. He has overseen the

🕐 Summer: Mon-Sat 11.00-23.00, Sun 11.00-22.30; Winter Mon-Fri 12.00-15.00 and 18.00-23.00, Sat 11.00-23.00, Sun 11.00-22.30

🍴 Lunchtime and evening menus; daily specials

£ All major credit cards

🛏 5 rooms (1 twin, 2 doubles, 2 family) en suite B&B

Ⓟ Car parking, beer garden

🎵 Weekly entertainment

❓ Country Park nearby, Monkey Sanctuary

building of a new extension so that the pub has a spacious restaurant and can offer high-quality accommodation. There are five guest bedrooms, all recently refurbished, all en suite and all comfortably furnished and tastefully decorated. The quiet, unspoilt cove itself – once, as the name suggests, a haunt for smugglers - is a delight for walkers and beach-lovers alike and right on the edge of a lovely country park.

Here in the oldest building in Seaton, guests can enjoy a range of fine ales as well as lagers, ciders, wines, spirits and soft drinks. Tempting bar snacks are available daily, while the restaurant menu offers a variety of delicious home-cooked meals for lunch and dinner.

For a taste of genuine Cornish natural beauty and hospitality, look no further.

THE TAVERN

MELLANVRANE LANE, TRENINNICK, NEAR NEWQUAY,
CORNWALL TR7 2LQ
TEL: 01637 873564 FAX: 01637 873325

Directions: From the A30, take the road to Newquay. The Tavern is on the outskirts of the town.

Steve, Karen and their friendly, helpful staff welcome all comers to **The Tavern**, a traditional pub in the best sense of the word. Steve is a local man who has been at the helm of this fine inn for several years. Set back from the road amid lovely gardens and sheltered by overarching trees, the exterior is festooned with beautiful hanging baskets and is a true home from home. This charming, relaxed ambience continues inside, where the main bar, family room and games room have plenty of cosy nooks and crannies, and where sofas and other soft furnishings complement the usual tables and chairs.

There are always three real ales available, together with a good compliment of lagers, ciders, spirits, wines and soft drinks.

Food is treated as a speciality here, with Wednesday nights being Curry Night, where guests are offered a choice of beef or chicken curry with all the trimmings. Saturday is steak night, where 8-oz rump steaks are served up for only £4.95. Mixed grills and chicken are also on the menu this night.

There's live music every Friday night, as local artists enhance the pub's lively and welcoming atmosphere by providing a high standard of entertainment. And on Sunday night, locals and visitors alike vie in the popular quizzes, as four different quizzes take place for cash prizes and gifts of wine.

For great atmosphere, food and drink and a warm welcome, don't miss this hidden gem.

- 🕐 Mon-Sun 11.00-23.00
- 🍴 Special menus, and by prior arrangement
- 🅿 Car parking, beer gardens
- 🎵 Darts and euchre, golf society, angling society, live music weekly
- @ tavern.inn@ntlworld.com, www.taverninn.co.uk, www.innsofcornwall.com
- ❓ Newquay, coastal walks, beaches

THREE TUNS

THE SQUARE, ST KEVERNE, CORNWALL TR12 6NA
TEL: 01326 280949

Directions: From Helston take the A3083, then turn left onto the B3293 direct to St Keverne. The Three Tuns is situated in the left corner of the square, next to the church

The Three Tuns is located in the heart of the village of St Keverne, on the village square. This charming unspoilt village is set in an area of outstanding natural beauty.

Built in approximately 1900, there are three acres of lovely grounds to the rear including a children's play area, extensive gardens and a beer garden – just the place to relax and enjoy a quiet drink or some of the great food on offer on fine days.

The interior is warm and has a welcoming ambience, and retains much of its original character, happily combined with the comforts of today.

The bar area is open-plan, while there's a separate dining area. From bar snacks and lunches to full evening meals,

complemented by daily specials, the menus boast a range of tempting dishes such as home-made pies, steaks, chicken and vegetarian choices. Fish and seafood are specialities.

Real ales – three at any one time – are on tap, together with a good range of lagers, ciders, spirits, wines, soft drinks, teas and coffees.

The six guest bedrooms are comfortable and well-appointed, providing the perfect base from which to explore this beautiful region.

Will Lea is a local man; he and his wife Lisa and their friendly staff are happy to offer all their guests a warm Cornish welcome.

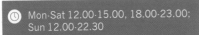

- Mon-Sat 12.00-15.00, 18.00-23.00; Sun 12.00-22.30
- Lunchtime and evening menus; daily specials
- All major credit cards
- 6 rooms en suite B&B
- Car parking, beer garden
- Music monthly, quiz nights, darts, pool table
- The Lizard Peninsula, beaches, coastal walks, diving

TREWARMETT INN

TREWARMETT, NEAR TINTAGEL, CORNWALL PL34 0ET
TEL: 01840 770460 FAX: 01840 779011

Directions: A30 into north Cornwall/Camelford, right to Slaughter Bridge, right onto the B3263

Driving along the B3263, The **Trewarnett Inn** is impossible to miss for its lively mural painted along one exterior wall, depicting a sailing ship, a pirate and Poseidon himself, lord of the sea. This cheerful and welcoming inn is over 300 years old and has been either an inn or a guest house ever since. In 1999 Edwina Chignell and her partner, Jamie Arnott, arrived and have created a pub of some standing. Jamie is a craftsman and artist and has used his talents to restore the pub. This excellent inn boasts real old-world style, with flagstone floors, low beamed ceilings and other wonderful traditional features that add to the pleasing and comfortable ambience.

Home-cooked food is another major draw here, as hearty favourites are prepared using the freshest local ingredients in season. Medieval banquets are held by arrangement for private and corporate groups, where up to 36 diners are served by costumed serving-folk. Whichever of the excellent meals guests choose, to accompany them there are two real ales, ciders, lagers, spirits and both local (Cornish) and international wines. The inn is featured in the CAMRA Good Beer Guide.

The comfortable and cosy accommodation comprises five spacious and welcoming guest bedrooms, all en suite and attractively furnished and decorated. A major attraction at the Trewamett are the Folk music sessions, which are advertised on the internet and include both local and national musicians. The music has been described as among the best in Cornwall.

Edwina and Jamie offer all their guests a warm and friendly welcome and provide a very high standard of service.

- Mon-Sun 12.00-14.30, 19.00-23.00
- Lunchtime and evening menus; daily specials
- All major credit cards
- 5 rooms (twins and doubles) en suite. B&B
- Car parking
- Live music twice-weekly

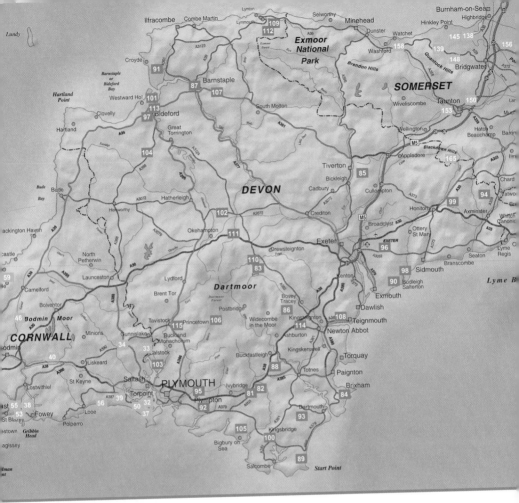

81	The Anchor Inn, Ugborough	**93**	The George Inn, Blackawton, Totnes
82	The Avon Inn, Avonwick, South Brent	**94**	The George Inn, Chardstock, Axminster
83	Bullers Arms, Chagford, Newton Abbot	**95**	The George Inn, Plympton, Plymouth
84	The Bullers Arms, Brixham	**96**	Halfway Inn, Aylesbeare, Exeter
85	The Butterleigh Inn, Butterleigh	**97**	Johnny's Bar, Bideford
86	Carpenters Arms, Islington, Newton Abbot	**98**	Kings Arms, Otterton
87	The Chichester Arms, Barnstaple	**99**	Kings Arms Inn, Stockland, Honiton
88	The Church House Inn, Rattery, Totnes	**100**	The Kings Arms Hotel, Kingsbridge
89	The Cricket Inn, Beesands, Kingsbridge	**101**	Kingsley Inn, Northam, Bideford
90	Dog & Donkey, Budleigh Salterton	**102**	The New Inn, Sampford Courtenay
91	Ebrington Arms, Knowle, Braunton	**103**	The Olde Plough Inn, Bere Ferrers
92	The Foxhound Inn, Brixton	**104**	The Old Union Inn, Stibbs Cross

Please note all cross references refer to page numbers

DEVON

Devon is a county of unsurpassed scenic attraction, from the high cliffs and deep valleys in the North to the chalk downland and oak woodland, and above all the glorious coastline. The North Devon Coast, from Hartland Point to Exmoor, offers spectacular scenery and fine sandy beaches. Several of the popular holiday resorts along the coast were developed when interest increased in sea bathing and sea water therapies, made fashionable by George III and later monarchs. The South West Coast Path takes in many interesting, picturesque places along the coastline including Bideford, Ilfracombe and the village of Clovelly, a quaint village that tumbles down a steep hillside in a series of terraces. Also on the route is Barnstaple, one of the country's oldest boroughs, a place, for many, associated with the tale of

PLACES OF INTEREST

Tarka the Otter. Opened in 1992 by Prince Charles, the Tarka Trail, a figure of eight long distance foot path and cycle path, takes in many of the towns and villages mentioned in the book by Henry Williamson.

Further inland, the countryside is characterised by small, unspoilt villages of thatched cottages and lonely farmsteads.

High, bleak and wild, Dartmoor is southern England's only true wilderness. It covers some 365 square miles, rising to a height of more than 2,000 feet. The tors are Dartmoor's most characteristic feature and these great chunks of granite have withstood the effects of the wind, rain and ice better than the less resistant rocks which once surrounded them. The

Burgh Island

moorland is littered with stone circles, menhirs, burial chambers and single, double or even triple rows of stones including a row of 150 stones on Stall Moor that is believed to be the longest prehistoric stone row in Europe.

In medieval times, the moorland was the scene of much commercial activity, as tin has been mined here since at least the 12th century. There is still evidence of mining on the moors and Devon has four stannary towns, where the metal was brought to be weighed and assayed. Later, the land here was exploited for lead, copper, iron and even arsenic. Today, Dartmoor's most famous, or infamous, building is its prison, right in the middle of the bleak moorland at Princetown. Originally built by French prisoners of war from granite quarried from the moor, it is a building as inhospitable as the countryside that surrounds it. It is also famed for its Dartmoor ponies that have roamed here freely since at least the 10th century. Sir Arthur Conan Doyle made the moorland even bleaker and wilder than it is in his mysterious and spine-chilling novel, *The Hound of the Baskervilles*.

Surrounding the National Park there are the charming and delightful towns of Okehampton, Tavistock, Ivybridge and Bovey Tracey, that have served the needs of those who lived and worked on the moors for centuries. In the less harsh landscape of the eastern area of Dartmoor lies Widecombe a wonderful, scenic village that is home to the famous fair.

The largest centre of population in the southwest peninsula, Plymouth developed at the end of the 12th century when its potential as a military and commercial port was recognised. But it was not until the 16th century that it became the main base for the English navy, when Sir Francis Drake famously finished his game of bowls before leading the fleet from Plymouth against the Spanish Armada.

To the east of Plymouth, as far as the River Dart and south of Dartmoor is the South Ham, a favoured area, well known for its mild climate, fertile soil and lush pasture. The rivers that drain Dartmoor and flow into the south coast cut right through the South Ham, acting, until relatively recent times, as a great barrier to communication and expansion. The only

Watersmeet, Devon

two towns are Totnes and Kingsbridge. The area is characterised by wonderfully picturesque ports and charming, sleepy villages, linked by narrow, winding country lanes.

West of the River Dart is a stretch of coastline called the English Riviera. The first palm tree arrived here in 1820; it took well to the mild climate and hundreds more were planted along the seafronts of the newly fashionable resorts along the coast, most notably, Torquay. East Devon is a beautiful and often overlooked part of Devon, as many pass through here on the motorway for destinations further southwest. However, the area has plenty to offer: interesting market towns, pretty villages, elegant resorts, spectacular coastline, ancient history and, of course, the county town – the city of Exeter. A Roman stronghold that had also been the home of a Celtic tribe, Exeter became a major ecclesiastical centre in the 7th century when an abbey was founded here. The Normans constructed the magnificent St Peter's Cathedral and, today, it remains one of the best examples of the Decorated style of church architecture. Further up the River Exe is Tiverton, a town built on the

Valley of the Rocks, Lynton

prosperity that it gained from the woollen trade. While Tiverton was built on wool, Axminster has become synonymous with carpets. Using a technique developed by a local weaver, Thomas Whitty, these luxurious and highly desirable carpets grace floors around the world as well as the floor of the town's St Mary's Church. In Honiton, a large proportion of the town's population, even children, were once involved in hand-made lace. Queen Victoria insisted on Honiton lace for her wedding dress, reviving interest in it during the 19th century, and lace continues to be made here, though on a smaller scale. East Devon has a Heritage Coastline that can be explored and walked, by taking the South West Coast Path. Apart from a wealth of bird, plant and wildlife, this stretch of coast is known for its genteel and elegant resorts, once the holiday preserve of the well-to-do, looking for British alternatives to a Napoleon dominated Europe. Old fishing villages such as Budleigh Salterton and Exmouth were thus saved from obscurity. Sidmouth, visited by Jane Austen and James Makepeace Thackeray, was really put on the map when the Duke of Kent moved here in 1819, with his daughter Princess Victoria (later Queen Victoria).

Appledore

This delightful old fishing village of narrow winding lanes and sturdy 18th and 19th century fishermen's cottages is a natural place to find the **North Devon Maritime Museum** in a former shipowner's residence. It contains a wealth of seafaring memorabilia, along with other historical aspects of the village and surrounding area.

Axminster

During the Middle Ages, Axminster was an important religious centre with a minster, but the town is most famous for its carpets, made here since 1755. Quality has always been the keynote, and so much time and labour went into the making of just one Axminster carpet that the completion of each carpet was celebrated by a procession to St Mary's Church, where a peal of bells would be rung. Carpets are still manufactured here using the latest computerised looms and the factory welcomes

visitors; **Axminster Museum** dedicates some of its exhibition space to the industry that made this modest town a household name around the world.

Barnstaple

Claiming to be Britain's oldest borough, Barnstaple, at the head of the Taw estuary, was the administrative and commercial capital of this region at the time of the Domesday Book. At that time, it had its own mint and a well-established market that still continues nearly 1,000 years later. The **Church of St Peter and St Paul**, the 17th century **Horwood's Almshouses** and the

Barnstaple Bridge

charming 15th century **St Anne's Chapel** are all worth a visit, as is **Queen Anne's Walk**, a colonnaded arcade with some lavish ornamentation and a statue of Queen Anne on top of its central doorway. The building stands on the old town quay from where, in 1588, five ships set sail to join Drake's fleet against the Spanish Armada. The building is now home to the **Barnstaple Heritage Centre**, a wonderful place where more can be found out about this ancient town.

One of the town's most enduring industries has been pottery, made here continuously since the 13th century, and the **Royal Barum Pottery** welcomes visitors to its workshop, museum and well-stocked shop. Barnstaple is the northern terminus of the **Tarka Line**, a wonderfully scenic 39-mile route that follows the gentle river valleys of the Rivers Yeo and Taw, where Tarka the Otter had his home. Walkers can discover the countryside that inspired the novel by taking the **Tarka Trail**, an unusual figure of eight long distance footpath of some 180 miles that crosses over at Barnstaple.

Bickleigh

This village in the Exe valley, a charming place of thatched cottages and lovingly tended gardens in a beautiful riverside setting is one of Devon's most photographed villages. It is also home to two of the area's most popular attractions. **Bickleigh Mill** has been converted into a craft centre and a farm stocked with rare breeds, while across the river stands **Bickleigh Castle**, a moated and fortified 14th century manor house. The interior houses some excellent Tudor furniture including a massive four-poster bed, some fine oil paintings and an armoury from the Civil War. Close to the castle is an even older chapel, dating from the 11th century.

Bideford

An attractive town set beside the River Torridge estuary, Bideford was once Britain's third busiest port. Many commodities passed through the dock, but the town specialised in tobacco from the North American colonies. Evidence of this golden age can still be seen around the town in the various opulent merchants' houses that have survived. While staying at the Royal Hotel, Charles Kingsley wrote *Westward Ho!*, the swashbuckling Elizabethan story based around Bideford, which he described as a "little white town".

An excursion from Bideford that should not be missed is the day trip to **Lundy Island**. This unique lump of granite rock, three miles long and half a mile wide, derives its name from the old Norse 'lunde ey', meaning puffin island. These attractive birds are still in residence today along with many other species - over 400 have been recorded. Undisturbed by cars, the island has a small village complete with a church, a pub and a shop that sells the famous Lundy stamps. Also on the island are the ruins of a 13th century castle.

Lundy Island

Bigbury on Sea

Just off the shore of this popular family resort is **Burgh Island**, which is an island only at high tide. When the tide recedes, it can be reached by walking across the sandbank or by taking an exciting ride on the vintage Sea Tractor. The whole of this 28-acre island, complete with its 14th century Pilchard Inn, was bought in 1929 by the eccentric millionaire Archibald Nettlefold. The extravagant Art Deco hotel that he built attracted many visitors including Noël Coward, the Duke of Windsor and Mrs Wallis Simpson and Agatha Christie.

Branscombe

This scattered village of farmhouses and cottages lies on one of the most spectacular stretches of Heritage Coast in east Devon. It is a vista of flat-topped hills, deep valleys leading down to the sea, shingle beaches, hedge-lined country lanes and thatched cottages. The **South West Coast Path** follows the coastline through this delightful landscape, which is a haven for rare plants and butterflies.

Branscombe is home to what was, before it closed in 1987, the last traditional working bakery in Devon. Now in the hands of the National Trust, the stone-built and thatched **Old Bakery** is a tearoom, and in the baking room the old baking equipment has been preserved.

Brent Tor

Brent Tor, a 1,100 foot volcanic plug that rears up from the surrounding countryside, is one of the most striking sights in the whole of Dartmoor. The **Church of St Michael of the Rocks** stands on the top of it. The fourth smallest complete church in England, St Michael's is only 15 feet wide and 37 feet long and has walls only 10 feet high but three feet thick.

Brixham

The most southerly of the three towns that make up the great Torbay conurbation, Brixham was, in the 18th century, the most profitable fishing port in Britain. Fishing is still the most important activity in this little town although the fishing fleet has to pick its way through flotillas of yachts and tour boats. On the quay, the stalls sell the boats'

Brixham Harbour

visit here so special. Veitch introduced many rare tress into the arboretum along with rhododendrons, magnolias and herbaceous borders; in the parkland are a number of interesting structures, including a 19th century chapel and the Dolbury Iron Age hill fort. Here, too, can be found Marker's Cottage dating from the 16th century, and Forest Cottage, originally a gamekeeper's home. Circular walks around the grounds provide ample opportunity to discover the wealth of plant, animal and birdlife that thrives in this large estate.

daily catch, wriggling fresh from the sea.

At only 15 feet high, Brixham's lighthouse has been called the 'highest and lowest lighthouse in Britain' because it stands at the top of the 200 foot cliffs at the most easterly point of **Berry Head**, a country park noted for its incredible views.

Broadclyst

Just to the north of the village and set within the fertile lands between the Rivers Clyst and Culm, lies the large estate of **Killerton**, centred around the grand 18th century mansion house that was the home of the Acland family. Furnished as a comfortable family home, the house contains the Paulise de Bush costume collection and visitors can also see a Victorian laundry.

While the house provides some interest it is the marvellous grounds laid out by John Veitch in the 1770s that make a

Buckfastleigh

Buckfastleigh is the western terminus and headquarters of the **South Devon Railway**, formerly called the Primrose Line, where steam trains continue to make the seven mile journey through the valley of the River Dart to Totnes.

Another popular attraction close to the town is the **Buckfast Butterflies and Dartmoor Otter Sanctuary**, where the exotic butterflies can be seen in a specially designed tropical rain forest environment and the otters can be watched from the underwater viewing area. **Buckfast Abbey** dates from the early 20th century and stands on the site of a monastic site founded in the 11th century.

Buckland Monachorum

Tucked away in a secluded valley above the River Tavy, **Buckland Abbey** was originally founded in 1278 by Amicia, Countess of Devon, and though small it became an influential Cistercian monastery. However, it is better known as the last home of Sir Francis Drake. It remained in the Drake family until 1946, when it was bought by Captain Arthur Rodd, who presented it to the National Trust. Of the many exhibits at the abbey, pride of place goes to Drake's Drum, which legend says will sound whenever England is in peril. The Drum was brought to England by Drake's brother Thomas, who was with the great seafarer when he died on the Spanish Main in 1596. Elsewhere at the Abbey, visitors can see a magnificent monastic barn, a craft workshop and a herb garden. Just a few miles away is one of the county's most popular visitor attractions **Morwellham Quay**, a historic site that recreates the busy atmosphere of the 1850s, when half the world's copper came through this tiny harbour.

Budleigh Salterton

A famous Victorian visitor to this pleasant, refined town was the artist Sir John Everett Millais, who stayed here during the summer of 1870 in a curiously shaped house known as the Octagon. It was beside the town's beach that he painted his best-known picture, *The Boyhood of Raleigh*, using his two sons and a local fisherman as models. On the seafront is **Fairlynch Museum**, one of the very few thatched museums in the country, home to numerous collections covering all aspects of life through the ages in the lower Otter Valley. It was built for a local ship-owner who could watch his boats bringing in their cargoes from the lookout tower.

Cadbury

Cadbury Castle is not made of chocolate, nor is it really a castle. Built high on a hilltop, about 700 feet above sea level, Cadbury Castle is actually an Iron Age hillfort and it is claimed that the views from here are the most extensive in Devon. On a good, clear day the landscapes of Dartmoor and Exmoor are in full view and, further away, the Quantocks and Bodmin Moor can also be seen. Just to the east of Cadbury stands **Fursdon House**, which has been the home of the Fursdon family since the 13th century. Among the fascinating memorabilia on display, which include old scrapbooks and some excellent 18th century costumes and textiles, is a letter written by Charles I during the Civil War. The exterior of the building shows a range of differing architectural styles reflecting the length of time that this family has lived here.

Clovelly

This wonderfully quaint and picturesque village, which tumbles down a steep hillside in terraced levels, is many people's idea of the typical Devonshire coastal village. The whitewashed cottages are decked with flowers right throughout the summer and from the little sheltered harbour, the enchanting view of this unique place is certainly worth a photograph or two. One of the reasons that Clovelly has remained so unspoilt right into

Clovelly Harbour

the 21st century is that it has belonged to the Rous family since 1738 and they have ensured that it has remained free of such modern defacements as telegraph poles and other street furniture. Charles Kingsley lived and attended school here in the 1820s and the **Kingsley Exhibition** explores the novelist's links with the village. The **Fisherman's Cottage**, next door, provides an insight into what life was like in Clovelly at that time. The village's award-winning **Visitor Centre** covers the history of Clovelly and the surrounding area from as far back as 2000BC to the present day.

Combe Martin

Situated on the banks of the River Umber, Combe Martin is a popular seaside resort with a good sandy beach and some delightful little secluded bays. The village is also home to a remarkable architectural curiosity, **The Pack o' Cards Inn**, built in the early 18th century by Squire George Ley with the proceeds of a

particularly lucrative evening at the card table, represents a pack of cards with four decks, or floors, thirteen rooms and a total of 52 windows. The inside has not been forgotten either and there are many features that represent the cards in each suit. On the southern outskirts of the village is the **Combe Martin Wildlife and Dinosaur Park**.

Croyde

This is a lovely little seaside village renowned for its excellent family-friendly beach. Just to the northwest of Croyde lies **Baggy Point**, a headland, made of Devonian rock (so named because it was first identified in this county) and a popular nesting place for seabirds. To the northeast of Croyde lies the village of **Georgeham**, where Henry Williamson settled and wrote his famous novel published in 1928, *Tarka the Otter*. Although in later life Williamson moved to Norfolk, he is buried in Georgeham churchyard.

Dartmouth

One of England's principal ports for centuries, it was at Dartmouth, in the 12th century, that crusaders on both the second and third crusades mustered before sailing. Here, too, in the shelter of the harbour, Queen Elizabeth's men o' war lay in wait to see off stragglers from the Spanish Armada. In 1620, *The Mayflower* put in here for repair before sailing for Plymouth and then the New World. However, it

The Old Front

was centuries earlier that Alfred the Great developed Dartmouth as a strategic base. In 1373, Geoffrey Chaucer, as Inspector of Customs, visited the town. He is believed to have modelled the Shipman in his *Canterbury Tales* on the then Mayor of Dartmouth, John Hawley. An enterprising merchant and seafarer, Hawley was responsible for building the first **Dartmouth Castle,** the dramatically sited fortress that guards the entrance to the Dart estuary. Dartmouth's most famous building is undoubtedly the **Britannia Royal Naval College**, a sprawling red and white building, constructed between 1899 and 1905, which dominates the northern part of the town.

Dawlish

By the time that Brunel's Great Western Railway arrived here in 1846, the town was already well known as a fashionable resort. To the northeast of the town is **Dawlish Warren**, a sand spit that almost blocks the mouth of the River Exe. As well as the golf course here there is a Nature Reserve that is home to many species of flowering plant including the Jersey Lily, which cannot be found elsewhere on mainland Britain. Further north again, at **Starcross**, the last surviving relics of Brunel's **Atmospheric Railway** can be seen. The engineer had intended that the railway between Exeter and Totnes should be powered by a revolutionary new system incorporating a third rail. This would be a long vacuum chamber that would draw the carriages along by air pressure. Brunel never thought small, and his visionary plan also included the building of ten great

Italianate engine houses along the line. The project failed, due partly to a lack of funds and partly to the effects of rain, salt and hungry rats on the leather seals of the vacuum pipes.

Drewsteignton

A place of thatched cottages grouped, along with its medieval church, around a village square, Drewsteignton is a much photographed village. To the south can be found **Prestonbury Castle** and **Cranbrook Castle**, not castles but Iron Age hill forts, while to the southwest lies **Castle Drogo**, a granite structure that looks every inch a medieval castle although it is not.

Exeter

A lively and thriving city with a majestic cathedral, many fine old buildings and a wealth of excellent museums. After the Romans withdrew from the country, the city became a major ecclesiastical centre and, in AD 670, King Cenwealh founded an abbey on a site where the Cathedral now stands. A wonderful example of the Decorated style, the 300 foot long nave has stone piers rising some 60 feet and then fanning out into sweeping arches. Equally impressive is the west front, where a staggering display of over 60 sculptures, carved between 1327 and 1369, can be seen. In the High Street stands the remarkable **Guildhall**. Used as a town hall ever since it was built in 1330, it is one of the oldest municipal buildings in the country. As well as being an ecclesiastical centre, Exeter was also an important port and this is reflected in its dignified **Custom House** built in 1681. It now forms the centrepiece of the **Exeter Historic Quayside**, where the old warehouses have been converted into a fascinating complex of craft shops and cafés. Here, too, can be found the **Seahorse Nature Aquarium**, which is dedicated solely these beautiful, delicate little creatures. To the southwest of the city lies **Exeter Racecourse**, one of the most scenic in the country and one that is considered to be Britain's favourite holiday course.

Exmouth

Dubbed the 'Bath of the West', this was a place developed for the very top ech-

Quayside and Maritime Museum

elons of society. Lady Byron and Lady Nelson came here and stayed at lodgings in The Beacon, an elegant Georgian terrace overlooking the Madeira Walk and Esplanade. However, this early success hit a setback in the mid 19th century when Isambard Brunel routed his Great Western Railway down the other side of the Exe estuary. It was not until a branch line reach the resort in 1861 that business began to pick up again. From Exmouth, the **East Devon Way**, signposted by a foxglove,

Hartland Point

is a middle distance footpath of 40 miles that travels through the county to Lyme Regis just over the border in Dorset. On the northern outskirts of the town is one of the most unusual houses in Britain – **A La Ronde** – a unique 16-sided house, built in the late 18th century on the instructions of two widely travelled spinster cousins.

Hartland

The most striking building here is the parish **Church of St Nectan** to the west of the village centre. While the exterior, with its 128-foot high tower, is certainly impressive, it is the interior and the glorious 15th century, exquisitely carved screen that makes this church one of the most visited in the county. In the churchyard is the grave of Allen Lane, who revolutionised publishing in 1935 by his introduction of Penguin Books –

paperback novels that were sold at sixpence (2.5p) each.

To the west of the village lies **Hartland Abbey**, founded in 1157 and given by Henry VIII, at the time of the dissolution in the 16th century, to William Abbott, Sergeant of the Royal wine cellars. Housed in the abbey is a wonderful collection of paintings, porcelain and furniture, acquired by the family over generations and, in the former Servants' Hall is a unique exhibition of documents dating right back to 1160.

Hatherleigh

This medieval market town continues to hold a weekly market and is also popular with fishermen trying their luck on the River Torridge and its tributary.

A good place from which to begin an exploration of Hatherleigh is the **Tarka**

Country Information Point at **Hatherleigh Pottery**, where there are exhibits and displays detailing the life and countryside in and around this 1000-year-old town.

Holsworthy

This old market town just four miles from the Cornish border serves a large area of rural Devon and each Wednesday it comes alive as its traditional street market continues to be held. In July, the town plays host to the three-day long **St Peter's Fair**, an ancient event first held here in 1185. Holsworthy's most striking architectural features are the two Victorian viaducts that once carried the railway line through to Bude. Situated high above the southern outskirts of the town, they now form part of a footpath along the old track bed, and those making the climb will be rewarded with some stunning panoramic views.

Honiton

The unofficial capital of east Devon, Honiton is perhaps best known for the delicate Honiton lace, which is still sought after today. The arrival of machine-made lace in the late 18th century almost wiped out the industry in Honiton. But when Queen Victorian insisted on wearing hand-made Honiton lace on her wedding day, she established a new fashion for the lace that was to persist throughout the 19th century. The lace is still made here today, but on a much smaller scale. It can be bought from local shops and can be seen in **Allhallows Museum**, which houses a unique collection of traditional lace and puts on demonstrations of lace-making.

Ilfracombe

As with so many resorts, Ilfracombe developed in direct response to the early 19th century craze for sea bathing and seawater therapies. The **Tunnel Baths**, with their extravagant Doric facade, were opened in 1836, by which time a number of elegant residential terraces had been built on the hillside to the south of the old town. Adjacent to the **Ilfracombe Museum**, housed in the disused laundry of the now long-forgotten Ilfracombe Hotel, is the town's **Landmark Theatre,** a superb multi-purpose theatre and arts centre with a

Ilfracombe

café and a spacious display area. At nearby Hele Bay is the lovingly restored **Old Corn Mill and Pottery**; the mill, which dates from 15125, still produces flour, and in the pottery visitors can watch master potter Robin Gray at work producing his unique pieces.

Kenton

Founded in Saxon times, this picturesque village is famed for its glorious 14th century church whose tower, standing over 100 feet tall, is decorated with a wonderful assortment of ornate carvings. But it is **Powderham Castle**, to the east of the village, which brings people to this particular part of Devon. Set in one of the finest deer parks in Devon beside the River Exe, the castle has been the home of the Courtney family, the Earls of Devon, since 1390, although the present building dates mostly from the 18th century. Along with the breathtaking grand staircase and impressive marble hall, the castle is home to many family portraits, including some by the Devon-born painter Sir Joshua Reynolds, and a longcase clock by Stumbels of Totnes that plays a tune at four, eight and 12 o'clock.

Lydford

Though it may be hard to believe today, in Saxon times Lydford was one of just four royal boroughs in Devon, along with Exeter, Barnstaple and Totnes. What made Lydford so important was its strategic position on the River Lyd. In the 11th century, the Normans built a fortification here that was superseded a hundred years later by the present **Lydford Castle**. This austere stone fortress, now in the hands of English Heritage, served for decades as a court and prison for the independent tin miners of Dartmoor. To the southwest of the village, the valley of the River Lyd suddenly narrows to form the mile and a half long **Lydford Gorge**, one of Dartmoor's most spectacular natural features. A circular walk round the gorge begins high up before passing through the enchanting riverside scenery and past the thrilling **Devil's Cauldron**.

Okehampton

Close to Okehampton are Dartmoor's great peaks, **High Willhays** and **Yes Tor**, rising to over 2,000 feet and officially designated mountains. From Celtic times Okehampton has occupied an important position on the main route to and from Cornwall, and situated on the top of a wooden hill, dominating the surrounding valley of the River Okement, are the remains of **Okehampton Castle**. The largest medieval castle in Devon, it was dismantled on the orders of Henry VIII after the owner, the Earl of Devon, had been found guilty of treason, but the remains are an evocative, romantic sight.

Ottery St Mary

This small town is justly proud of its magnificent 14th century **Church of St Mary**, looking part cathedral and part Oxford college. The striking exterior is mirrored by the beautiful interior and

Church of St Mary

there are several medieval treasures including a 14th century astronomical clock, showing the moon and planets, that still functions with its original machinery.

Paignton

In the early Victorian era this was a little farming village, noted for its cider, but the two superb sandy beaches and the development of Torquay saw Paignton become a popular family holiday resort, complete with pier and promenade. One of the main attractions here is **Paignton Zoo**, set in beautiful botanic gardens and home to some 300 species of animals from around the world.

The **Paignton and Dartmouth Steam Railway** follows the coastline along the bottom of Tor Bay before travelling through the wooded slopes that border the Dart estuary to Kingswear. Here passengers alight and catch a ferry to Dartmouth. The locomotives and carriages all bear the chocolate and gold livery of Brunel's Great Western Railway and, on certain services, passengers can dine in luxurious Pullman style on the Riviera Belle Dining Train.

Plymouth

The most famous part of this historic city is undoubtedly **Plymouth Hoe**: it was on The Hoe, overlooking **Plymouth Sound**, on Friday 19th July 1588, that Sir Francis Drake was playing bowls when he was told of the approach of the Spanish Armada. In true British fashion, Drake completed his game before boarding the *Golden Hind* and sailing off to intercept the Spanish ships.

Plymouth's oldest quarter, the **Barbican,** is today a lively area of restaurants, pubs and an innovative small theatre, but it was once the main trading area of the town, where merchants exported wool and imported wine. Close by is **The Citadel**, a massive fortress, built as a defence against a seaborne invasion by Charles II. Near here is a reminder that Plymouth was the departure point for the Pilgrim Fathers who sailed off to a new life in Massachusetts. The **Mayflower Stone** stands at the point where they boarded their ship. A number of other interesting buildings from Plymouth's past, which survived the devastating bombing raids of World War II, can be seen in the Barbican district. The city is also home to **Jacka's Bakery,** which claims to be the oldest commercial bakery in the country and it is reputed to have supplied *The Mayflower* with ship's biscuits. Here, too, is the

Plymouth Hoe

Princetown

Situated at the heart of the Dartmoor, some 1,400 feet above sea level, Princetown is an isolated and bleak settlement surrounded by some spectacular scenery. It is notorious for its atrocious weather and is the home of one of the country's best-known and most forbidding prisons – **Dartmoor**. Princetown is also home to the National Park's **Moorland Visitors' Centre**, which contains some excellent and informative displays about the moor and a wide-ranging stock of books, maps and leaflets.

National Marine Aquarium, where state-of-the-art techniques allow visitors to travel through the oceans of the world to encounter brilliantly coloured fish, seahorses and even Caribbean sharks.

Postbridge

The village is, perhaps, best known for its **Clapper Bridge**, probably dating from the 13th century and the best preserved example of its kind in Devon. Spanning the East Dart River, a few yards down stream from the road bridge, the clapper bridge is a wonderful example of medieval minimalist construction with just three huge slabs of granite laid across solid stone piers. To the west of Postbridge are the ruins of **Powder Mills**, a 19th century gunpowder factory. The abundance of space was about the only safety feature at the factory, where the batches of powder were tested by firing a proving mortar that can still be seen near the cottages.

Salcombe

Sheltered from the prevailing west winds by steep hills, the town basks in one of the mildest micro-climates in England. Like many other small ports along the southwest coast, Salcombe developed its own special area of trading. While Dartmouth specialised in French and

Clapper Bridge

Spanish wine, clipper ships brought the first fruits of the West Indies' pineapple harvest and oranges from the Azores to Salcombe. Although all that traffic has now ceased, the harbour throngs with pleasure craft and the small fishing fleet operates from **Batson Creek**, a picturesque location where the fish quay is piled high with lobster creels. The town's seafaring history is interestingly displayed at the **Salcombe Maritime and Local History Museum**, housed in the old Customs House on the quayside.

Sidmouth

The village's spectacular position at the mouth of the River Sid, with its dramatic red cliffs and broad pebbly beach, assured its popularity with visitors and a grand esplanade was constructed lined with handsome Georgian houses. One of the town's early visitors was Jane Austen, who came here on holiday in 1801. In the 1830s Thackeray visited the town and during the Edwardian age Beatrix Potter was a visitor on several occasions. A stroll around the town reveals a wealth of attractive Georgian and early Victorian buildings and, surprisingly for a town of this size, Sidmouth has nearly 500 listed buildings.

Tavistock

This handsome old town is one of Devon's four stannary towns (a name that come from the Latin word for tin – stannum). These towns (the others are Ashburton, Chagford and Plympton) were the only places licensed to weigh and stamp the metal extracted from the moor. In the 1840s, Francis, the 7th Duke, used some of the family's profits from their copper mines to build the imposing **Guildhall** and several other civic buildings. One of the legacies of the ancient abbey is the annual three-day fair, granted its charter in 1105. It has evolved into the **Goose Fair**, a marvellous traditional street fair held each October. Tavistock was also permitted to hold a weekly market, which, 900 years later, still takes place every Friday in the Pannier Market, a building that was another gift to the town from the 7th Duke. A statue of the Duke stands in Bedford Square, and elsewhere in town in statue to Sir Francis Drake.

Teignmouth

There are two distinct sides to this town – the popular holiday resort and the working port – and these two parts seldom meet. On the coastal side of Teignmouth is the seaside resort, with its two-mile long sandy beach, promenade and pier, which draws many visitors throughout the year. On the northern bank of the River Teign, the working port is reached by a narrow channel with currents so fast and powerful that boats can only enter the harbour with a Trinity House pilot on board.

Tiverton

Tiverton is the only town of any size in the Exe valley and a strategic point on the river. In 1106, Henry I ordered the

Tiverton Castle

building of **Tiverton Castle**, around which the town began to develop and grow. Rebuilt and expanded over the years, the castle was besieged during the Civil War by the Parliamentarian General Fairfax who successfully took the stronghold in 1645. Later it was decreed that the castle should be destroyed beyond any use as a fortress and Cromwell's troops carried these instructions out to the letter leaving a mutilated but substantial structure with no defences.

A wealthy merchant, Peter Blundell, endowed Tiverton with a school. It was in the **Old Blundell's School** building of 1604 that the author RD Blackmore received his education. He later used the school as the setting for the first chapter of his novel *Lorna Doone*. Now a highly regarded public school, Blundell's moved, in 1880, from its original position beside Lowman Bridge to its present location on the edge of the town. On the southeastern outskirts of the town is a quay that marks the western end of the **Great Western Canal**. This was a branch of a rather grand scheme that proposed the building of a canal from Topsham to Taunton to link the Bristol and English Channels. Work began on the Tiverton to Lowdwells section in 1810 and finished just four years later, but no more work was carried out for 13 years, and plans for the rest of this ambitious project were scrapped. The completed section, never profitable and closed in 1869, was not allowed to deteriorate completely and has recently been re-opened as a country park with charming rural canalside walks.

A few miles north of Tiverton, up the Exe Valley, lies **Knightshayes Court**, a striking Victorian Gothic house with grand and opulent interiors, blending medieval romanticism with lavish Victorian decoration. The house is surrounded by extensive grounds that include a water-lily pond, topiary and rare shrubs.

Torquay

The undisputed premier resort of southwest England, Torquay enjoyed royal patronage from its early days. Edward VII came here on the royal yacht *Britannia*, which anchored in the bay, and each evening he would travel discreetly to the Imperial Hotel to his waiting mistress, Lily Langtry.

Torquay was the birthplace, in 1890, of Agatha Mary Clarissa Miller (later Agatha Christie), and one of the town's most popular attractions can be found in the Abbot's Tower at Torre Abbey which houses the **Agatha Christie Memorial Room** where a wonderfully personal collection of her memorabilia, donated by her daughter, is on display. At the **Torquay Museum**, there is an exhibition of photographs recording the life of Dame Agatha as well as a pictorial record of Torquay over the last 150 years. Among the museum's treasures are many items discovered at **Kents Cavern**, a complex of caves that were first excavated in the 1820s and from where an amazing collection of animals bones was extracted. Just to the north of the centre of Torquay is **Babbacombe Model Village** created by Tom Dobbins. As well as over 400 beautifully crafted models, with amusing names such as Shortback and Sydes for the barbers, the village also has delightful gardens, with 500 types of dwarf conifers, a model railway and an ornamental lake.

Totnes

The impressive remains of **Totnes Castle** include what is generally recognised to be the best preserved motte and bailey castle in Devon. Among the many exhibits in **Totnes Museum** is one honouring one of the town's most famous sons, Charles Babbage (1791-1871), whose analytical machine was the forerunner of the modern computer. On the quayside is **Totnes Motor Museum**, where a private collection of vintage, sports and racing cars covering some 80 years is on display. Many of the cars are still raced by the family who own them.

Westward Ho!

When, in 1855, Charles Kingsley's novel of Elizabethan derring-do was published it caught the rising tide of Victorian patriotism brought on by the on-going war in the Crimea and *Westward Ho!* became a great success. So much so that a company was formed to develop this spectacular site, with its rocky cliffs and two miles of sandy beach, and so the resort was created.

Now very much established as a bustling holiday resort, the village is also home to the unusual **Pot Walloping Festival** that takes place here every spring. Local people along with visitors join together to throw the pebbles, dislodged during the winter storms, back on to the famous ridge.

Widecombe in the Moor

Enjoying a delightful setting in the valley of the East Webburn River, Widecombe in the Moor is a very pleasant village with a grand old church that has been dubbed the **Cathedral of the Moors**. Dedicated to St Pancras, the church was built with funds raised by the tin miners of the 14th century. Though enlarged during the next two centuries, its massive 120-foot granite tower with the backdrop of the high moorland, remains its most impressive feature. Widecombe is most famous for its fair. Taking place each September, this jolly affair is known the world over from the song that tells of the adventures of Uncle Tom Cobleigh, his friends and the old grey mare on their way to attend the fair.

THE ANCHOR INN

LULTERBURN STREET, UGBOROUGH, DEVON PL21 0NG
TEL: 01752 892283 FAX: 01752 690722

Devon

Directions: From Plymouth take the A38 east to Ivybridge. From Ivybridge turn off the main road on to the B3213 and follow the signs to Ugborough.

The hillside village of Ugborough looks north over the main road to Ugborough Beacon and the southern reaches of Dartmoor. This is home to **The Anchor Inn**, a particularly pretty place with bench seating to the front and festooned with hanging baskets of flowers. Originally built as three cottages in the 14th century, the interior retains many traditional features such as the low oak-beamed ceilings, leaded windows and open fireplaces. Throughout, the atmosphere is cosy and friendly. As well as the lounge area, with its thatched bar, there is a separate restaurant, where one of the ceiling beams is adorned with a charming collection of bells in all shapes

and sizes.

Managed by Sheelagy Jeffreys, the inn is locally renowned for the excellent quality and range of dishes served here. The a la carte menu, served in either the bar or restaurant, is supplemented by an ever-changing specials board. The excellent cuisine has a distinctly international flavour, with French, Canadian, South American and Italian dishes rubbing shoulders with local Devon beef, ostrich, wild boar, alligator and bison, as well as tempting vegetarian meals. The wine list also provides an interesting selection from around the globe. There's also a good choice of real ales, lagers, ciders, wines, spirits, soft drinks, teas and coffees.

To the rear of the inn there are seven gorgeous self-contained cabine providing ideal accommodation for a peaceful and relaxing break.

🕐 Mon-Sun 10.30-15.00, 17.00-22.30

🍴 A la carte served in the bar and restaurant

💷 All major credit cards

🛏 7 double cabins all en suite and self-contained

🅿 Bench seating to the front, large car park

🎵 Occasional live music

❓ Dartmoor National Park (1 mile), Dartmoor Wildlife Park (6 miles), beaches (7 miles), walking, riding, sailing

THE AVON INN

AVONWICK, NEAR SOUTH BRENT, DEVON TQ10 9NB
TEL: 01634 73475

Directions: Main junction off the A38 to Avonwick

The Avon Inn takes its name from its location, in the charming village of Avonwick. This handsome and distinguished pub is open afternoons and evenings every day, offering a taste of genuine hospitality, excellent service and quality food and drink. This large and welcoming inn is cosy and comfortable inside.

The traditional décor includes brasses and prints of local scenes adorning the walls. Mark and Natasha Benfield and their friendly, helpful staff are enthusiastic about providing a warm welcome to all their guests. Drinks on tap include a range of real ales, together with a good complement of ciders, wines and spirits, soft drinks, teas and coffees. Meals can be enjoyed in the elegant restaurant or in the attractive garden.

The menus offer the best of traditional English fare with a Continental twist. The Sunday roast is delicious and gaining a well-deserved reputation for quality and value. Here in this corner of Devon, this attractive and cosy inn is well worth seeking out both for its relaxed ambience and for the excellent food and drink on offer.

- Mon-Sat 12.00-14.00, 18.00-21.30; Sun 12.00-14.30
- Lunchtime and evening menus; daily specials
- All major credit cards
- Car parking, beer garden, children's play area
- @ mbenfield@talk21.com
- ? Totnes, South Hams

BULLERS ARMS

7 MILL STREET, CHAGFORD, NEAR NEWTON ABBOT,
DEVON TQ13 8AW

Directions: From junction 31 on the M5, take the A38 and then the A382
towards Morehamptonstead. Passing through the town, continue for 3 miles
before turning left onto the B3192. Go into the village of Chagford, turn right at
the T-junction and the Bullers Arms is on the right.

At the heart of this charming and typical
Devon village, the **Bullers Arms** is a
very attractive inn dating back in parts
to the 1700s. The interior has been
sympathetically modernised over the
years, to effect a stylish and tasteful
result while retaining many original
features such as the ceiling beams and
large stone fireplace which enhance the
traditional feel of this welcoming inn.

The large beer garden to the rear is a
pleasant and secluded oasis of
tranquillity in which to enjoy a peaceful
drink or meal on fine days.

There are always four, Cask Marque
awarded real ales on tap, together with a
good selection of lagers, ciders, spirits
and soft drinks, and an extensive wine
list.

🕐 Mon-Thur 11.00-15.00, 17.00-
23.00; Fri-Sat 11.00-23.00; Sun
12.00-22.30

🍴 Bar meals and snacks, a la carte

💷 All major credit cards

🛏 1 double room, 2 twin rooms, all en
suite

🅿 Street parking, beer garden

🎵 Darts, chess

@ bullersarms@hotmail.com

❓ Dartmoor National Park, Castle
Drago (3 miles), Finch Foundry (6
miles) Hound Tor Medieval Village
(6 miles), walking, cycling, horse
riding, fishing, birdwatching

Licensees Alex and Karen offer all
their guests a warm welcome and
genuine hospitality, combined with
excellent service. Both trained with
major brewers and in London hotels.
Alex, originally from Australia, is head
chef and prepares a very good range of
home-made favourites. The tasty bar
meals and snacks are supplemented by a
splendid list of dishes that include not
only hearty traditional meals such as
steaks and fresh fish but also a range of
curries and vegetarian options. Children
have their own menu, so that all the
family can enjoy the delights of this
superior inn.

THE BULLERS ARMS

4 THE STRAND, BRIXHAM, DEVON TQ5 8EH
TEL: 01803 853329

Directions: From Paignton follow the coast road south to Brixham. The Bullers Arms is on the harbour front.

John Noblett at **The Bullers Arms** is a man who wants to give the public what it wants - and succeeds. Located at The Strand in Brixham overlooking the harbour and Sir Francis Drake's ship *The Golden Hind*, this fine pub has been tastefully refurbished to a high standard of comfort and quality.

There are two distinct bars: The Boat has a bar which has been built in the style of half a clinker-built boat and pew-type seating as well as the usual tables and chairs, a timber dado and open fireplace. This is a no-smoking area, while the main bar offers equally comfortable seating, an open fireplace and traditional décor, where smoking is permitted. There is also a large-screen tv and pool table in another area for those who like sport. John also offers live music all year round.

Both attractive bars offer the full range of beers, ciders, wines, spirits, real ales and guest ales, and soft drinks. At lunchtime, tempting bar meals and sandwiches are available, while in the evenings the menu is devoted to seafood, crab and steaks along with a range of daily specials, all home-cooked and home-prepared to order. Sunday lunch, justly popular with locals and visitors alike, consists of a choice of roasts complete with vegetables and all the trimmings.

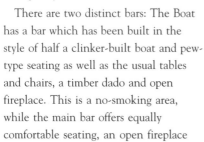

- Mon-Sat 11.00-23.00; Sun 12.00-22.30
- Lunchtime and evening menus; daily specials
- Car parking
- Occasional live music, pool, large-screen tv

THE BUTTERLEIGH INN

BUTTERLEIGH, COLLUMPTON, DEVON EX15 1PN
TEL: 01884 855407 FAX: 01884 855600

Devon

> **Directions:** Take junction 28 from M5 into Collumpton, turn right at the Manor
> Hotel crossroads, follow the signs to Butterleigh and The Butterleigh Inn lies in
> the village centre.

The Butterleigh Inn is a splendid 400-year-old traditional Devonshire cob building that has been a delightful country inn for many years. Purchased by David and Suzanne Reed in 2002, this is very much a friendly family pub and a labour of love – David's local for many years, when the opportunity came to buy it he gave up the farming life to become licensee. Both locals and visitors enjoy the relaxed and homely atmosphere. Full of character, the inn has several small, cosy bar areas, each of which offers the perfect place for customers to settle down and savour some fine hospitality, great food and drink and good

conversation. The feeling of time having stood still is enhanced by the flagstone floors, ancient fireplacecs and the interesting array of local memorabilia decorating the walls.

Customers can expect a good selection of real ales – Tawny and Barn Owl from the local Cotleigh Brewery and a changing guest ale – as well as keg beers, lagers and ciders, and a fine range of international wines from which to choose. Well known for the excellent food, Suzanne cooks up a range of tempting dishes, at lunchtime and dinner, including delicious daily specials. Booking is advised for Friday and Saturday evening and Sunday lunchtime at this justly popular and welcoming inn. On fine days, the excellent food and drink can be enjoyed outdoors in the attractive beer garden.

- 🕐 Mon-Thurs 12.00-14.30, 18.00-23.00; Fri 12.00-14.30, 17.00-23.00; Sat 11.00-23.00; Sun 12.00-15.00, 19.00-22.30
- 🍴 Lunchtime (12.00-14.30) and evening (19.00-21.45) menus; daily specials
- £ All major credit cards
- 🅿 Beer garden, children under 14 welcome lunchtimes, dogs welcome
- 🎵 Darts, cribbage, cards, shove ha'penny, chess, dominoes
- @ www.thebutterleighinn.co.uk
- ❓ Bickleigh Castle and Bickleigh Mill Visitor Centre (3 miles), Tiverton (3 miles), Fursdon (4 miles)

CARPENTERS ARMS

ILSINGTON, NEWTON ABBOT, DEVON TQ13 9RG

TEL: 01364 661215

Devon

Directions: Take the A38 to the Drum Bridges roundabout, taking the turn-off to Ilsington continue for approx 5 mins. Carpenters Arms is situated behind the Church

The picturesque Dartmoor village of Ilsington, birthplace of the famed Jacobean playwright John Ford (1586-1639), stands some 500 feet up on the edge of Dartmoor, surrounded by woodland. It boasts an impressive medieval church with some fine carvings and a lovely old traditional inn, **The Carpenters Arms**, which opened as a simple alehouse in the early 19th century.

The building itself is much older than that, however, as the ancient dark beams attest. Adorned with gleaming horse brasses, other traditional features include an open log fire. The pub is run by Julie Southcombe, who has been here since 2002; she has long experience in the trade and brings this expertise to bear on providing an excellent standard of service and friendly hospitality to all her guests. She stocks a good range of reals ales, together with lagers, ciders, wines and a selection of spirits, soft drinks, teas and coffees. The lunchtime and evening menus offer a tempting selection of snacks and meals. Guests can enjoy their relaxing drink or meal anywhere throughout the inn, hough there's a special area for families with children. For parties of six or more, booking is requested.

Central to village life, several local football and darts teams meet here regularly, and the pub hosts regular theme nights when food of a particular place, region or style takes centre-stage.

- Mon-Sat 12.00-15.00, 18.00-23.00; Sun 12.00-15.00, 19.00-22.30
- Bar snacks to a la carte; lunchtime and evening menus; daily specials
- Car parking, beer garden
- Quiz nights, theme nights, darts
- Bovey Tracey (3 miles), Haytor Rocks (2 miles)

THE CHICHESTER ARMS

28 PILTON STREET, BARNSTAPLE, DEVON EX31 1PJ
TEL: 01271 375285

Devon

Directions: From Barnstaple A39 (north) left at Pilton Park, sharp right to Pilton Street. From Ilfracombe A361 (south), left at Fairview Junction 200yds sharp left to Pilton Street.

Located down a quiet street a quarter-mile from the town centre in Pilton, a neighbourhood which retains an exclusive 'village' feel within the town, **The Chichester Arms** presents a delightful face to the world: pristine and festooned with flowers, the gracious 18th-century exterior hints at the welcome waiting here. Inside, this welcome is confirmed: comfortably and handsomely furnished and decorated, with many traditional features, this is just the place to enjoy a quiet drink or delicious meal in friendly, relaxed surroundings.

From snacks to a la carte, and from morning coffees and cream teas to lunch

and evening meals, the tempting food on offer include sandwiches, burgers, grills, fish, fowl, beef and pork dishes and vegetarian options, all expertly prepared using the freshest local ingredients to create a range of both traditional and more innovative dishes. The changing daily specials are well worth sampling, while the Sunday lunches are justly famous.

Run by Christopher Hewitt, accompanied by his friendly, helpful staff, the pub attracts a mature and discerning clientele. Guests can be assured of finding a good choice of well-kept ales here, along with draught lagers, a good wine list, spirits, ciders, soft drinks, teas and coffees.

This attractive pub is well worth seeking out.

- ⏰ Mon-Thur 12.00-15.00, 17.00-23.00; Fri-Sat 11.00-23.00; Sun 12.00-22.30
- 🍴 Bar snacks to a la carte and speciality buffets
- 💷 All major credit cards
- 🅿 Beer garden, parking in Street or Fairview carpark
- 🎵 Quiz nights (Wed), charity draws (Fri), skittles, darts, pool, euchre, shove ha'penny, party bookings
- ❓ Historical ancient priory church, pottery & ceramics, 5 mins walk from Tarka Cycleway and town centre

THE CHURCH HOUSE INN

RATTERY, NEAR TOTNES, DEVON TQ10 9LD
TEL: 01364 642220 FAX: 01364 642220

Directions: From Exeter take the A38 south towards Plymouth. One mile after Dean Prior take the minor road to the left, signposted Rattery, and The Church House Inn can be found approximately 1 mile away.

The Church House Inn, a listed building, dates back to 1028 and is one of Englands most historic and Devons oldest Inn. Originally a home to the monks today its proud owner is Ray Hardy, who together with his friendly and conscientious staff offer genuine hospitality to all their guests, locals and visitors alike.

This splendid free house, as befits a venerable building of this age, has open log fires and sturdy oak beams, and plenty of cosy nooks and crannies. Those interested in history will enjoy a look at the list of local vicars displayed on one wall. Opening for morning coffee, the inn also stocks a good range of real ales (always three at least), lagers and spirits, and a good cellar of wines from around the world.

The superb menu of traditional English fare offers everything from snacks, light meals and sandwiches to full a la carte in the spacious and elegant restaurant. Daily specials complement guests' range of delicious choices. There's something here to suit everyone's tastes, and to be enjoyed in a truly relaxing and welcoming atmosphere.

- ⏱ Mon-Thur 11.00-14.30, 18.00-23.00; Fri-Sat 11.00-23.00; Sun 12.00-22.30. Seasonal adjustments to all day opening times stated

- 🍴 Bar meals and snacks to a la carte, lunchtime and evening; daily specials

- 💷 All major credit cards

- 🅿 Outside terrace and garden with seating, dining room also available for private functions. Children welcome; pets welcome

- ❓ Dartington Crystal and Cider Press Centre (3 miles), South Devon Railway (3 miles), Totnes (4 miles), walking, birdwatching, sailing

THE CRICKET INN

BEESANDS, KINGSBRIDGE, DEVON TQ7 2EN
TEL: 01548 580215

Directions: From Kingsbridge take the A379 towards Dartmouth and at Chillington turn right for Beesands

Stop and ask a local on your way to **The Cricket Inn**, and you'll be told it's the place to find 'the best seafood on the coast'.

Rachel Simon and Nigel Heath are your friendly hosts at this distinguished inn. Famed for generations for its crab sandwiches and other seafood specialities, the pub had fallen into disrepair when Rachel and Nigel rescued it in 2001 and undertook careful renovations and refurbishment. Today it is comfortable and welcoming, offering excellent en suite accommodation complete with double portions of everything at breakfast.

The seafood could hardly be fresher – it practically jumps over the sea wall and straight into the frying pan! The famous crab sandwiches remain on the menu, complemented by sweet scallops and also a range of favourites including steaks and the hearty traditional Sunday roast. Breakfast, lunch or dinner, guests can be assured of the best and freshest home-cooked dishes.

The inn is decorated with old maps, charts and local photographs, dating back to the late 1800s. A centre of village life, the inn has a horseshoe-shaped bar with the pub on one side and the restaurant on the other, and carries a full selection of real ales, lagers, ciders, wines and spirits.

- 🍴 Bar snacks to a la carte; daily specials
- £ All major credit cards
- 🛏 En suite B&B
- Ⓟ Car parking, garden
- 🎵 Games, darts, pool table
- @ tbc/ www.thecricketinn.co.uk

DOG & DONKEY

24 KNOWLE VILLAGE, BUDLEIGH SALTERTON, DEVON EX9 6AL

TEL: 01395 442021

Directions: Exeter to Budleigh Salterton, turn left at Knowle Village. The Dog & Donkey is 150 yards further on the right-hand side

At the start of the new millennium, Ian and Yvonne McFarlane took over as new owners of **The Dog & Donkey** and decided that locals and visitors alike deserved something more than just a drinking pub. They have introduced accommodation and food, and have really turned this inn into something special.

The accommodation on offer at present comprises two rooms, one with a large balcony, both commanding pleasant views and boasting all the facilities and amenities one could ask for. Ian and Yvonne are planning to add more rooms as time goes on.

The food, like the drink on offer, is very good and sourced locally. The Sunday lunch has become an institution and the pub's function room, which seats 100, is always full for this weekly treat. Through the week most diners choose to take their meals in the intimate, charming dining room or in the bar itself. The menu includes steaks, ham, chicken, lamb, local seafood and vegetarian dishes, while there are also daily blackboard specials. Food can be accompanied with wines chosen to complement the food or one of the full range of beers, spirits or soft drinks available. Bass is probably the most popular real ale here, though there are a range of ever-changing guest ales on offer.

Ian is a qualified chef, so all the dishes are expertly prepared and presented.

Among the many other features that recommend this fine inn are the handsome, cosy interior and relaxed, welcoming atmosphere.

- Mon-Fri 11.00-14.30, 18.00-23.00; Sat 11.00-15.00, 18.00-23.00; Sun 12.00-15.00, 19.00-22.30
- Lunchtime and evening menus; daily specials
- 2 rooms
- Car parking, beer garden
- Music Wednesday nights, Games, skittles, pool table
- Donkey Sanctuary, Bicton Gardens

WINSHAM ROAD, KNOWLE, NEAR BRAUNTON, DEVON EX33 2LW
TEL: 01271 812166 FAX: 01271 816088

Directions: From junction 27 on the M5 take the A361 to Barnstaple and continue on this road towards Ilfracombe. Ebrington Arms can be found by turning right in the village of Knowle into Winsham Road, 2 miles after passing through Braunton.

Ebrington Arms is a charming village Freehouse serving real ales, fine wines and an extensive bar menu – seven days a week. This delightful inn has been tastefully extended over the years to increase its comfort and spaciousness, though much of the original 18th-century building remains. The cosy snug bar is well frequented by regulars, while there is also a comfortable lounge bar and a separate restaurant. The cellar at Ebrington Arms is well stocked and, apart from the three real ales on tap and the usual beers and lagers, there is a choice of 15 malt whiskies and an

extensive wine list.

The bar menu offers a tasty range of superb homecooked hot and cold dishes, while the magnificent evening a la carte menu is served in the intimate restaurant. In fine weather, the attractive beer garden is the place to relax wth a drink or meal. The house speciality is fish and mouthwatering seafood and fish dishes are complemented by an ever-changing list of imaginative daily specials, expertly prepared by the inn's chef. Becoming increasingly well known for their excellent menus, landlords Phil and Dee Lurcook have certainly put their years of experience in the hotel trade to good use here. A charming place to find that will definitely satisfy the whole family, Ebrington Arms is well worth a visit.

- Mon-Sat 12.00-15.00, 16.00-23.00; Sun 12.00-15.00, 19.00-23.00
- Bar meals and snacks. A la carte
- Visa, Mastercard, Delta, Switch, Amex, Diners
- Children's play area, car parking, functions catered for
- Traditional pub games, skittles, pool table
- ebringtonarms@aol.com
- Marwood Hill 3 miles, Braunton Burrows Nature Reserve 4 miles, Ilfracombe 6 miles, beach 4 miles, Barnstaple 7 miles, walking, fishing, bird watching

THE FOXHOUND INN

KINGSBRIDGE ROAD, BRIXTON, DEVON PL8 2AH
TEL: 01752 880271 FAX: 01752 881974

Directions: A379 Kingsbridge Road from Plymouth

Chris and Jean Joseph have since April 2002 taken over as licensees of **The Foxhound Inn** and, complemented by Carol Cocklin as manager and her husband Dan as chef, this charming establishment has moved forward in leaps and bounds.

The exterior is stonebuilt and whitewashed, impressive and wecloming. Established as a pub in the late 18th century, it has offered warm hospitality to locals and visitors alike every since.

The interior is comfortable and cosy, with traditional features such as exposed beams and open fires. There's a nautical décor here, in both the public bar and the lounge, and a separate non-smoking dining room. There are five cask ales on offer at all times and a full range of beers, wines, ciders and spirits, together with soft drinks, teas and coffees.

The excellent drink is complemented by a fine menu of bar snacks and full meals created using local fresh seafood, specials such as steaks, chicken and lamb dishes, as well as vegetarian options.

All this, together with the charming surroundings, make this superb inn a welcome break for the weary traveller or tourist, a place to be included on any visit to the area.

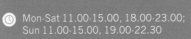

- Mon-Sat 11.00-15.00, 18.00-23.00; Sun 11.00-15.00, 19.00-22.30
- Lunchtime and evening menus; daily specials
- £ Visa, Access, Delta, Switch, Mastercard
- Car parking
- @ Occasional live entertainment
- ? Kitley Caves, Plymouth, Newton Ferris, yachting

THE GEORGE INN

BLACKAWTON, TOTNES, DEVON TQ9 7BG
TEL:01803 712342

Directions: Off the A3881 Dartmouth-Totnes Road

Vic Hall, co-licensee of **The George Inn** in Blackawton, was educated locally but moved away for some years to work elsewhere. When he met Ruth Coe, they often came here on holidays, and a few years ago bought some cottages and made them self-catering accommodation. When the village pub came up for sale they bought it and successfully maintaining it as a classic local pub. No fruit machines, no jukeboxes, just good wholesome food, real ales, great accommodation and excellent company. The true heart of the village, this Free House offers an extensive and varied menu, as well as seasonal and local fare on the daily specials board in the lounge bar. Guests with special dietary

requirements are happily catered for. All dishes are freshly cooked to order – good food, not fast food, is the order of the day here! Appetites large and small are also happily accommodated, with extra portions available free on request. A brief sample of the menu includes jumbo mussels, chicken skillets, home-cooked classics such as liver, bacon, onions and gravy, and meat pies, as well as a good range of tempting vegetarian dishes. There are always four real ales on tap, as well as Belgian beers, two local ciders, lagers, spirits and soft drinks.

The lovely beer garden commands excellent views down the valley towards the sea, and is just the place to enjoy an al fresco meal or drink on fine days. The interior is comfortable and cosy, with attractive furnishings and a relaxed, homely feel. The Gallery area of the pub features the work of local artists.

- 🕐 Mon 18.30-23.00; Tues-Sat 12.00-14.30, 18.30-23.00; Sun 12.00-15.00, 18.30-22.30
- 🍴 Lunchtime and evening menus; daily specials
- 💷 Delta, Switch, Visa, Mastercard
- 🛏 4 rooms (twins and doubles) en suite B&B; self-catering cottages
- 🅿 Car parking, beer garden
- 🎵 Monthly jazz nights
- @ george@barncourt.com, www.barncourt.com

THE GEORGE INN

CHARDSTOCK, AXMINSTER, DEVON EX13 7BX
TEL: 01460 220241

Directions: Off the A358 between Chard and Axminster

Resembling a fairytale cottage, **The George Inn** is a beautiful thatched stonebuilt inn festooned with window-boxes. Potted plants and traditional wooden picnic tables dot the front patio area, while the interior boasts numerous nooks and crannies with settles and other supremely comfortable seating. Dating back over 700 years, the inn began life as the parish house serving the local church. A close look at the stone window frames in the snug reveals graffiti written in 1648! The pub also boasts at least one resident ghost.

Here amid these charming surroundings, guests come to enjoy the excellent home-cooked food and excellent drink. There are two house chefs, both of international standing, and they create a wonderful menu of everything from lobster and salmon Thai style through pan-fried chilli chicken, roasted fillet of beef and glazed rack of lamb to crisp fresh salads and vegetarian choices such as a wild mushroom millefeuille and spinach and ricotta tortellini.

To wash down your meal there are always three real ales on tap, together with a good wine list and a selection of lagers, ciders, spirits, soft drinks, teas and coffees.

For those wishing to linger in the area – and there are plenty of sights and attractions in the region – the inn also offers very cosy and comfortable accommodation.

- Mon-Sat 12.00-14.30, 18.00-23.00; Sun 12.00-15.00, 19.00-22.30
- Lunchtime and evening menus; daily specials
- All major credit cards
- 4 rooms (twins and doubles) en suite B&B
- Car parking, beer garden
- Skittles, darts, pool table
- Axminster, Lyme Regis, Sidmouth, Exeter, Honiton

THE GEORGE INN

191 RIDGEWAY, PLYMPTON, NEAR PLYMOUTH,
DEVON PL7 2HJ
TEL: 01752 336623

Directions: A38 Expressway – off to Plympton town centre; The George is found just before the shopping centre

The George Inn is a delightful 18th-century coaching inn. This thriving, bustling local for all ages offers a warm and friendly atmosphere amid very pleasant traditional surroundings. From the clapboard exterior to the ceiling friezes, pannelled walls and open fires, there's a wealth of traditional features that add to the relaxed and comfortable ambience.

The range of delicious home-cooked food includes everything from snacks to steaks and chicken, seafood and vegetarian dishes, complemented by the daily specials. Tuesday nights are Curry

Night. Meals can be enjoyed in the dedicated Family Room or in the main bar. Three different CAMRA-recommended real ales are served here, along with a good choice of lagers, ciders, wines, spirits, soft drinks and tea and coffee.

Upstairs there's a fine function room that seats up to 100 people. With its own bar and dancing area, bookings of over 30 are free when taking one of our buffets. The George can provide a range of buffets from which to choose.

Known as Plympton's premier eating house, this excellent pubic house and restaurant is run by Bill and Elaine Goodwin. They've been here since 2000 and take pride in providing all their guests with warm hospitality and great service, to accompany the fine food and drink.

- 🕐 Mon-Sat 11.00-23.00; Sun 12.00-22.30. Food serving times: Mon 12.00-14.30, 18.00-20.00; Tues-Sat 12.00-14.30, 18.00-20.30; Sun 12.00-15.30
- 🍴 Lunchtime and evening menus; daily specials
- 💷 All major credit cards
- 🅿 Car parking
- 🎵 Live music Fridays and Saturdays; free jukebox; big-screen live football
- @ enquiries@thegeorgeinn.org; www.thegeorgeinn.org
- ❓ Plymouth; Stag Lodge Country

HALFWAY INN

SIDMOUTH ROAD, AYLESBEARE, NR EXETER, DEVON EX5 2JP
TEL: 01395 232273 FAX: 01395 232273

Directions: On A3052 Exeter to Sidmouth road.

Personal service and comfortable accommodation, great food and drink and a warm welcome – **Halfway Inn** has it all. Owner Brian Ewing is a friendly and conscientious host who always ensures his guests have everything they

need. He is also a chef, and together with manager Ian Roberts, who is also a chef, and additional chefs in the kitchen, he offers an excellent and varied menu of steaks (a speciality), chicken, duck, lamb, seafood and vegetarian dishes, as well as daily specials. Both at lunch and dinner time there's a full range of choices, from light meals to elaborate and hearty dishes.

To accompany the meal, or have on their own, there's a full range of local and international beers, wines and spirits, ciders and real ales, soft drinks, teas and coffees. Spending the night here is another treat, as each of the four guest bedrooms is supremely comfortable and well-appointed. Guests wake to a delicious home-cooked breakfast, just the thing to set them up for a day's touring. Brian has chosen the menu and staff with an eye towards quality, service and providing real home comforts. More a restaurant offering drink and accommodation than your average pub, this delightful hidden place is well worth seeking out. Locals and visitors alike return again and again to sample the excellent food, drink and hospitality.

- Mon-Sat 11.00-23.00; Sun 12.00-22.30
- Lunchtime and evening menus; daily specials
- Visa, Access, Switch, Delta, Mastercard
- 4 rooms en suite
- Car parking, beer garden

JOHNNY'S BAR

36 MILL STREET, BIDEFORD, DEVON EX39 2JJ
TEL: 01237 421105

Directions: North Devon link road from junction 29 of the M5 to Bideford town centre

A labour of love brought **Johnny's Bar** in Bideford back from the brink of ruin. This distinctive establishment has been tastefully and thoroughly converted and refurbished from its original shell up, and is now a sophisticated venue attracting a lively and friendly

clientele. This welcoming pub is pristine and stylish throughout, from its bright frontage to its charming interior. Inside, blonde wood flooring, gracious décor, chrome fixtures and fittings and very comfortable seating enhance the pleasant ambience.

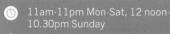

- 🕐 11am-11pm Mon-Sat, 12 noon-10.30pm Sunday
- 🍽 Bar meals and a la carte
- 💷 All major credit cards
- 🅿 Parking
- ❓ Bideford museums, markets, shopping, Saunton Sands, Barnstaple, beaches, golf, walking, bird watching

The bar offers an excellent range of bottled beers and juices, ciders, spirits and soft drinks, and boasts an impressive wine list, with French, Chilean and Australian vintages heading the list.

To the rear there is a split-level dining area, where guests can enjoy a selection of expertly prepared and presented dishes. The accent is on continental/international fare.

John and Sue Taylor, who are also the licencees at The Tavern in the Port in Bideford, together with their friendly staff make any visit here a very pleasant experience. This excellent pub is well worth seeking out.

KINGS ARMS

FORE STREET, OTTERTON, DEVON EX9 7HB
TEL: 01395 568416   FAX: 01395 568425

Directions: Right in the heart of Otterton

John and Katie Collingwood have their customers' comfort and happiness in mind in everything they offer at the **Kings Arms** in Otterton.

The impressive whitewashed exterior includes not just this handsome pub but also a 24-hour shop (amusingly named 'Arkwright's' as in the popular old television programme, *Open All Hours*) and post office.

The menus at this welcoming inn range from light snacks such as ploughman's, burgers and jacket potatoes to ever-changing dinner options and daily specials including scampi, plaice, steaks, curries and more, all home-cooked and using the freshest local ingredients.

John and Katie insist on their ales being in perfect condition; the range includes local and imported beers, wines and spirits with an excellent selection of locally produced real ales, including, of course, Otter ale. There are also soft drinks, teas and coffees to accompany the fine food on offer.

There is luxurious accommodation available at very affordable prices in one of nine well-appointed, comfortable and inviting guest bedrooms, designed to incorporate all amenities and facilities guests have come to expect.

This truly hidden place is well worth seeking out and calling back at time after time.

- Mon-Sat 11.00-23.00; Sun 12.00-22.30
- Lunchtime and evening menus; daily specials
- Visa, Access, Delta, Switch, Mastercard
- 9 rooms en suite B&B
- Car parking, shop and post office on site
- Regular live music
- @ kings@transuk.co.uk; www.kingsarmsotterton.com
- Bicton Park

KINGS ARMS INN

STOCKLAND, HONITON, DEVON EX14 9BS
TEL: 01404 881361 FAX: 01404 881732

> **Directions:** Between the A303 and A35 to the east of Honiton

The **Kings Arms Inn** is a traditional pub in the best sense of the word. From its thatched and whitewashed exterior to the comfortable and cosy interior which comprises The Farmers Bar and the Cotley Restaurant Bar, this inn is the perfect place to enjoy the great food and drink on offer. In fine weather locals and visitors can enjoy their meal or pint in the attractive and sun-filled garden/patio area.

The ambience is warm and welcoming throughout this charming inn, and the superb choices on the menu include all the usual traditional hearty favourites, expertly prepared and presented using the freshest local ingredients.

Four real ales are available at all times, together with a good range of lagers, ciders, spirits and soft drinks. The comprehensive wine list features 100 different vintages from all over the globe.

Run since 1987 by Paul Diviani, Heinz Kiefer and John O'Leary who, together with their helpful, friendly staff, meet customers' every requirement, this attractive inn offers a warm welcome, genuine hospitality and great food and drink in convivial surroundings to all comers.

There's also accommodation available for guests wishing to linger in this delightful part of the country, with three guest bedrooms (one twin and two doubles), all en suite and very comfortably furnished and decorated.

- 🕐 Mon-Sat 12.00-15.00, 18.30-23.00; Sun 12.00-15.00, 18.30-22.30
- 🍽 Lunchtime and evening menus
- £ All major credit cards
- 🛏 3 rooms (twin and doubles) en suite B&B
- Ⓟ Car parking, beer garden
- 🎵 Skittles, darts, live music at weekends and Bank Holidays
- @ info@kingsarms.net, www.kingsarms.net
- ❓ Honiton, Axminster, Exeter

THE KINGS ARMS HOTEL

93 FORE STREET, KINGSBRIDGE, DEVON TQ7 1AB
TEL: 01548 852071 FAX: 01548 852799

Directions: Take the A381 from Totnes or the A379 from Plymouth

The James family took over at **The Kings Arms Hotel** in August 2002. Graham, his wife Ros, son Darren, daughter Leanne and her fiance Matthew, who is the chef, have already made improvements at this well-established hotel, as they share a belief in personal service and quality. The excellent accommodation consists of 12 rooms, most with four-poster beds, all en suite and supremely comfortable, with a feel of yesteryear when hotel rooms were spacious and distinctive.

This former coaching inn dates back to 1776 and features exposed beams, timber panelling and a large open fireplace in the main bar – as well as not just one but two resident ghosts.

There's an excellent range of local and imported beverages available in the bar. Along with three real ales – Speckled Hen, Bass and a changing guest ale –

there are lagers, ciders, spirits, soft drinks and a good selection of wines from the world over. Chef Matthew insists on using only the freshest local ingredients and so the menu offers an impressive and tempting array of seasonal specialities, with an emphasis on seafood and steaks on the dinner menu. The bar food on offer at lunchtime is all guests would expect of a quality country hotel. Ideal for the businessperson or holiday-maker alike, the James family make all their guests feel most welcome.

- 11.00-23.00
- Lunchtime and evening menus; daily specials
- All major credit cards
- 12 en suite rooms
- Car parking, garden

KINGSLEY INN

FORE STREET, NORTHAM, BIDEFORD, DEVON EX39 1AW
TEL: 01237 474221

Directions: On the main road, sign posted from Bideford to Northam, Kingsley Inn is on the left.

Totally refurbished throughout to provide a happy mix of traditional features and modern comforts, **Kingsley Inn**, located in the handsome village of Northam, is well worth seeking out.

Run by Tony and Sue Wilson, this welcoming inn enjoys a reputation for quality and service. Tony, Sue and their friendly, conscientious staff make every guest feel welcome. Tony is a local man who is happy to provide information to visitors on local sights and attractions.

To quench your thirst, the pub has two real ales and a changing guest ale, as well as a good complement of lagers, ciders, wines, spirits, soft drinks, teas and coffees.

Tony is a gifted cook and the cuisine has a distinctly international flavour, with dishes ranging from traditional favourites to more innovative modern creations. Meals such as lobster tails, vegetable lasagne, steaks, lamb and more are freshly prepared. The changing daily specials will often include tempting choices such as Cumberland sausage and plaice stuffed with prawns. There is also a children's menu. The Sunday roast is justly popular - booking recommended.

Outside there's a very attractive garden with patio and flourishing floral borders – just the place to enjoy a quiet drink or delicious snack or meal.

- Mon-Sat 11.00-23.00; Sun 12.00-23.00
- Bar snacks and meals, a la carte
- All major credit cards
- Beer garden, car parking
- Live music Sunday afternoons, pool table, darts
- Bideford, Appledore, Barnstaple, Saunton

Devon

THE NEW INN

SAMPFORD COURTENAY,NEAR OKEHAMPTON,DEVON EX20 2TB
TEL: 01837 82247   FAX: 01837 89211

Directions: Off **A30** towards the Moor and Moretonhampstead, turn right at Whiddon Down to North Tawton, at cross roads turn left follow signs to Hatherliegh, pub is on right as you pass through Sampford Courtenay.

The New Inn at Sampford Courtenay is well worth seeking out. This distinguished coaching inn is estimated to be some 500 years old, and is a happy marriage of traditional features and modern refurbishment. The exterior is whitewashed and cheery, with a traditional thatched roof. The interior is warm and welcoming, painted in attractive pastels, with low, heavily beamed ceilings (carved with witty ditties), open fires and a cosy mixture of sofas and tables and chairs. Tenants Stephen and Lynn Tickner, who are friendly and enthusiastic hosts, ensure that the atmosphere at this marvellous inn is

always relaxed and welcoming.

The chef is highly and justly acclaimed for his skills. The lunch menu offers a range of fresh-cut granary sandwiches and snacks, while the dinner menu presents a tempting selection of expertly prepared and presented dishes, from favourites such as steak and ale pudding and fresh local sausages to chargrilled Cajun chicken salad and spinach, tomato and mozzarella pudding.

Real ales, straigh from the cask, lagers, ciders, soft drinks, teas and coffees are available at this excellent inn, which also prides itself on its superb wine list.

For a taste of genuine Devon hospitality, do not miss this superb inn. Families and children are always welcome.

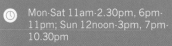

- 🕐 Mon-Sat 11am-2.30pm, 6pm-11pm; Sun 12noon-3pm, 7pm-10.30pm
- 🍴 Bar meals and snacks, a la carte, dining room
- £ All major credit cards
- 🅿 Garden, car parking, play area. Children welcome, Dogs welcome.
- @ stevetickner1@hotmail.com

THE OLDE PLOUGH INN

FORE STREET, BERE FERRERS, DEVON PL20 7JG
TEL: 01822 840358

Directions: From Tavistock follow directions to Bere Alston then turn off to Bere Ferrers just before village, follow road until you see pub on the right.

Just 100 yards from the River Tavy, here in Bere Ferrers which is set between the River Tamar and the River Tavy, **The Olde Plough Inn** is a small and pristine inn. Painted in a pale buff with red doors and windows and festooned with hanging baskets, it presents a welcoming face to the world. The inside

is no less charming, with exposed stonework walls, beamed ceilings, and open fireplace and a cosy, intimate ambience.

Dating back to the 1600s, it was once three cottages and has had a varied history, becoming a pub in 1857. Adrian

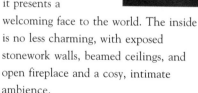

- 🕐 Mon-Sat 12.00-15.00,19.00-23.30. Sunday 12.00-15.00, 19.00-22.30
- 🍴 Lunchtime and evening menus; daily specials
- 💷 All major credit cards
- Ⓟ Car parking, beer garden
- 🎵 Quiz nights, darts, euchre

and Jools Keightley are the friendly and considerate hosts, who offer all their guests a warm welcome. Popular with locals and visitors alike, this relaxed pub is well-known for the quality of the food. Traditional favourites such as fishcakes and steak and ale pie share the menu with chicken curry and pate. All are home-cooked and home-prepared to order.

And to drink? A good range of beers, including two real ales and a changing guest ale, lagers, ciders, wines, spirits, soft drinks, teas and coffees. The charming beer garden is filled with urns and tubs of flowers, and offers a lovely riverside view.

THE OLD UNION INN

STIBB CROSS, TORRINGTON, DEVON EX38 8LH

TEL: 01805 601253/601158 FAX: 01805 601158

Directions: From Bideford take the A386 then the A388 towards Holsworthy. The Old Union Inn lies on the A388 at the crossroads with the B3227.

The Old Union Inn is a large and attractive pub dating back to the 1600s. Full of character and charm, the inn occupies pride of place in the centre of the village. This typically attractive north Devonshire pub has lost none of its age-old feel over the years, and today's guests can enjoy the warmth of the inglenook fireplace just as people have over the last few centuries. Cosy and comfortable whatever the time of year, the pub walls are decorated with all manner of interesting and unusual memorabilia – prints and photographs of local scenes, and a wealth of brassware and copperware - sure to encourage much conversation.

The pub is owned and personally run by Ray and June Oliver and their son, Sam. All have the happy knack of making people feel instantly at ease.

As well as the excellent selection of real ales, key beers, stouts, lagers and spirits served from the bar, The Old Union also offers customers a delicious menu of home-made bar snacks and meals. All cooked to order – and perfection – the pies in particular are a house speciality well worth taking time over. Mouth-watering traditional puddings are also on the menu. A place for good conversation, as well as good food, drink and hospitality, those looking for a traditional inn need look no further.

- Summer - Mon-Sun 12.00-23.00; Winter – Mon-Sun 12.00-15.00, 17.00-23.00
- Bar meals and snacks all day
- All major credit cards
- 4 rooms en suite
- Car parking, beer garden, children's play area, dogs welcome
- Darts, bar billiards, quiz nights, large-screen satellite TV
- fishing, shooting, walking, North Devon coast 8 miles

PICKWICK INN

ST ANN'S CHAPEL, BIGBURY-ON-SEA, DEVON
TEL: 01548 810241   FAX: 01548 810241

Directions: Take the A379 Plymouth to Kingsbridge road and the Inn is on the B3392 road to Bigbury On Sea.

Pickwick Inn is a charming family-run pub in the capable hands of Tony Bell and his son Jonathan, and offers everything guests could want: excellent accommodation and good food and drink. More a restaurant which offers accommodation and drink than a pub that offers food, this convivial place is worth seeking out.

There are four guest bedrooms (three standard and one family room), all attractively and comfortably furnished and decorated. The 110-seater restaurant includes a lovely conservatory area. The bar has pew-type seating – which is very apt as it is located in the 15th-century former chapel of St Anne's church; the original beams form part of the bar.

There is also a children's play area and a patio garden where guests can have a relaxing drink or meal when the weather is fine.

The extensive menu ranges from sandwiches and simple basket meals such as sausages, chicken and scampi, to the 16-ounce T-bone steak or roast duck. Specials can include lasagne, steak and kidney pie, beef curry and other hearty favourites. Everything is home-made and has that wonderful individually home-cooked flavour. Alongside the full carvery there is also a bar menu every night and at Sunday lunchtime.

- Mon-Sat 11.00-3.00, 5.30-11.00; Sun 11.00-3.00, 5.30-10.30
- Lunchtime and evening menus; daily specials
- All major credit cards
- 4 rooms
- Car parking, beer garden
- tonybell@pickwickinn.freeserve.co.uk; www.pickwick-inn.co.uk

THE PLUME OF FEATHERS

THE SQUARE, PRINCETOWN, YELVERTON, DEVON PL20 6QQ
TEL: 01822 890240 FAX: 01822 890780

Directions: The Plume of Feathers is located in the village square, next to Highmoorland Visitor Centre.

The Plume of Feathers Inn is Princetown's oldest building. Built in 1785, this traditional, family-run inn is set in the heart of Dartmoor. With its copper-topped bars, log fires and oil lamps, it has plenty of atmosphere and also retains many charming original features. It was built to house some of the workmen who came to build Tor Royal, the estate of Sir Thomas Tyrwhitt. When the building first became an inn, it is believed to have been called The Princes Arms. As the arms of the Prince of Wales include three ostrich feathers, the inn soon became known by its current name.

Proud of its high standards of service and quality, this distinguished and welcoming pub offers many amenities

including two main bars, a large family/function room, children's play area, picnic area and large open courtyard.

It's the fine food and drink that draw visitors and locals alike, with an impressive range of everything from tempting bar snacks and sandwiches to delicious main courses. Booking is recommended for the Sunday roast lunch. And to accompany your meal there's a selection of real ales, lagers, ciders, wines, spirits, teas and coffees.

Owner James Langton has been here since 1973, and is a well-known and respected figure in the community. He and his family and staff offer all their guests genuine hospitality.

Accommodation is also available, for anyone wishing to stay and explore this area of great natural beauty and rugged grandeur.

- Mon-Sat 11.00-23.00; Sun 12.00-22.30
- Mon-Fri 11.00-14.00 (snacks until 14.30), 17.00-21.30; Sat-Sun and school holidays all day
- £ All major credit cards
- 2 bunkhouses B&B, campsite
- P Car parking, chiildren's play area, picnic area
- ? Highmoor Visitors Centre, Dartmoor

RING O' BELLS

MANOR ROAD, LANDKEY, NEAR BARNSTAPLE, DEVON EX32 0JL
TEL: 01271 830364

Devon

Directions: Leave Barnstaple on the A361 towards Tiverton. Turn left at the first junction - sign posted Landkey. Drive into the village and turn right at the War Memorial, into Manor Road. The Ring O' Bells is down the road on the right hand side, under the church.

Kevin and Kathryn Burgess welcome all guests to **Ring o Bell** with genuine hospitality. This friendly inn is located on the outskirts of this village community. Located next to the village church, it is believed to have been built originally to house the stonemasons who crafted the church. Inside all is warm and cosy, with a spacious open-plan public bar and an equally attractive and welcoming lounge bar/restaurant area. Handsome original features include the exposed beamwork, and brasses adorn the walls. Entertainment in the form of tried-and-true pub games such as skittles and shove ha'penny add to the traditional and

comfortable ambience.

Food is one of this fine pub's many highlights. The lunch menu offers a wide choice of bar snacks, sandwiches, omelettes, jacket potatoes and home-made main dishes such as lasagne, steak and kidney pie, and Stilton and vegetable crumble, as well as a selection of fish dishes. For evening meals the choice is just as varied, and the options just as delicious: steaks, fish and seafood, poultry and vegetarian dishes, all expertly prepared and presented. The desserts are truly mouth-watering, and there is a special children's menu. Kathryn and Kevin take well-deserved pride in maintaining excellent standards of quality and hospitality. This hidden inn is well worth seeking out.

- Mon-Fri: 11.30-14.30, 18.30-23.00; Sat: 11.30-23.00; Sun: 12.00-15.00, 19.00-22.30
- Lunchtime and evening menus; daily specials
- All major credit cards
- Parking available on Street
- Skittle Alley, Games, Shove ha'penny, darts, pool table

RING OF BELLS

FORE STREET, BISHOPSTEIGNTON, TEIGNMOUTH, DEVON TQ14 9QP
TEL: 01626 775468

Directions: Just off the Teignmouth to Newton Abbot Road, turn opposite Jack's Patch Garden Centre

Margaret and Graeme Doble and their son Jay, who is the licensee, took over the **Ring of Bells** in early 2002 and are the toast of the village by virtue of their attention to traditional values and service. In fact one of the locals says that the Sunday lunch is 'just like eating Mum's roast,' and that just about sums it all up. The

food is home-cooked, generous and wholesome. There is of course a children's menu which offers burgers and other children's favourites, while other delights at lunchtime (12.00-14.00) include delicious, hearty soups and rolls, sausage and mash, seafood and steaks as well as simple sandwiches. Dinner is served from 18.00-21.00 and offers all you would expect of this charming inn –

meat, fish, fowl and vegetarian dishes, graciously prepared and presented. Dating back to the 1600s and possibly much older, this notable pub was originally a beer-house with a cottage next door that once housed the local Liberal Club before both were transformed into the present hostelry.

The interior boasts ancient beams, stone walls, open fireplace and interesting local memorabilia dotted around the walls. While enjoying the friendly and relaxed ambience you can savour a meal and/or one of a full range of beers, lagers, wines, spirits, soft drinks and hot beverages. There are always three real ales on tap, including a changing guest ale.

- 🕐 Mon-Sat 11.00-23.00; Sun 12.00-22.30
- 🍴 Lunchtime and evening menus; daily specials
- 💷 All major credit cards
- 🎵 Quizzes, live music

THE ROCKFORD INN

BRENDON, NEAR LYNTON, DEVON EX35 6PT
TEL: 01598 741214 FAX: 01598 741265

Directions: Barnstaple A39 to Lynmouth/Lynton, on to Brendon

Friends old and new are given a hearty welcome by Elaine, Nicola and Barrie, proprietors of **The Rockford Inn**, a traditional Exmoor pub dating back to the 17th century. This fine country inn, within the spectacular Exmoor National Park and on the banks of the East Lyn River, has many attributes to recommend it. This family-run pub offers genuine hospitality. A convivial atmosphere pervades the spacious open-plan bars, enhanced by traditional open fireplaces, beamed ceilings and attractive décor.

Delicious food is on the menu both at lunchtime (12.00-14.30) and dinner (19.00-21.00), home-made by Elaine, who oversees a range of meals freshly cooked to order, such as fish and seafood dishes, steaks, vegetarian choices and more. The desserts are mouth-watering, and there is also a separate children's menu.

Real ales on tap include Rockford ale (brewed at St Austell), Barn Owl, Golden Arrow and Tawny Owl. There is also a good selection of malt whiskies, ciders, lagers, wines, soft drinks and teas and coffees.

Accommodation comprises six guest bedrooms (1 single, 3 doubles and 2 family rooms). Each room is comfortably and handsomely furnished and decorated, with a real home-from-home ambience.

With its oustanding riverside location, there is good fishing available, as well as some superb walking in the area. Children and well-behaved pets are welcome at this superior inn.

- Mon-Thurs 12.00-15.00, 18.00-22.30; Fri-Sat 12.00-23.00; Sun 12.00-16.00, 18.30-22.00
- Bar snacks and evening meals
- All major credit cards
- 6 rooms
- Car parking, pool table, darts. Dogs welcome
- @ enquiries@therockfordinn.com www.therockfordinn.com
- Lynton, Watersmeet House (1 ½ miles), Doone Valley (4 miles), coastal paths, North Devon Forest

THE SANDY PARK INN AND RESTAURANT

SANDY PARK, CHAGFORD, NEWTON ABBOT, DEVON TQ13 8JW
TEL: 01647 432236 FAX: 01647 432236

> **Directions:** M5 south to Drumbridges roundabout, right onto the A382, to just beyond Moretonhampstead. From the North - 2 miles south of Whiddon Down on A382

Real ales, fine wines, superb food and a warm welcome await visitors to **The Sandy Park Inn and Restaurant**, a lovely and charming thatched 16th-century inn. The interior has three main areas: the bar, restaurant and a cosy snug. The atmosphere is relaxed and convivial.

All the dishes on the excellent menu are home-cooked to order. There's fresh fish every day, and a range of tempting daily specials. Tasty choices from the extensive menu include prime British steaks, tenderloin of pork, Gressingham duck, rack of lamb and wild mushroom stroganoff. Diners will also want to leave room for one of the mouth-watering desserts such as sticky toffee pudding or apple and blackberry pie.

Westcountry Micro-Breweries supply the real ales, and there's also a good complement of lagers, ciders, spirits, soft drinks, teas and coffees, together with domestic and international wines by the bottle or glass.

Owners Paul and Marilyn Codlin and their friendly, helpful staff provide a very high standard of service and quality. This traditional Devon inn has all the ingredients for a delightful and relaxing drink or meal, amid the lovely surroundings of Dartmoor National Park, with its outstanding views and walks.

- 🕐 Tues-Thurs 18.30-23.00; Fri-Sat 12.00-14.00, 18.30-23.00; Sun 12.00-14.00, 19.00-22.30
- 🍴 Lunchtime and evening menus; daily specials
- 💷 All major credit cards
- 🅿 Car parking, beer garden
- ❓ Dartmoor National Park

THE SEVEN STARS INN

FORE STREET, SOUTH TAWTON, NEAR OKEHAMPTON,
DEVON EX20 1LW   TEL: 01837 840292 FAX: 01837 849010

Devon

> **Directions:** From junction 31 on the M5 take the A30 towards Launceston. After passing Okehampton turn right into South Tawton. The Seven Stars Inn is on Fore Street, near the village centre.

Built in the 17th century, **The Seven Stars Inn** is located in the heart of the village of South Tawton close to the village shops and the impressive village church. A beautiful stonebuilt inn almost covered in creeper, it is a traditional pub in the best sense of the word. The interior summons up an atmosphere of gracious charm, with the characteristic separate bar, lounge and a spacious restaurant area. Exposed beams, large stonebuilt fireplace, original features and the tasteful traditional décor all add to the olde worlde ambience. The chef-prepared lunchtime menus feature a tempting range of classic and more innovative fare, all cooked fresh to order. Blackboard daily specials complement the fine variety of

meat, fish and salad dishes. At weekends there are also evening meals served, with an emphasis on a range of tempting choices created using the freshest local ingredients available. There are always at least two real ales on tap, together with a good selection of draught lagers, wines, ciders, spirits and hot and cold beverages.

Landlady Judy Bostock and her staff are friendly and welcoming, with many years experience of offering warm hospitality and excellent food and drink.

The accommodation available comprises two very comfortable rooms, and this attractive, cosy inn makes for a fine base from which to explore this part of Devon.

- 🕐 Mon 20.00-23.00, Tue-Sat 11.00-23.00, Sun 11.00-22.30
- 🍴 Bar meals and snacks (except Mondays). A la carte
- 💷 Visa, Mastercard, Switch, Delta, Amex, Diners, Eurocard, Solo
- 🛏 2 rooms en suite
- 🅿 Car parking
- 🎵 Quiz nights, special themed nights, darts
- ❓ Exeter xx miles, North Devon xx miles, Dartmoor National Park xx miles, walking, horse riding, fishing, bird watching

THE STAG HUNTERS HOTEL

BRENDON, NEAR LYNTON, DEVON EX35 6PS
TEL: 01598 741222 FAX: 01598 741352

Directions: From junction 25 on the M5 take the A358 to Williton and then the A39 to Minehead and on towards Lynton. One mile before Countesbury, turn left and The Stag Hunters lies a short distance away.

Found in the gloriously unspoilt valley of the River Lyn, **The Stag Hunters Hotel** is a handsome and traditional family-run hotel which offers superb old-fashioned hospitality. Surrounded by five acres of paddocks and a delightful garden, the nearby river can be fished for salmon and trout. This ancient stone-built hotel is well placed for many of north Devon's historic attractions.

The welcoming bar serves a wide choice of beers, ales, wines and spirits, including the highly regarded local Exmoor real ale. The food here is very much influenced by the hotel's location, and the splendid a la carte menu, served in the atmospheric restaurant, offers seasonal Devon fare along with locally caught seafood. The less formal bar menu is equally tempting and offers a wonderful range of homecooked dishes.

The décor features beamed ceilings and attractive prints and paintings. The residents lounge is comfortable and welcoming. Guests enjoy a pleasant and relaxing night's sleep in one of the comfortable and well-appointed bedrooms and there is stabling for eight horses. Well-behaved dogs can be accommodated in their owners' rooms. The charm of this magnificent Devon country hotel with its splendid setting is a place well worth seeking out, with it's special appeal for those looking for old-fashioned, high-quality hospitality.

- (🕐) Mon-Sat 11.00-15.00, 17.00-23.00; Sun 12.00-15.00, 19.00-22.30
- (🍴) Bar meals and snacks. A la carte
- (£) Visa, Mastercard, Switch, Delta, Amex, Diners, Eurocard, Solo
- (🛏) 12 double rooms en suite
- (P) Beer garden, car parking, stabling, paddocks, dogs welcome
- (🎵) Regular music and sing-alongs
- (@) www.staghunters.com, enquiries@staghunters.fsnet.co.uk
- (?) Watersmeet Ho 1 mile, Foreland Point 2 miles, Lynton and Lynmouth Cliff Railway 3 miles, Exmoor National Park 2 miles, coast 1 mile, walking, fishing, horse riding, bird watching

THE TAVERN IN THE PORT

1 BRIDGE STREET, BIDEFORD, DEVON EX39 2BU
TEL: 01237 423334 FAX: 01237 473142

Directions: North Devon link road from junction 27 of the M5 to Bideford town centre.

The Tavern in the Port is a large and welcoming town-centre pub up a typically sloping Devonshire street. This fine establishment dates back to the very early 19th century and was originally three separate properties. Now blended into one, inside, open-plan bars lead into each of three distinct parts of the inn; all boast a wealth of attractive features such as the exposed beamwork and stonework, complemented by faithful period replica furnishings and fittings. The atmosphere throughout is relaxed and friendly, while the seating and ambience are sure to encourage guests' comfort.

The Tavern is the first part of this inn. Here can be found a good range of real ales, lagers, ciders, wines, spirits, soft drinks, teas and coffees, to be enjoyed in one of the Tavern's cosy nooks.

At The Chandler's Restaurant, a variety of tempting home-cooked snacks and meals – everything from sandwiches to a la carte dishes – is served. The delicious and innovative snacks, starters, main courses (where meat and vegetarian dishes complement the selection of fish courses) and mouth-watering sweets are well worth a try.

Corkers is a bar and evening club, open late. This lively venue attracts a friendly crowd of regulars and visitors.

Nothing is too much trouble for welcoming hosts John and Sue Taylor and their children, Lisa and Steven, who treat every one of their guests to some genuine hospitality.

- Mon-Sat 11.00-23.00; Sun 11.00-22.30 (special promotions/'Happy Hours' 11.00-12.30 and 17.00-19.00)
- Bar meals and a la carte
- All major credit cards
- Parking, garden
- Occasional live music
- @ carlsbergtetley@aol.com
- ? Bideford museums, markets, shopping, Saunton Sands, Barnstaple, beaches, golf, walking, bird watching

THE TOBY JUG INN

BICKINGTON, NEAR NEWTON ABBOT, DEVON TQ12 6JZ
TEL: 01626 821278

Devon

Directions: From Exeter take the A38 towards Plymouth and, at the Drum Bridges roundabout, turn on to the old A38 following the signs to Bickington. The Toby Jug Inn lies approximately 3 miles down the road.

Dating back to the 1600s, **The Toby Jug Inn** is an impressive building lying on the main road through the village of Bickington. Looking very much like the traditional old coaching in that it is, The Toby Jug is a delightful place where a warm welcome is certainly the order of the day. Full of character and charm, the interior boasts stone floors, exposed stone walls and a mass of fascinating local memorabilia adorning the walls and ceiling beams. Divided into three distinct areas – the main bar, Stable bar and dining room, each room has a wonderful fireplacee with cosy rustic

seating and a convivial ambience - just the place to relax after a day out in the glorious countryside.

Mike Barron is a genial host who is popular with locals and visitors alike and who welcomes everyone to his establishment with genuine warmth. Guests from near and far come to sample the excellent food and drink. The menu of freshly prepared home-cooked food – there are two chefs hard at work in the kitchen – offers everything from tasty sandwiches to three-course gourmet meals. Fresh locally-caught fish is the house speciality. The range of liquid refreshment includes real ales, ciders, lagers, soft drinks, a good wine list, and teas and coffees.

With its proximity to the A38, there really is no excuse not to call in at this marvellous and welcoming inn.

- 🕐 Winter: Sat-Sun all day (Sun until 22.30); Summer: Mon-Fri 11.00-15.00, 17.00-23.00; Sat-Sun all day (Sun until 22.30)
- 🍴 Bar meals, snacks and a la carte in bar or dining room
- 💷 Visa, Access, Delta, Switch
- 🅿 Beer garden, car parking, small animal enclosure, children welcome, dogs welcome
- 🎵 Occasional music evenings, darts, cards
- ❓ Dartmoor National Park (3 miles), Gorse Blossom Miniature Railway and Woodland Park (1½ miles), walking, golf, fishing

THE WHITCHURCH INN

CHURCHILL ROAD, WHITCHURCH, TAVISTOCK, DEVON PL19 9ED
TEL: 01822 612181

Directions: A386 Plymouth to Tavistock Road, turn right to Whitchurch
approaching Tavistock and beyond Horrobridge

The Whitchurch Inn
combines the best of
traditional features with
modern style and comfort.
Dating back to the 12th
century and directly adjacent
to the village church, this
warm and welcoming inn is a
cosy retreat. Rachel
Newphry, who runs this fine
establishment, has been here
since 1999 and has totally
refurbished the interior with
taste and style. There's an open-plan bar
and restaurant (including a non-smoking
eating area) complemented by the
original ceiling beams, thought to have
been crafted from ships' timbers. The pub
is adorned with prints, coppers and
brasses, and there are cosy nooks and
crannies for a quiet, relaxing drink or
meal.

The food on offer is nothing short of
superb. Everything from bar snacks to
hearty dishes at lunchtime and evenings
is here (Mon-Fri 12.00-14.30 and 18.30-
21.45; Sat-Sun 12.00-21.45), together
with a range of tempting daily specials.
Seafood is just one speciality, alongside a
good selection of char-grilled steaks,
chicken dishes, vegetarian options and
more.

Real ales are here, too, as well as a
good range of lagers, ciders, wines,
spirits, soft drinks and excellent coffees
and teas.

Rachel and her friendly, efficient staff
offer all their guests the best in warm
hospitality and superb service.

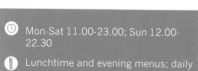

- 🕐 Mon-Sat 11.00-23.00; Sun 12.00-22.30
- 🍴 Lunchtime and evening menus; daily specials
- 💷 All major credit cards
- 🅿 Car parking, beer garden
- ❓ Dartmoor, Tavistock (1 mile), Plymouth (14 miles)

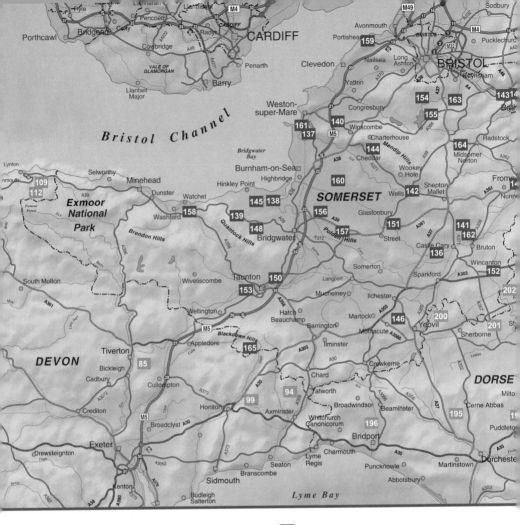

136	Alhampton Inn, Alhampton, Ditcheat
137	The Anchor Inn, Bleadon
138	The Anchor Inn, Combwich, Bridgwater
139	The Ancient Mariner, Nether Stowey
140	The Bell Inn, Banwell, Weston-Super-Mare
141	The Bell Inn, Evercreech
142	The City Arms, Wells
143	Englishcombe Inn, Bath
144	The Gardener's Arms, Cheddar
145	The Greyhound Inn, Stogursey, Bridgwater

146	The Halfway House, Chilthorne Domer
147	King William IV, Combe Down, Bath
148	The Lamb Inn, Spaxton, Brigwater
149	The Masons Arms, Frome
150	The Merry Monk, Monkton Heathfield
151	The Mitre Inn, Glastonbury
152	The Nog Inn, Wincanton
153	The Old Inn, Bishops Hull, Taunton
154	The Pelican Inn, Chew Magna
155	The Red Lion, Bishop Sutton, Bristol

Please note all cross references refer to page numbers

SOMERSET

The high moorland plateau of Exmoor National Park straddles both Somerset and Devon, though seventy per cent of the land lies within Somerset. It borders the Bristol Channel coast and is sometimes seen as Dartmoor's poor relation but this would be a mistake for visitors to make. An area with a character all its own, Exmoor is a wonderful blend of moor and heath, swift flowing streams, deep wooded valleys and the high cliffs of its coastline. Many of the settlements here are ancient, dating back to well before the Norman Conquest. Throughout the National Park, there are relics from the Bronze and Iron Ages such as hut circles, standing stones and barrows. This is also the land of the wild Exmoor pony and herds of red deer, matched by the wealth of bird and plant life. The moor is criss-crossed by a network of paths and bridleways providing superb opportunities for discovering the hidden delights of this glorious area on foot or on horseback.

Romantic Exmoor has become inextricably linked with Richard Doddridge Blackmore and his novel *Lorna Doone*, published in 1869.

Of the ancient towns and villages along the Exmoor coast, Lynmouth is one of the most interesting, dubbed the "English Switzerland" by the poet Robert Southey in 1812. This small fishing village developed into an early seaside resort and is still popular today. Minehead, too, is a

Watchet Lighthouse

popular place today but anyone visiting the holiday village, originally created by Billy Butlin in 1962, will find it hard to believe that the town was once a busy Celtic port.

Once a major port to rival Bristol, Bridgwater's docks have not withstood the test of time as, gradually, the River Parrett silted up. However, this particular cloud had a silver lining for the people of the town as the mud, when baked, was a very effective scourer and it was used up until the early 20th century to clean stone. To the west of Bridgwater lie the Quantock Hills, an Area of Outstanding Natural Beauty that extends from just outside Taunton to the coast at Quantoxhead.

South Somerset is characterised by ancient Saxon towns and villages, willows that grow on the old marshlands of the Somerset Levels and warm honey-coloured building stone. Despite having been founded in the 8th century, Taunton did not finally become the county town until the 1930s. Many of its buildings dating back as far as Tudor times, and it is an excellent starting point to begin an exploration of the southern part of the county. To the north and east of the town lie the Somerset Levels, an area of marshland that, from medieval times onwards, has continued to be drained to provide rich and fertile farmland.

Over the centuries, land rising above the wetlands has been settled, and two hills in particular were settled in ancient times and have given rise to local legends. Burrow Mump is said to have been the site of an ancient fortification belonging to King Alfred and it was at a nearby village, Althelney, that the King is said to have burnt the cakes. The Iron Age hill fort at Cadbury Castle is thought to have been the location of King Arthur's Camelot. Excavations have confirmed that there was indeed a fortification here from that period and the remote and romantic setting has enhanced this belief.

Yeovil, the only other large town in the southern area, dates back to the time of the Romans but, despite its age, it is a modern place perhaps best known as the home of Westland Helicopters. However, it is the area's ancient villages and old market towns, such as Norton Fitzwarren, Muchelney, Langport and Ilminster, that provide the real source of interest here. Glorious old buildings, some dating back to the Norman era, can still be found but what makes these places so attractive is the honey-coloured limestone - hamstone - used in their construction. The rich farmland is littered with magnificent country and manor houses including the late medieval stone manor house of Lytes Cary, the Palladian Hatch Court and Montacute House, built in the late 16th century for Elizabeth I's Master of the Rolls. The fine houses are often overshadowed by their gardens: there are some splendid examples here, particularly those, such as Barrington Court, Hestercombe Gardens and Tintinhull House Gardens, that have been influenced by the early 20th century landscape gardener, Gertrude Jekyll.

Elegant cities such as Bath, charming old market towns, the glorious countryside of the Mendip Hills, connections with the legends of King Arthur and coastal resorts like Weston-super-Mare are all part of the charm of the northeastern region of Somerset. Running from Weston-super-Mare to Frome, the limestone Mendip Hills cut across this area in a spectacular fashion. Although even at their highest point they only reach just over 1,000 feet, there are some magnificent panoramic views out across the flat lands of the Somerset Levels and over the Bristol Channel to South Wales. A wealth of prehistoric remains have been found here but two of the hills most popular and famous attractions are both natural – Cheddar Gorge and the caves at Wookey Hole. The Mendips are also the home of the smallest city

Hestercombe Gardens

in England, Wells, where a cathedral was founded in the 12th century on the site of a Saxon church. Wells is dominated by its cathedral, a magnificent building that contains a wonderful 14th century Astronomical Clock. Glastonbury, with an Abbey said to have been founded by

Allerford Bridge

Joseph of Arimathea in AD 60, is the earliest seat of Christianity in the British Isles. It is also believed to have been the last resting place of King Arthur and Queen Guinevere.

To the north of the Mendips lies the city of Bath, which in the 18th century became the most fashionable spa town in the country. Close by is the West Country's largest city, Bristol, which dates back to Saxon times when a settlement was founded here at the strategically important bridging point of the Avon gorge. The gorge is spanned by one of the city's most famous constructions, the Clifton Suspension Bridge, which was completed after the death of its designer Isambard Kingdom Brunel. Down by the old wharf can be seen another of Brunel's masterpieces, the SS *Great Britain*, the first iron-hulled passenger liner, launched in 1843.

Barrington

To the east of the village is the beautiful National Trust owned **Barrington Court**, famous for its enchanting garden influenced by the great 20th century garden architect Gertrude Jekyll.

Bath

Since time immemorial over half a million gallons of water a day, at a constant temperature of 46°C, have bubbled to the surface at Bath. The ancient Celts believed the mysterious steaming spring was the domain of the goddess Sulis and they were aware of the water's healing powers long before the invasion of the Romans. However, it was the Romans who first enclosed the spring and went on to create a spectacular health resort that became known as Aquae Sulis. By the 3rd century, Bath had become so renowned that high ranking soldiers and officials were coming here from all over the Roman Empire. Public buildings and temples were constructed and the whole city was

Roman Baths, Bath

enclosed by a stone wall. By AD 410, the last remaining Roman legions had left and, within a few years, the drainage systems failed and the area returned to marshland. Ironically, the ancient baths remained hidden throughout the entire period of Bath's 18th century renaissance and were only discovered in the late 19th century. The restored Roman remains centre round the **Great Bath**, a rectangular lead-lined pool standing at the centre of a complex system of buildings that took over 200 years to complete. **Bath Abbey** is now considered to be the ultimate example of English Perpendicular church architecture. Inside, there is a memorial to the Richard 'Beau' Nash, one of the people responsible for turning Bath into a fashionable Georgian spa town. The elegant and stylish Beau Nash, who had only come to the town to earn a living as a gambler, became the Master of Ceremonies and, under his

pressure, the town became a relaxing place for the elegant and fashionable of the day's high society. Among the entrepreneurs and architects who shared Nash's vision was the architect John Wood who, along with his son, designed many of the city's fine neoclassical squares and terraces. Among these is the **Royal Crescent**, John Wood the Younger's Palladian masterpiece and one of the first terraces in Britain to be built to an elliptical design.

Famed for its wealth of Georgian architecture Bath is a delightful city to wander around and marvel at the buildings. Beside the original Roman Baths is the **Pump Room**, which looks much as it did when it was completed in 1796. The National Trust owned **Assembly Rooms**, one of the places

Royal Crescent

where polite 18th century society met to dance, play cards or just be seen, were severely damaged during World War II and not re-opened until 1963. Spanning the River Avon, in the centre of the city, is the magnificent **Pulteney Bridge**, designed by Robert Adam and inspired by Florence's Ponte Vecchio. The city boasts a number of fine museums, including **Holburne Museum** with a superb collection of decorative and fine art; the **Museum of East Asian Art** display artefacts from China, Japan, Korea and Southeast Asia; and the **Bath Postal Museum** with a reconstruction of a Victorian sorting office.

Bridgwater

Situated at the lowest bridging point of the River Parrett in medieval times, Bridgwater is an ancient inland port and industrial town. Before the construction of a canal dock in the early 19th century, the ships arriving at Bridgwater used to tie up on both sides of the river below the town's medieval bridge and here, too, can be seen the last remnant of the castle, **The Water Gate**, on West Quay. After a long period of decline in the textile industry and as the river was beginning to silt up, Bridgwater underwent something of an industrial renaissance as new industries were established here during the early 19th century.

Bristol

Situated at a strategically important bridging point at the head of the Avon gorge, Bristol was founded in Saxon times and soon became a major port and market centre. Situated just to the west of the old castle site stands **Bristol Cathedral** founded in around 1140 by Robert Fitzhardinge as the great church of an Augustinian abbey. While the abbey no longer exists, several original Norman features, such as the chapter house, gatehouse and the east side of the abbey cloisters, remain. Among the treasures, is a pair of candlesticks donated to the cathedral in 1712 by the rescuers of Alexander Selkirk, the castaway on whom Daniel Defoe based his hero Robinson Crusoe. Much of

Clifton Suspension Bridge

Bristol's historic waterfront has now been redeveloped for recreation and has a number of visitor attractions. Also in the old port area of the city is the **Bristol Industrial Museum**, which presents a fascinating record of the achievements of the city's industrial and commercial pioneers including household names such as Harvey (wines and sherries), McAdam (road building), Wills (tobacco) and Fry (chocolate). The city's connections with the sea are remembered at the **Maritime Heritage Centre** dedicated to the history of shipbuilding in Bristol; a number of historic ships line the wharf, including Brunel's mighty *SS Great Britain*, the world's first iron-hulled passenger liner launched in 1843. For many visitors, Bristol's most famous feature is another Brunel masterpiece, the graceful **Clifton Suspension Bridge** that spans the Avon gorge to the west of the city centre. Opened in 1864, five years after the death of its designer, the bridge continues to be a major route into the city. Suspended more than 200 feet above the river, it provides magnificent views over Bristol and the surrounding countryside. The land just to the west of the bridge is now the **Avon Gorge Nature Reserve**.

Bruton

This remarkably well-preserved former clothing and ecclesiastical centre, beside the River Brue, is more like a small town than a village. The priory was first established here in the 11th century and although much of this has now gone the former priory church is now the parish church. Across the river from the church is the **Patwell Pump**, a curious square structure that was the parish's communal water pump that remained in use until well into the 20th century. Further downstream a 15th century packhorse bridge can be seen near the site of the famous King's School. **The Dovecote**, arguably Bruton's most distinctive building, can be seen on the crest of a hill to the south of the bridge. Built in the 15th century, it is thought to have doubled as a watchtower.

Burnham-on-Sea

In the late 18th century, mineral springs were discovered and an attempt was made to turn Burnham-on-Sea into a spa town to rival Cheltenham and Bath. However the efficacious effects of its waters were never properly realised and, in the end, the town depended on its wide sandy beach to attract visitors. Burnham's most distinctive landmark is the **Low Lighthouse**, a curious square structure raised above the beach on tall stilts. To the southeast of Burnham is the small town of **Highbridge** once a busy coastal port on the Glastonbury Canal. To the northeast, lies **Brent Knoll**, a conspicuous landmark that can be seen from as far away as South Wales. Brent Knoll's southern slopes are said to have been the site of a battle that King Alfred fought and won against the Danes. The summit, which can be reached by footpaths beginning near the churches at East Brent and Brent Knoll, offers walkers a spectacular view out over the Bristol Channel, the Mendips and the Somerset Levels.

Castle Cary

Once the site of an impressive Norman castle, this lovely little town has an atmosphere of mature rural calm as well as some interesting old buildings. There is a handsome 18th century post office, a tiny lock-up gaol called the **Round House** dating from the 1770s and a splendid Market House with a magnificent 17th century colonnade.

Chard

Chard has expanded rapidly since World War II, but the centre of this light industrial town still retains a pleasant village-like atmosphere that is most apparent in its broad main shopping street. At the western end of the town's High Street, housed in the attractive thatched Godworth House, is the award winning **Chard Museum**, which is an ideal place for visitors to find out more about this town's eventful past.

To the northwest of the town is a 200-year-old corn mill, **Hornsbury Mill**, whose impressive water wheel is still in working order. To the northeast, **Chard Reservoir Nature Reserve** is a conservation area that is an important habitat for wildlife. Kingfisher, great crested grebe and other rare species of birds have made their home in and around the lake.

Charterhouse

Rising, in some places, to over 1000 feet above sea level, the **Mendips** form a landscape that is like no other in Somerset and, although hard to imagine today, lead and silver were once mined from these picturesque uplands. The Mendip lead-mining activity was centred around the remote village of Charterhouse and the last mine in the district, at Priddy, closed in 1908. Charterhouse takes its name from a Carthusian monastery, **Witham Priory**,

which owned one of the four Mendip mining sectors, or liberties. This area has been known for its mineral deposits since the Iron Age and such was its importance that the Romans declared the mines here state property within just six years of their arrival in Britain. A footpath from Charterhouse church leads up onto **Black Down** that is, at 1067 feet, the highest point in the Mendips. From here, to the northwest, the land descends down into **Burrington Combe**, a deep cleft said to have inspired the Rev Augustus Toplady to write the hymn *Rock of Ages*.

Cheddar

This sprawling village is best known for its dramatic limestone gorge, **Cheddar Gorge**, which is one of the most famous

Cheddar Gorge

and most often visited of Britain's many natural attractions. It is characterised by its high vertical cliffs, from which there are outstanding views out over the Somerset Levels, the Quantock hills and, on a clear day, across the Bristol Channel to south Wales. The National Trust owns most of the land around this magnificent ravine, which is a Site of Special Scientific Interest. Numerous rare plants grow here and it is also a haven for butterflies. There is a circular walk through the area that takes in plantations, natural woodland and rough downland. A place that draws rock climbers, the less ambitious may like to take the 322 steps of **Jacob's Ladder** that lead up the side of the gorge to the site of **Pavey's Lookout Tower**, a novel vantage point that offers yet more spectacular views of the surrounding area.

The village is also renowned for its caves and, of course, its cheese. Although much embellished by modern tourist paraphernalia, its two main show caves, **Gough's Cave** and **Cox's Cave**, are worth seeing for their sheer size and spectacular calcite formations.

Claverton

Just to the west of the village lies the 16th century country mansion, **Claverton Manor**, best known now as the **American Museum and Gardens**. Founded in 1961, it is the only establishment of its kind outside the United States and the rooms of the house have been furnished to show the gradual changes in American living styles from the arrival of the Pilgrim Fathers in the 17th century to New York of the 19th century.

Crewkerne

A thriving agricultural centre during Saxon times, Crewkerne even had its own mint in the decades leading up to the Norman invasion. Evidence of this ancient former market town's importance and wealth can still be seen in the magnificence of its parish Church of St Bartholomew built using money generated by the late medieval boom in the local wool industry. Unlike many other towns in Wessex, whose textile industries suffered an almost total decline in later years, Crewkerne was rejuvenated in the 18th century when the availability of locally grown flax led to an expansion in the manufacture of sailcloth and canvas webbing. Among the many thousands of sails made here were those for HMS *Victory*, Admiral Nelson's flagship at the Battle of Trafalgar.

The town lies close to the source of the River Parrett and from here the 50-mile long **River Parrett Trail** follows the river through some of the country's most ecologically sensitive and fragile areas, the Somerset Levels and Moors.

Just a couple of miles southwest of Crewkerne, close to the village of **Clapton**, are the varied and interesting **Clapton Court Gardens**. Among the many beautiful features of this 10 acre garden are the formal terraces, the rose garden, the rockery and a water garden.

Dunster

The village is dominated by **Dunster Castle** standing on top of the wooded Conygar Hill. The castle was one of the last Royalist strongholds in the West Country to fall in the Civil War and the garrison only surrendered after a siege lasting 160 days. Some of its finest date from the 17th century, in particular the superb plasterwork in the dining room and the magnificent balustraded main staircase with its delicately carved flora and fauna. The parkland of Dunster Castle is also home to another National Trust property, **Dunster Working Watermill,** built in the 18th century on the site of a pre-Norman mill. The village's principal religious house, **Dunster Priory**, was an outpost of Bath Abbey. It is now largely demolished, and the only parts of the priory to survive are the splendid priory church and an unusual 12th century dovecote that can be seen in a nearby garden.

Exmoor National Park

The characteristic heartland of the Exmoor National Park, seventy per cent of which lies within Somerset, is a high, treeless plateau of hard-wearing Devonian shale carved into a series of steep-sided valleys by the prolonged action of the moor's many fast-flowing streams. Whereas the upland vegetation is mostly heather, gorse and bracken, the more sheltered valleys are carpeted with grassy meadows and pockets of woodland. The deep wooded combes provide shelter for herds of shy red deer, which roam at will, but are seldom seen. Easier to spot are the hardy Exmoor ponies, now almost all cross-breeds, which often congregate at roadside parking areas where there can be rich pickings from holidaymakers.

Exmoor is crisscrossed by a network of paths and bridleways, which provide superb opportunities for walking and pony-trekking. Many follow the routes of the ancient ridgeways across the high moor and pass close to the numerous hut circles, standing stones, barrows and other Bronze and Iron Age remains which litter the landscape. Among the finest examples are the stone circle on **Porlock Hill, Alderman's Barrow** north of Exford, and the delightfully named **Cow Castle** near Simonsbath. The

Cow Castle

remarkable medieval packhorse bridge known as **Tarr Steps** lies to the north of the village of Hawkridge, near Dulverton.

Frome

Frome prospered during the Middle Ages on the back of its cloth industry but competition from the

Glastonbury Tor

woollen towns of the north in the 19th century saw the industry begin to decline, although the trade did not vanish completely until the 1960s. The town's old quarter is an attractive conservation area where among the shops and restaurants, can be found the **Blue House**.

Built in 1726 as an almshouse and a boy's school, it is one of the town's numerous listed buildings; in fact, Frome has more listed buildings that any other town in Somerset.

Glastonbury

Today this ancient town of myths and legends, of tales of King Arthur and the early Christians, is an attractive market town still dominated by the ruins of its abbey, which continues to attract visitors. The dramatic remains of **Glastonbury Abbey** lie in the heart of the old town and, if the legend of Joseph of Arimathea is to be believed, this is the site of the earliest Christian foundation in the British Isles. However, it is

the abbey's connection with King Arthur and his wife Queen Guinevere that draws most visitors to Glastonbury. During the Middle Ages, Glastonbury Abbey was an internationally renowned centre of learning and scholars and pilgrims, from all over Christendom, made their way here.

To the east of the town lies another site renowned for its ecclesiastical, secular and legendary connections. **Glastonbury Tor** is a dramatic hill that rises above the surrounding Somerset Levels. The 520-foot tor has been inhabited since prehistoric times and excavations on the site have revealed evidence of Celtic, Roman and pre-Saxon occupation. The striking tower at the summit is all that remains of the 15th century **Church of St Michael**, an offshoot of Glastonbury Abbey.

Hatch Beauchamp

Hatch Beauchamp is a pleasant village that has managed to retain much of its rural atmosphere despite being on the major route between Ilminster and Taunton. One of the finest country houses in the area is **Hatch Court**, a magnificent Palladian mansion built of honey coloured limestone and completed in 1755. Among its finest features are the hall with its cantilevered stone staircase, the curved orangery with its arched floor-to-ceiling windows and the semicircular china room with its elegant display of rare porcelain and glass. There is also a fine collection of 17th and 18th century English and French furniture, 19th and 20th century paintings and a small military museum commemorating Britain's last privately raised regiment, the Princess Patricia's Canadian Light Infantry. The extensively restored grounds incorporate a walled kitchen garden, rose garden, arboretum and deer park.

Hinkley Point

Hinkley Point is perhaps best known for its two great power stations. At the **Hinkley Point Visitor Centre** there are exhibitions and displays that outline the natural history of the Earth. The environment around the power station teems with wildlife and should not be forgotten. The **Hinkley Point Nature Trail** leads walkers through a wide diversity of habitats and, along with the many species of birds and the wild flowers, some visitors may be lucky enough to see glow worms on the guided night-time walks. The trail also includes

an early Bronze Age mound, known locally as **Pixie's Mound**, which dates back to 1500 BC and was excavated in 1906.

Ilchester

It was during the 13th century that Ilchester reached its peak as a centre of administration, agriculture and learning, and like its near neighbour Somerton, its was, for a time, the county town of Somerset. Three substantial gaols were built here, one of which remained in use until the 1840s. The tiny **Ilchester Museum** is in the centre of the town, by the Market Cross, and here the story of the town from is told through a series of exhibits that include a Roman coffin and

Fleet Air Arm Museum

skeleton. Ilchester was the birthplace, in around 1214, of the celebrated scholar, monk and scientist, Roger Bacon, who went on to predict the invention of the aeroplane, telescope and steam engine.

At **Yeovilton**, just to the east of this pleasant small town, is one of the world's leading aviation museums, the **Fleet Air**

Arm Museum, which contains a unique collection of aircraft, of which around half are on permanent display.

Lynmouth

For centuries Lynmouth was a village scraping a living from the land and the sea, and just as the herring shoals were moving to new waters this part of the north Devon coast began to benefit from two great enthusiasms: romantic scenery and sea bathing. Coleridge and Wordsworth came here on walking tours in the 1790s and Shelley visited in 1812. Robert Southey, later to become the Poet Laureate, first used the phrase "English Switzerland" to describe the dramatic scenery that Gainsborough considered the "most delightful" for a landscape painter. However, by the mid 19th century the steep cliff between Lynmouth and its neighbour along the coast, Lynton, was affecting the growing tourist trade. Bob Janes, a local engineer, designed the **Lynton-Lynmouth Cliff Railway,** and this ingenious railway, opened in 1890 and still running today, rises some 450 feet in just 900 feet and is powered by water. Often mentioned in the same breath as Lynmouth, **Lynton,** just half a mile along the coast to the west and reached by the cliff railway, is home to the **Exmoor Museum** housed in a restored 16th century dwelling. Here an intriguing collection of tools and the bygone products of local craftsmen can be seen along with other exhibits that recount the area's history. To the west of Lynton is one of the most remarkable natural features in Devon, the **Valley of the Rocks**.

Martock

The old part of Martock is blessed with an unusually large number of fine buildings and among these can be found the National Trust's **Treasurer's House**, a small medieval house of two stories built in the late 13th century. Visitors can see the Great Hall, an interesting wall painting and the kitchen added to the building in the 15th century. To the west of Martock, **Lambrook Manor Garden** was laid out by the writer and horticulturist, Margery Fish, who lived at the medieval Hamstone manor house from 1937 until her death in 1969. Her exuberant planting and deliberate lack of formality created an atmosphere of romantic tranquillity that is maintained to this day. Now Grade I listed, the garden is also the home of the National Collection of cranesbill species geraniums.

Minehead

A popular seaside town, lying at the foot of the wooded promontory known as **North Hill**. It is one of the oldest settlements in Somerset. At one time, ships arrived here with wool and livestock from Ireland, crops from the plantations of Virginia, coal from the South Wales' valleys and day trippers from Cardiff and Bristol. The merchants and paddle steamers have gone and nowadays the harbour is the peaceful haunt of sailing dinghies and pleasure craft.

There is a good view of the old port from the **North Hill Nature Reserve** and a three-mile-walk starting near the lifeboat station on the harbour side is an excellent way to explore this area of Minehead and its surroundings. The town is the terminus of the **West Somerset Railway**, the privately owned steam railway that runs for 20 miles between the resort and Bishop's Lydeard, just northwest of Taunton.

Montacute

This charming village of golden Hamstone houses and cottages is also home to the magnificent Elizabethan mansion, **Montacute House**, built in the 1590s for Edward Phelips, Queen Elizabeth's Master of the Rolls, probably by William Arnold, the architect of Wadham College, Oxford. Constructed of Hamstone, the house is adorned with characteristic open parapets, fluted columns, twisted pinnacles, oriel

windows and carved statues. The long gallery, one of the grandest of its kind in Britain, houses a fine collection of Tudor and Jacobean portraits on permanent loan from London's National Portrait Gallery. Other noteworthy features include the stone and stained glass screen in the great hall and Lord Curzon's bath, an Edwardian addition concealed in a bedroom cupboard. Montacute village is the home of the **TV and Radio Memorabilia Museum**, where a vast collection of vintage radios, wireless receivers and television sets, from the 1920s through to the present day, is on display.

Muchelney

During medieval times **Muchelney Abbey** grew to emulate its great rival at Glastonbury. After the Dissolution in 1539, the buildings, mainly dating from the 15th and 16th centuries, gradually fell into disrepair. Much of its stone was removed to provide building material for the surrounding village. In spite of this, a substantial part of the original structure, including the south cloister and abbot's lodge, can still be seen today. The abbey is now under the custodianship of English Heritage.

Nunney

This picturesque old market town is dominated by its dramatic moated

Montacute House

Castle begun in 1373 and thought to have been modelled on the Bastille. The castle came under attack from Parliamentarian forces during the English Civil War and, despite having a garrison of only one officer, eight men and a handful of civilian refugees, the castle held out for two days. However, the bombardment damaged the building beyond repair and it had to be abandoned, leaving the romantic ruins that can still be seen today. One of the 30 pound cannonballs that were used by Cromwell's forces can be seen in the village's 13th century church.

Selworthy

Selworthy

This picturesque and much photographed village is situated on the side of a wooded hill. Just to the northwest lies **Selworthy Beacon**, one of the highest points on the vast **Holnicote Estate**. Covering some 12,500 acres of Exmoor National Park, it includes a four-mile stretch of coastline between Minehead and Porlock Weir. **Dunkery Beacon**, the highest point on Exmoor, rises to 1,700 feet.

Virtually the full length of the River Horner lies within the Dunkery Estate, from its source on the high moorland to the sea at Bossington Beach, one of the best examples of a shingle storm beach in the country. The whole area is noted for its diversity of wildlife and plant life.

Shepton Mallet

This town on the banks of the River Sheppey was an important centre of woollen production and weaving, and in the 15th century the town's most striking building, its magnificent parish church, was constructed. Other reminders of Shepton Mallet's past can be seen around its market place where there is a 50 foot high **Market Cross**, dating from around 1500 and restored in Victorian times. Today, Shepton Mallet is a prosperous light industrial town with a good selection of shopping and leisure activities. Each year the town plays host to two agricultural shows. The **Mid-Somerset Show** is in August and, in May, the **Royal Bath and Wells Show** has a permanent showground to the southeast of the town.

Somerton

At one time the capital of Somerset under the West Saxons, the settlement here grew up around an important

Market Cross

constructed demonstration track.

Just to the southeast of the village lies Cadbury Castle, a massive Iron Age hill fort believed by some to be the location of King Arthur's legendary Camelot.

crossroads. Expansion towards the end of the 13th century altered this old town's original layout creating the present open market place that is home to the distinctive **Market Cross** and town hall.

Between 1278 and 1371, Somerton was the location of the county gaol and the meeting place of the shire courts as well as continuing to develop as a market town, reflected in the delightfully down-to-earth names of some of its streets such as Cow Square and Pig Street (now Broad Street). Today, Somerton is a place of handsome old shops, inns and houses and its general atmosphere of mature prosperity is enhanced by the presence of a number of striking ancient buildings.

Sparkford

The **Haynes Motor Museum** is thought to hold the largest collection of veteran, vintage and classic cars and motorbikes in the United Kingdom. This unique collection has over 200 exhibits and each one is driven or ridden at least once every six months around a specially

Street

Much of the growth of Street was due to one family, the Clarks. In the 1820s, the Quaker brothers Cyrus and James Clark began to produce sheepskin slippers from the hides of local animals. Many of the town's older buildings owe their existence to the family and, in particular, there is the **Friends' Meeting House** of 1850 and the building that housed the original Millfield School. The oldest part of the Clark's factory has now been converted into a fascinating **Shoe Museum** and, although the company is one of the largest manufacturers of footwear in Europe, it continues to keep its headquarters in the town.

Tatworth

A short distance to the southeast of Tatworth lies **Forde Abbey**, founded in the 12th century by Cistercian monks. Over the years it became one of the richest and most learned monasteries in the country but it had already declined greatly by the time of the Dissolution in 1536. Today, in its beautiful setting beside the River Axe, it is one of the most charming country houses in Britain and is also famous for its glorious gardens.

Taunton

Despite a settlement being founded here by the Saxon King Ine in the 8th century, Taunton, the county town of Somerset, has only been its sole centre of administration since 1935. Before that date, both Ilchester and Somerton had been the of architect Sir Edwin Lutyens and landscape designer Gertrude Jekyll, the Edwardian formal garden was restored to its former glory in the 1980s whilst the landscape garden was first laid out over 150 years earlier.

Washford

Washford is dominated by **Cleeve Abbey**, the only monastery in Somerset that belonged to the austere Cistercian order founded in 1198 by the Earl of Lincoln. The most impressive feature is the Great Hall – a magnificent building with tall windows, a wagon roof decorated with busts of crowned angels and medieval murals, and a unique set of floor tiles with heraldic symbols. The village is also the home of the diesel locomotive workshops of the West Somerset Railway and the **Bakelite Museum**, a fascinating place providing a nostalgic look at the 'pioneer of plastics'.

Wellington

This pleasant old market town was once an important producer of woven cloth and serge and it owes much of its prosperity to Quaker entrepreneurs and, later, the Fox banking family. Fox, Fowler and Co were the last private bank in England to issue notes and they only ceased in 1921 when they were taken over by Lloyds. The broad streets around the town centre are peppered with fine Georgian buildings, including the neoclassical **Town Hall**. To the south of the town stands the **Wellington Monument**, a 175-foot high obelisk erected not long after the duke's great victory at Waterloo.

Wells

The first church in England's smallest city is believed to have been founded by King Ine in around 700 and, after a diocesan tussle with Bath, the present **Cathedral of St Andrew** was begun in the 12th century. Taking over 300 years to complete, this magnificent cathedral demonstrates the three main styles of Gothic architecture. Its 13th century west front, with over 100 statues of saints, angels and prophets gazing down on the cathedral close, is generally acknowledged to be its crowning glory, although it was defaced during the English Civil War. Inside there are many superb features including the beautiful scissor arches and the great 14th century stained glass window over the high altar. However, the cathedral's most impressive sight is its 14th century **Astronomical Clock**, one of the oldest working timepieces in the world.

To the south of the cathedral's cloisters is the **Bishop's Palace**, a remarkable fortified medieval building, enclosed by a high wall and surrounded by a moat fed by the springs that give the city its name.

Weston-super-Mare

This popular seaside resort, whose greatest asset is undoubtedly its vast expanse of sandy beach, has, in recent years, also developed as a centre of light industry. Weston-super-Mare was, as late as 1811, just a fishing hamlet with only 170 residents. Within 100 years, it grew to become the second largest town in Somerset. Despite is relatively modern appearance, this area has been inhabited since prehistoric times and the wooded promontory at the northern end of Weston Bay was the site of a sizeable Iron Age hill settlement known as **Worlebury Camp**. The development of Weston began in the 1830s around the Knightstone, an islet joined to the shore at the northern end of the bay, and here was eventually built a large theatre and swimming baths. The arrival of the railway in 1841 saw the town's expansion increase rapidly and, in 1867, a pier was built on the headland below Worlebury Camp connecting Birnbeck Island with the mainland. The **Grand Pier** now stands at the centre of an area crammed with souvenir shops, ice cream parlours, cafés and assorted attractions that are part and parcel of a British seaside resort. There are also the indoor attractions of the **Winter Gardens**, along the seafront, and the fascinating **Time Machine** Museum.

Just to the southeast of the town lies Weston Airport, home to the world's largest collection of helicopters and autogyros. The only museum in Britain dedicated to rotary wing aircraft, the **International Helicopter Museum** has over 40 exhibits ranging from single-seater autogyros to multi-passenger helicopters. Visitors can see displays on the history and development of these flying machines and a conservation hangar where the aircraft are restored.

Wincanton

This attractive old cloth-making town was also a bustling coaching town as it lies almost exactly half way between London and the long-established naval base at Plymouth. In the heyday of stagecoaches, up to 20 a day would stop here. Modern day Wincanton is a peaceful light industrial town whose best known attraction, **Wincanton National Hunt Racecourse**, harks back to the days when horses were the only form of transport. Horse racing began in the area in the 18th century and the racecourse moved to its present site to the north of the town centre in 1927. This is the course where the great Desert Orchid often had his first race of each season during his dominance of steeple chasing in the 1980s.

Wiveliscombe

An ancient and isolated village where the Romans once had a fort - a quantity of 3rd and 4th century coins have been uncovered in the area. Later, in medieval times, the local manor house was used as a summer residence of the bishops of Bath and Wells. The remains, including a striking 14th century archway, have now been incorporated into a group of cottages. To the northeast of

The Great Cave

Wiveliscombe, close to the village of **Tolland**, is the delightful **Gaulden Manor**, which once belonged to the Turberville family whose name was borrowed by Thomas Hardy for use in his novel, *Tess of the D'Urbervilles*.

Wookey Hole

The village, in the rolling uplands of the Mendip Hills, is a popular place with walkers, cavers and motorised sightseers who are drawn by the natural formations found here. Throughout the centuries, the carboniferous limestone core of the hills has been gradually dissolved away by the small amount of acid in rainwater. This erosion has created over 25 caverns around Wookey Hole, of which only the largest half dozen or so are open to the public. The **Great Cave** contains a rock formation known as the Witch of Wookey that casts a ghostly shadow and is associated with gruesome legends of child-eating. During prehistoric times, lions, bears and woolly mammoths lived in the area. In a recess known as the **Hyena's Den**, a large cache of bones was found, many of them showing signs of other animal's toothmarks.

Yeovil

Yeovil's parish **Church of St John the Baptist** is the only significant medieval structure to survive, as most of its other early buildings were destroyed by the series of fires that struck the town in the 17th century. During the 18th century, Yeovil developed into a flourishing coaching centre due to its strategic position at the junction of several main routes. Industries such as glove-making, leather working, sailcloth making and cheese producing were established here, and today, Yeovil retains its geographical importance and is south Somerset's largest concentration of population. It is a thriving commercial, shopping, and market town best known perhaps as the home of Westland Helicopters.

ALHAMPTON INN

ALHAMPTON, NEAR DITCHEAT, SOMERSET BA4 6PY
TEL: 01749 860210

Directions: From Shepton Mallet on the A37 turn right at the sign for Ditcheat. At Ditcheat turn left at sign for Alhampton-1 mile.

Set in four acres of lovely grounds, **Alhampton Inn** is a gracious and traditional hostelry dating back to the 17th century. The impressive, Virginia Creeper-clad exterior gives one a taste of the comforts awaiting inside, where original features include the beamed ceilings and open fireplaces. Both bars are cosy and welcoming, with settees and easy chairs complementing the table-and-chair seating, paintings by local artists adorn the walls, and there's a relaxed and pleasant atmosphere throughout.

The food on offer combines the best of traditional English fare with more innovative dishes, including a good range of everything from snacks and sandwiches to hearty main courses using the freshest local ingredients. Beef, pork, lamb, chicken and fish dishes are supplemented by vegetarian options and daily specials.

To drink there are always two real ales together with farmhouse ciders, a good range of lagers, spirits and wines, and soft drinks, teas and coffees. Meals and drink can be enjoyed in either bar or, on fine days, out in the lawned garden where attractive thatched parasols shelter the tables. Barbecues are a regular feature in season.

Mark Jales runs this fine establishment, ably assisted by his friendly and conscientious staff. For genuine hospitality amid very pleasant surroundings, look no further.

- 🕐 Mon-Thurs 12.00-15.00, 18.00-23.00; Fri-Sat 11.00-23.00; Sun 12.00-22.30
- 🍴 Lunchtime and evening menus; daily specials
- 💷 All major credit cards
- 🅿 Car parking, beer garden, children's play area
- 🎵 Games, darts, quiz nights, jazz evenings
- @ alhampton@alhamptoninn.freeserve.co.uk
- ❓ Bath and Wells Showground, Shepton Mallet, Wells.

THE ANCHOR INN

BRIDGWATER ROAD, BLEADON, NR WESTON-SUPER-MARE, BS24 0AW
TEL: 01934 812352

Somerset

Directions: From junction 22 on the M5 take the A38/A370 road towards Weston-Super-Mare. The Anchor is on the left 4 miles from this junction.

The **Anchor Inn** in Bleadon is a charming and cosy traditional Somerset inn well worth seeking out. This welcoming establishment has a wealth of handsome features including the open fires and stonebuilt walls that add to the comfortable and homely ambience. Owners Steve and Sue Evans have been here since 2000, and have over 12 years' experience in the trade. They offer all their guests a warm welcome and great food and drink. Sue is the cook, putting together a varied menu of delicious meals and snacks such as steaks, home-

made pies and a tempting range of meat, fish and vegetarian dishes. The Sunday lunch is particularly popular – booking is recommended. Meals are available at lunch time and evenings Monday to Saturday, and in summer throughout the day. Guests can enjoy their food in either the lounge bar, the cosy non-smoking restaurant or, on fine days, in the lovely beer garden.

Drinks on tap at this excellent Free House include two real ales – Bass and a changing guest ale – along with locally-produced Thatcher's cider, Worthington Creamflow, Carling, Stella Artois, Grolsch, Dry Blackthorne and Guinness, as well as wines, spirits, soft drinks and teas and coffees. The décor and furnishings throughout are attractive and comfortable, the atmosphere always friendly and hospitable. Sue, Steve and their staff go out of their way to provide a high standard of service. Coach parties welcome with bookings.

- 🕐 Mon-Sat 11.00-23.00; Sun 12.00-22.30
- 🍴 Bar meals, a la carte 12.00-14.30 and 18.00-21.00 Mon-Sat; traditional Sunday lunch; food served all day in summer
- 💷 All major credit cards
- 🅿 Off-road parking, beer garden, children's room, horse/pony & cart riding available (bookings taken)
- 🎵 Darts, skittle alley, pool; music,comedy and kareoke nights Fridays and Saturdays; live music Sunday from 4.30 and the last Friday of the month
- ❓ Weston-Super-Mare (5 miles), Middle Hope Nature Reserve (5 miles), Clevedon Court (5 miles), Bristol (14 miles), walking, cycling, horse riding, fishing, bird-watching

THE ANCHOR INN

RIVERSIDE, COMBWICH, NEAR BRIDGWATER, SOMERSET TA5 2RA
TEL: 01278 653612

Somerset

> **Directions:** A39 Bridgwater-to-Minehead Road sign posted from Cannington. Six miles from Bridgwater

As befits its name, features of the exterior of **The Anchor Inn** resemble a twin-funnel paddle steamer. This charming exterior bodes well for what's inside: welcoming, cosy bar areas, snug and main bar, all fully refurbished in 2002 to provide the very best in comfort. On fine days there's also the enclosed and lawned beer garden. In these attractive surroundings, locals and visitors alike can enjoy great food and drink.

The menu of home-cooked favourites caters for everything from sandwiches, snacks and light meals to dishes to satisfy the heartiest appetite. Steaks, chicken, pork, lamb, seafood and vegetarian dishes are all home-cooked and home-prepared to order. The Sunday roasts are a treat worth seeking out. All use fresh local ingredients.

To accompany your meal there's a range of real ales, lager, ciders, spirits, wines, soft drinks, teas and coffees.

Licencees Daniel and Jessica Whyte and Carrie Anne Bennett bring a wealth of enthusiasm to providing all their guests with the best in warm hospitality and excellent service. This convivial, friendly inn is popular with locals and visitors alike, and boasts live music at weekends. The atmosphere every day is relaxed and welcoming, and this fine inn is just the place to enjoy a great meal or drink amid very pleasant surroundings.

- ⏰ Winter: Mon-closed; Tue-Fri 12.00-14.30, 18.30-23.00; Sat 12.00-23.00; Sun 12.00-22.30. Summer: Mon-Fri 12.00-23.00; Sat11.00-23.00; Sun 12.00-22.30
- 🍴 Lunchtime and evening menus; daily specials
- 💷 All major credit cards
- 🅿 Car parking, beer garden
- 🎵 Games, darts, pool table, quiz night (Thurs), live music at weekends
- ❓ Bridgwater, Parrott Trail walk, Nature Reserve

THE ANCIENT MARINER

42 LIME STREET, NETHER STOWEY, SOMERSET TA5 1NG
TEL: 01278 733544

> **Directions:** From junction 23 on the M5 take the A38 to Bridgwater and then the A39 towards Minehead. Nether Stowey is midway between Bridgwater and Minehead just off the A39.

Once housing a blacksmith's – an integral part of any 17th-century coaching inn – **The Ancient Mariner** in Nether Stowey has a long and distinguished history of offering comfort and great food and drink to weary travellers. This history is proudly upheld today by Sylvia and Dave Merton and their friendly, attentive staff, who offer

all their guests genuine hospitality.

The interior of this excellent Free House is cosy and welcoming.

Specialities include steaks, fish and seafood dishes, and the menu and specials board features some innovative dishes as well as traditional favourites. The inn has tea room facilities open in summer for morning breakfasts and cream teas in the afternoons. There are always five real ales on tap, including local brew Butcombe Gold as well as four changing guest ales. Guests can also choose from among four draught lagers and three draught ciders, one of which is a rough cider brewed locally by Coombes. Spirits, wines, soft drinks, teas and coffees complete the list of beverages available. Popular with locals and visitors alike, this fine pub is well worth a visit for its great food, well-kept ales and convivial atmosphere.

- 🕐 Mon-Thurs 11.00-14.30, 18.00-23.00 (closed Mon lunch in winter); Fri-Sat 11.00-15.00, 18.00-23.00 (winter), 11.00-23.00 (summer); Sun 12.00-15.00, 19.00-22.30 (winter), 12.00-22.30 (summer)

- 🍴 Lunchtime (Tues-Sun 11.00-14.30 winter; Mon-Sun 11.00-14.30 summer) and evening (18.00-23.00) menus; daily specials; tea room mornings and cream tea afternoons every day in summer

- 🅿 Car parking, large beer garden; children welcome; dogs welcome; 90 ft outside play area

- 🎵 Long skittle alley, darts, fruit and quiz machines, quiz nights alternate Sundays from 8 p.m.; steak night Thursdays

- @ ancientmariner@supanet.com

- ❓ Coleridge Cottage (opposite), beaches (4 miles), at foot of Quantock Hills, Bridgwater (8 miles), Minehead (8 miles), walking, cycling, horse riding, fishing, bird watching

Somerset

THE BELL INN

1 THE SQUARE, BANWELL, NR WESTON-SUPER-MARE,
SOMERSET BS29 6BL
TEL: 01934 822331

Directions: From junction 21 on the M5 take the A370 towards Weston-Super-Mare and then the A371 towards Wells. Banwell lies where the A371 meets the A368, east of Weston-Super-Mare. The Bell Inn is in the heart of the village.

The father-and-son team of Bob and Robert Wareham offer a cheerful welcome to all their guests at **The Bell Inn** in Banwell. Dating back to the 1750s, this excellent inn has always been a hub of the community and a welcome stop on the way for travellers since that time. And ever since the 1960s, The Bell has been a major venue for well-known folk and rhythm and blues bands. This tradition is maintained with the inn showcasing live bands every other week, usually on Sundays (ring or email for details).

In addition to the lively and

welcoming ambience, the inn offers great food and drink.

Food is available seven days a week, with a choice of dishes listed on the specials blackboard. The menu is chosen in direct response to the clientele's requests, and changes seasonally.

Among the four real ales on offer at this fine Free House there are two changing guest ales, together with a good complement of lagers, cider, wines, spirits, soft drinks and hot drinks.

There are two cosy and comfortable guest bedrooms, both doubles, one en suite, and are available all year round for anyone wishing to use this charming village as a base from which to explore Bath, Bristol or the many scenic delights of the region.

🕐 Mon-Fri 15.00-23.00; Sat 12.00-23.00; Sun 12.00-22.30

🍴 Lunchtime and evenings, seven days a week

🛏 2 double rooms, one en suite, available all year round

🅿 Parking, beer garden

🎵 Traditional long alley skittles, live music regularly

@ yeoldebellinn@aol.com

❓ King John's Hunting Lodge (3 miles), Cheddar Gorge (5 miles), Wells (10 miles), beach, walking, fishing, sailing, horse riding

THE BELL INN

BRUTON ROAD, EVERCREECH, SOMERSET BA4 6HY
TEL: 01749 830287 FAX: 01749 831296

Somerset

> **Directions:** From junction 23 on the M5, take the A39 to Glastonbury and then the A361 towards Shepton Mallet. Just south of the town, turn right onto the A371 towards Castle Cary and then left onto the B3081. The Bell Inn lies through the village, opposite the church.

The Bell Inn, found in the heart of this pretty Somerset village, lies opposite the village church and close to the delightful main square at Evercreech where the village cross still stands. Built during the 1700s, this splendid stone edifice has been added to over the years, and the various extensions have complemented earlier parts of the inn so that the long façade makes a particularly pleasing sight. Inside, the inn is open plan and spacious, warmed by the woodburning stove that stands in one of the inn's two original stone fireplaces. Numerous

pictures adorning the walls add to the home-from-home ambience. There is a separate cosy and intimate restaurant area that is just as relaxed and comfortable as the rest of the inn.

An excellent place to come for a taste of real Somerset rough cider, there are also four real ales available, together with many other beers, lagers and spirits and a good selection of wines served from the bar. The extensive menu is supplemented by delicious daily specials, and includes everything from mouth-watering freshly cut sandwiches and pasta dishes through to old favourites such as shepherd's pie and peppered duck breast.

In addition to the great food and drink on offer, the inn also has superb accommodation that is ideal for families.

- 🕐 Mon-Sat 11.30-23.00; Sun 12.00-22.30
- 🍴 Bar snacks and meals, a la carte
- 💷 Visa, Mastercard, Delta
- 🛏 3 rooms (twins and double) en suite B&B
- 🅿 Car parking, beer garden, functions catered for
- 🎵 Regular live music or karaoke, darts, pool, skittles
- ❓ Royal Bath and Wells Showground (1 mile), East Somerset Railway (3 miles), Hadspen House (5 miles), Wells (8 miles), Glastonbury (9 miles), walking, cycling, riding

THE CITY ARMS

69 HIGH STREET, WELLS, SOMERSET BA5 2AG
TEL: 01749 673916 FAX: 01749 670405

Directions: From junction 21 on the M5 take the A370 towards Weston-Super-Mare and then the A371 to Wells.

Situated in the heart of the smallest city in England, **The City Arms** is a spacious and delightful inn offering a great range of liquid refreshment and food in convivial and welcoming surroundings. Dating back to the Civil War, the pub began life as the city gaol, becoming an inn during the 19th century. Just a few yards from the lovely church of St Cuthbert's, the outer walls of the pub were built in the early 1500s – and a testament to its time as the city gaol exists in the small barred windows and low entrances which can be seen from the courtyard, as well as the old ceiling beams in the upstairs dining

hall, where the guards and keepers once took their meals. Nowadays the courtyard is festooned with hanging baskets and is a lovely place to enjoy a drink or meal on fine days. The interior is similarly attractive and comfortable.

There are six rotating ales available, plus keg bitter and a selection of lagers, local draught ciders, stout, spirits, soft drinks and a very good wine list. From snacks and sandwiches to hearty grills, seafood, pork, chicken and vegetarian dishes, the menu offers a good variety of tempting morsels. All the food is freshly prepared to order.

Locals and visitors alike return again and again for the unique ambience and excellent service available at this superior inn, which is well worth seeking out during any visit to this charming city.

- (clock) Mon-Sat 10.00-23.00; Sun 12.00-22.30
- (food) Mon-Fri 8.00-22.00; Sat 9.00-22.00; Sun 9.00-21.00
- (£) Visa, Mastercard, Access, Switch, Delta
- (P) Car parking, beer garden
- (@) hahapurveyingco@btconnect.com
- (?) Wells Cathedral, Bishop's Palace, Wookey Hole Caves (2 miles), Glastonbury (5 miles), Cheddar Gorge (8 miles), walking, cycling, horse riding, fishing

ENGLISHCOMBE INN

ENGLISHCOMBE LANE, BATH, SOMERSET BA2 2EL

TEL: 01225 425251

> **Directions:** Take the M4 to junction 18, Bath. Follow the A46 to Bath city centre and then take the A367 towards Exeter. Follow the road uphill and out of Bath to Bear Flat, taking the right fork at the shops into Bloomfield Road. The third right takes you into Englishcombe Lane.

The **Englishcombe Inn** is an impressive and handsome pub and restaurant offering great food and drink in very welcoming and pleasant surroundings. Recently completely refurbished, this fine inn marries the best of traditional features with modern comfort, including facilities for people with disabilities. Set in a quiet area, with a garden of some 2.5 acres featuring lawns, shrubs, trees and flowering plants overlooked by an attractive verandah, inside and out this inn makes the perfect place to enjoy a quiet drink or savour a tasty meal.

The interior boasts an open-plan layout, with comfortable seating and a convivial atmosphere. The friendly, helpful staff offer all their guests a warm welcome and genuine hospitality. The snacks and dishes on the menu are all home-cooked, making use of the freshest local ingredients to produce a broad range of tempting traditional favourites. There are also daily specials and a delicious Sunday lunch.

To drink, there's a good variety including three real ales together with lagers, ciders, wines and spirits, soft drinks, teas and coffees. The relaxed atmosphere makes any stop here a very pleasant one, which is why this excellent inn is popular with locals and visitors alike.

- 🕐 Mon-Sat 12.00-23.00; Sun 12.00-22.30
- 🍴 Lunchtime and evening menus; daily specials
- 💷 All major credit cards
- 🅿 Car parking, beer garden
- 🎵 Skittles, darts, pool
- ❓ Bath, golf, walking

Somerset

THE GARDENER'S ARMS

35 SILVER STREET, CHEDDAR, SOMERSET BS27 3LE
TEL: 01934 742235 FAX: 01934 740069

Directions: From junction 21 of the M5 take the A370 towards Weston-Super-Mare and then the A371 towards Wells until you reach Cheddar. The Gardeners Arms is located just to the north of the town on Silver Street.

Just a short walk from the gorge and well worth seeking out, **The Gardener's Arms** in Silver Street began life as several traditional cottages, dating back in parts to 1560. Believed to be the oldest drinking house in Cheddar, it takes its current name from the freshness and delectability of its food. The inn's renowned chef, Tim Collins, expertly prepares and presents an impressive range of tempting dishes. The menus are designed to allow guests to choose any combination to suit their

- ⏰ Mon-Sat 11.00-23.00; Sun 12.00-22.30
- 🍴 Lunchtime (12.00-14.00) and evening (18.00-21.00) menus; daily specials
- 💷 All major credit cards
- 🅿 Car parking, beer garden, children's play area
- 🎵 Quiz nights in winter (Sundays from 8 p.m.)
- @ e-mail: info@gardeners-arms.com website: www.gardeners-arms.com
- ❓ Cheddar and Cheddar Gorge (1 mile), Wookey Hole (5 miles), Wells (6 miles), beach, walking, cycling, horse riding, fishing, gliding, go-karting, pot-holing

appetite and inclination, with a range of starters and main courses to pick from and create their own light meal or feast. The popularity of the food means it's a good idea to book in advance at all times. Meals can be taken in the bar or in the non-smoking restaurant.

To wash down your meal, or enjoy on their own, there are three real ales to choose from, as well as a good selection of lagers, ciders, spirits and soft drinks. The wine list is excellent.

Landlord Will Nicholls has been in charge here since September of 2002. Born and bred locally, he is a font of knowledge about sights and attractions in the area. He and his helpful, friendly staff ensure that all their guests receive excellent service and genuine hospitality.

THE GREYHOUND INN

1 LIME STREET, STOGURSEY, NR BRIDGWATER SOMERSET TA5 1QR
TEL: 01278 732490

> **Directions:** From junction 23 on the M5 take the A38 to Bridgwater and then the A39 towards Minehead. Approximately 5 miles out of Bridgwater turn right onto a minor road signposted Stogursey. Enter the village and turn right into Lime Street just beyond the village church. The Greyhound Inn lies on the left.

Found tucked away in this historic village, **The Greyhound Inn** is a typically charming and welcoming Somerset inn run by Kaz Hill with able assistance from husband Tim. Kaz is a warm and friendly host who has been here since 2000, before which the inn had been closed. She has given it a new lease of life by offering a high standard of food, drink, accommodation and hospitality.

There are two real ales on tap –

Bombadier and Abbot, as well as a good selection of bitters, lagers, cider, stout, wines, spirits and soft drinks.

The menu and daily specials, too, offer something for everyone. Kaz is the cook and serves up a good range of homemade favourites. Booking is advised for Sunday lunch and at all times in the summer months. The non-smoking restaurant is cosy and comfortable.

The atmosphere here is convivial and relaxed, enhanced by the traditional décor – the inn dates back to the 1700s, though has recently been tastefully refurbished, to combine the best of old-world charm with modern convenience. The three guest bedrooms available are on the first floor. One is en-suite and one a family room. All are handsomely decorated and furnished, and offer quality accommodation.

- 🕐 Mon-Fri 12.00-15.00, 17.30-23.00; Sat 12.00-23.00; Sun 12.00-15.00, 19.00-22.30
- 🍽 Bar snacks, lunchtime and evening menus; Sunday morning breakfasts children's menu, daily specials
- 🛏 3 letting rooms
- Ⓟ Beer garden, children's play area and games room, car parking, functions catered for
- 🎵 Live music every Friday, skittles, darts, pool, quiz night every other Sunday; Fun Day every August Bank Holiday Sunday (all proceeds to charity)
- @ kaz@thegreyhound.freeserve.co.uk
- ❓ Coleridge Cottage (2 miles), beaches (3 miles), Quantock Hills (5 miles), Bridgwater (7 miles), walking, cycling, horse riding, fishing, bird watching

THE HALFWAY HOUSE INN

CHILTHORNE DOMER, NEAR YEOVIL, SOMERSET BA22 8RE
TEL: 01935 840350 FAX: 01935 849005

Directions: Off the A30/A37 and A303 between Yeovil and Ilchester

Here at the charming and impressive **Halfway House Inn Country Lodge**, Paul Roswell and his staff offer a standard of 3 diamond accommodation which is the envy of many hotels. They have created 12 purpose-built en suite guest rooms furnished and decorated with style and taste, and offering every comfort and amenity. One unit offers facilities for wheelchair-users; others offer cooking facilities.

This fine inn can be seen as a modern and upmarket motel with its own private courtyard parking; plans are also in progress for the addition of an outdoor heated swimming pool. Most rooms command excellent views over the surrounding countryside; there is also a camping and caravan park on site. Paul also hopes to develop a fishing lake beside the accommodation, and is creating a new silver service restaurant. The inn is a Free House and carries an excellent range of beers and spirits, cask ales and a superb selection of wines by the glass, as well as a fine wine list chosen to complement the varied menu.

There are two welcoming and attractive dining rooms (one non-smoking) in which guests can enjoy delicious meals at any time of day, choosing from the imaginative and varied menu which caters for all tastes and are created by expert chefs using only the freshest and best of local produce. In addition to the daily menu there are blackboard specials and, on Sunday, an excellent roast.

- 🕐 Mon-Sat 08.00-23.00; Sun 08.00-22.30
- 🍴 Lunchtime and evening menus; daily specials
- £ All major credit cards
- 🛏 12 rooms en suite B&B
- Ⓟ Car parking, skittle alley
- @ e-mail: paul@halfwayhouseinn.com website: www.halfwayhouseinn.com

KING WILLIAM IV

54 COMBE ROAD, COMBE DOWN, NEAR BATH, SOMERSET BA2 5HY
TEL: 01225 833137 FAX: 01225 833137

Somerset

> **Directions:** On the outskirts of Bath off the A36 Bath to Warminster road.

Run by Susie and Alan Barrow, the **King William IV** is a charming and welcoming inn at the heart of the beautiful village of Combe Down. Popular with locals and visitors alike, this delightful inn combines the best of traditional comforts with modern service and quality. Built as a beerhouse (brewery) in the early 19th century, this fine establishment was created to quench the thirst of local masons building cottages in the village.

The interior has a large open-plan bar and separate non-smoking restaurant. Adorned with prints of local scenes, many of them depicting the area's proud heritage as a mining district, the décor is attractive and the ambience relaxed and welcoming.

The delicious food is home-cooked by Alan. From sandwiches and baguettes to steaks and chicken, pork, lamb, seafood, fish and vegetarian dishes, there's something here to satisfy every appetite.

To quench your thirst there are always two or three real ales, along with ciders, lagers, wines, spirits, soft drinks, teas and coffees.

From the lovely gardens to the rear of the inn there are stunning views across rolling countryside.

The inn makes a perfect rest-stop for those exploring the Combe Down Heritage Trail, a one-hour walk round Combe Down and its environs.

🕐 Mon-Sat 11.00-23.00; Sun 12.00-22.30

🍴 Lunchtime: Mon-Fri 12.00-14.00; Lunchtime:Sunday 12.00-16.00- Evening meals available with 48 hours notice (Set price- 3 courses). Roasts available during the week with 24 hours notice. Booking advisable.

🅿 Car parking, beer garden

🎵 Darts, skittles, shove ha'penny, cribbage

❓ Prior Park Gardens (¼ mile), Bath (1 ½ miles), Heritage Trail

THE LAMB INN

BARFORD ROAD, FOUR FORKS, SPAXTON, NEAR BRIDGWATER,
SOMERSET TA5 1AD
TEL: 01275 671350

Directions: Bridgwater-to-Minehead Road, A39 turn left at the sign for Spaxton. The Lamb Inn is 1½ miles further down this road

The Lamb Inn is a gracious and welcoming inn offering great food and drink. The extensive exterior presents a friendly face to the world, whitewashed and adorned with window boxes. Inside, attractive original features include the beamed ceilings. The open-plan bar has a woodburning stove and is adorned with a fascinating collection of brasses, agricultural implements and handsome prints, all adding to the cosy, traditional ambience. The lovely lawned garden to the rear boasts a plethora of flowers and is just the place to enjoy a relaxing drink or meal on fine days.

Food is a highlight here, with a menu boasting a selection of home-cooked meals, from snacks and sandwiches to hearty favourites such as steaks, pies and grills complemented by vegetarian dishes. The Sunday roasts are delicious and justly popular – booking advised. All dishes use the freshest local ingredients available to create tempting and satisfying results.

To drink there are always two real ales, lagers, ciders, spirits, soft drinks, teas and coffees, together with an excellent wine list of international vintages.

Jacqueline Cremins has been running this fine inn since 2000. She is convivial and welcoming, and she and her capable, conscientious staff make sure every guest has an enjoyable and pleasant drink or meal.

🕐 Winter: Mon-Thurs 18.00-23.00, Fri-Sat 11.00-15.00, 18.00-23.00; Sun 12.00-15.00, 19.00-22.30. Summer: Mon-Sat 11.00-23.00; Sun 12.00-22.30

🍴 Lunchtime and evening menus; daily specials

🅿 Car parking, beer garden

🎵 Skittles

@ kings@transuk.co.uk; www.kingsarmsotterton.com

❓ Minehead, coastal and countryside walks, golf, National Trust/Coleridge cottage

THE MASONS ARMS

MARSTON GATE, FROME, SOMERSET BA11 4DJ
TEL: 01373 464537 FAX: 01373 455071

Somerset

Directions: From junction 18 on the M4, take the A36 around Bath to Frome. From the town, follow the A361 towards Glastonbury and The Masons Arms lies on the outskirts of Frome, just after Sainsbury's supermarket.

Found on the road to Glastonbury, **The Masons Arms** is a particularly attractive inn which began life as three charming cottages, built in the 17ᵗʰ century – a fact attested to by the three front doors, which remain as a reminder of its origins. The addition of colourful flower-filled award winning hanging baskets further increases the homeliness of this delightful inn. Entering by any of the three doors, guests are greeted by the charming interior, which is a labyrinth of cosy rooms and areas where the original cottage beams

and fireplaces remain in situ.

Here in this inviting place, guests are treated to an excellent selection of real ales, including those from Wadworth & Butcombe, together with lagers, beers and an extensive international wine list. Landlord Graham Mustow and his staff, winners of several customer service awards, enjoy a justly deserved reputation for superb food, and serve up a menu of tasty home-cooked dishes, from the sumptuous grills served on the hot skillet to an a la carte list of favourites supplemented by daily specials. The traditional Sunday lunches are justly popular and ideal for all the family. Booking is advised.

Outside there's an attractive beer garden. Graham also keeps an aviary which everyone is sure to find charming.

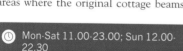

🕐 Mon-Sat 11.00-23.00; Sun 12.00-22.30

🍴 Bar meals and snacks, a la carte 12.00-14.30, 18.30-21.30 (Mon-Sat), 12.00-21.00 Sun including traditional Sunday lunchs

💷 All major credit cards (excluding Amex & Diners)

🅿 Car parking, beer garden, functions catered for

🎵 Occasional live music

❓ Longleat House and Park (3 miles), Witham Friary (4 miles), East Somerset Railway (7 miles), walking, cycling, riding, fishing

THE MERRY MONK

MONKTON HEATHFIELD, TAUNTON, SOMERSET TA2 8NE

TEL: 01823 412213 FAX: 01823 413887

Somerset

Directions: From junction 25 on the M5 take the A38. Monkton Heathfield is situated on the A361 close to its junction with the A38.

The Merry Monk is a handsome and friendly public house offering a high standard of food, drink and hospitality.

Wally and Sue Clayton have 30 years' experience in the licensing trade in Devon, Dorset and Somerset, and have been at The Merry Monk since 1997. Their experience shows in the expert and friendly service they offer all their guests.

Wadsworth 6X and a changing guest ale are the real ales on tap, as well as a

range of keg bitters, lagers, cider, stout, a good wine lists, spirits, soft drinks, teas and coffees.

Well known for the quality of its food, this excellent inn offers a choice of delicious meals and snacks. Home-made dishes such as steak-and-ale pies, beef and mushroom stroganoff and chicken korma are a speciality here, and can be chosen from the extensive menus or daily specials board. Booking is advised for Saturday evening and Sunday lunch. Children are welcome if dining. Meals can be taken throughout the pub or in the separate non-smoking restaurant, a large and tastefully furnished and decorated venue where the ambience is relaxed and homely. There's also an attractive conservatory, added in 2001. On fine days, the lovely beer garden is just the place to enjoy a pleasant drink or meal, and is has a children's play area.

- 🕐 Mon-Sat 11.00-15.00, 18.00-23.00; Sun 12.00-15.00, 19.00-22.30

- 🍺 Lunchtime (Mon-Sun 12.00-14.00) and evening (Mon-Sat 18.00-22.00; Sun 19.00-21.30) menus; daily specials

- 💷 All major credit cards except Diners

- 🅿 Disabled access, car parking, beer garden, children's play area, small function room

- 🎵 Quiz night first Wednesday of the month from 8 p.m.

- @ e-mail: wally@merrymonk.freeserve.co.uk, website: www.merrymonk.co.uk

- ❓ Hestercombe (2 miles), Fyne Court (3 miles), Taunton (4 miles), Durleigh Reservoir (6 miles), walking, cycling, horse riding, fishing, bird watching

THE MITRE INN

27 BENEDICT STREET, GLASTONBURY, SOMERSET BA6 9NE
TEL/FAX: 01458 831203

Directions: From junction 23 on the M5 take the A39 to Glastonbury.

Taking its name from the fact that it's located just steps away from the cathedral, seat of the bishops of Glastonbury over the centuries, **The Mitre Inn** is a pristine and delightful place to enjoy a quiet drink or meal amid comfortable and friendly surroundings. Run with the expertise that comes of many years' experience in the licensing and catering trades by Julia Wilson and Mary Manning, this excellent pub in the heart of Glastonbury is relaxing and welcoming.

With two locally brewed real ales plus three keg bitters, three lagers, cider, stout, wines, spirits, soft drinks, teas and coffees, there's something to quench every thirst. Well known for the quality

of its food, Julia and Mary share the cooking. They prepare a tempting variety of dishes at lunch and dinner, with a menu of traditional English, vegetarian, Italian and Indian dishes such as steak, Stilton and Guinness pie, mushroom stroganoff, spinach and ricotta cannelloni or lamb rogan josh, as well as a range of daily specials. Booking is recommended for Saturday evening and Sunday lunch. Children are welcome.

Every other Friday from 8 p.m. this convivial pub hosts a folk club, where all are welcome to bring their own instruments and join in. Anyone wishing to take a break from sightseeing in the area could hardly do better than to choose this fine inn as their stopping-off place.

- 🕐 Mon-Fri 11.00-15.00, 18.00-23.00; Sat 11.00-23.00; Sun 12.00-22.30
- 🍴 Lunchtime (12.00-14.00) and evening (18.00-21.30) menus; daily specials
- 💷 Visa, Mastercard, Access, Switch, Delta
- 🅿 Car parking, beer garden
- 🎵 Folk club, skittle alley
- ❓ Glastonbury/Glastonbury Tor, The Shoe Museum at Street (2 miles), Wells (7 miles), Cheddar Gorge (9 miles), walking, cycling, horse riding, fishing

THE NOG INN

Somerset

SOUTH STREET, WINCANTON, SOMERSET BA9 9DL
TEL: 01963 32159 FAX: 01963 824576

> **Directions:** From junction 18 on the M4 take the A36 and then the A361 to Frome. From the town take the A361, A359 and then the A371 to Wincanton. Wincanton is also just off the A303 London to the South West arterial road.

Set in the heart of Wincanton, **The Nog Inn** is very much a family-run establishment, offering a warm welcome and genuine hospitality to all guests. This Free House is run by Terry and Jan O'Meara together with their daughter Laura and son Martin. They have been here since 1991, and Terry and Jan have been in the trade some 32 years. Homely and convivial, it's just the place to relax and enjoy a quiet drink, great meal, and good company.

The Georgian exterior belies the size of the pub, which is quite extensive inside. The rear of the building is older, dating back some 400 years. Guests can dine throughout the inn, but there is also a separate dining area. Terry, Jan and Laura share the cooking. Booking is advised on Sundays. Guests can make their selection from the menu or specials board. All the dishes are home-cooked. Specialities of the house include home-made pies, pasta dishes and other hearty and satisfying favourites. Children are welcome if eating. Such is the renown of the meals here that other local pubs send their clientele this way to dine.

This fine pub boasts three real ales – Bass, Greene King IPA and a changing guest ale – along with one keg bitter, two draught lagers, a draught cider, two draught stouts and a good range of spirits, wines and soft drinks.

The hidden beer garden to the rear, accessible only through the pub, is a delightful retreat.

- 🕐 Mon-Fri 11.00-15.00, 17.00-23.00; Sat 11.00-23.00; Sun 12.00-22.30
- 🍴 Mon-Fri 12.00-14.30, 17.00-22.00; Sat 12.00-22.00; Sun 12.00-21.00
- £ All major credit cards
- Ⓟ Car parking, beer garden
- @ thenoginn@btopenworld.com
- ❓ Bickleigh Castle and Bickleigh Mill Visitor Centre, Tiverton, Fursdon, Stourhead, Hadspen House, Yeovilton

THE OLD INN

BISHOPS HULL ROAD, BISHOPS HULL, TAUNTON, SOMERSET TA1 5EG
TEL: 01823 284725 FAX: 01823 323425

Somerset

Directions: From junction 25 on the M5 take the A38 into Taunton and then through Taunton on the A38 towards Wellington. Bishops Hull is approximately 1 mile west of Taunton town centre.

The Old Inn, as befits its name, dates back in parts some 400 years – the whitewashed part of the building is from this earlier era - with a later, stonebuilt addition that itself goes back to the 1750s. This traditional coaching inn continues to the present day its long legacy of offering fine food, drink, hospitality and accommodation.

Father-and-son team Trevor and Paul have run this excellent inn since 1999.

Guests can dine anywhere in the pub, although there is also a dedicated dining area. Most of the enticing dishes on the menu and specials board are home-made, and there is a broad range of choice. Children are welcome and there's a special Seniors menu Monday to Saturday lunchtime. On fine days guests can make use of the beer garden located to the rear of this venerable pub.

This fine inn boasts two real ales: Butcombe Bitter and a changing guest ale, as well as keg bitters, lagers, cider, stout, wines, spirits and soft drinks.

The service is always friendly and attentive, as Trevor, Paul and their helpful staff make every effort to ensure guests enjoy their stay.

The accommodation comprises eight comfortable and attractive guest bedrooms, all located upstairs. Paul cooks the hearty breakfasts awaiting guests in the morning – just the thing to set you up for a day's sightseeing in the area.

- ⏰ Mon-Sat 11.00-23.00; Sun 12.00-22.30
- 🍴 Mon-Sat 12.00-14.00 and 19.00-21.00; Sun 12.00-14.00
- 💷 All major credit cards except Diners
- 🛏 8 letting rooms
- ♿ Disabled access, car parking, beer garden
- 🎵 Quiz night Wednesday once a month; long skittle alley, darts
- ❓ Taunton (1 mile), Hestercombe (3 miles), Fyne Court (4 miles), Durleigh Reservoir (7 miles), walking, horse riding, fishing, bird watching

THE PELICAN INN

SOUTH PARADE, CHEW MAGNA, SOMERSET BS40 8SL
TEL: 01275 332448

Directions: From Bristol, take the A38 towards Weston-Super-Mare. Take the B3130 on the left after about 3 miles.

The Pelican Inn is a wonderful old coaching inn dating back to the early 1600s. There's a wealth of original features such as the leaded lights and exposed beamwork. Other charming and unique details that make this a special placec are the enclosed courtyard that leads to a secluded lawned garden with shrubs and decorative borders. Inside and out, it's a relaxing and welcoming place. There are two bars – one guests can swear in, and one where they can't! – in which to enjoy the good range of real ales, lagers, ciders, wines, spirits, soft drinks, teas and coffees on offer.

- 🕐 Mon-Sat 11.00-23.00; Sun 12.00-22.30
- 🍴 Lunchtime and evening menus; daily specials
- 💷 All major credit cards
- 🅿 Car parking, beer garden
- 🎵 Games, darts, pool, quiz nights, occasional live music
- ❓ Chew Reservoir and Lakes, fishing, walking

Kerry and Richard, together with their able, friendly staff, run this delightful inn with the aim of providing the best in hospitality and comfort to all their guests. Kerry won the regional Bar Food Award for 2002, as attested to by the delicious range of home-cooked and home-prepared dishes on the menu. From sandwiches and light bites to steaks, chicken, pork, lamb, pies and vegetarian dishes, there's something to tempt every appetite. All are made with the freshest local ingredients.

Everything guests could want to ensure a relaxed and comfortable meal or drink amid very pleasant surroundings can be found here at this traditional pub.

THE RED LION

SUTTON HILL ROAD, BISHOP SUTTON, NEAR BRISTOL,
SOMERSET BS39 5UT
TEL: 01275 332689

Somerset

Directions: From Bath take the A39 road towards Wells. Afeter about5 miles turn right onto the A368 to Bishop Sutton.

The Red Lion in Bishop Sutton is a large, handsome inn dating back some 150 years. The interior is open-plan with a long bar. Light, airy and spacious, it is at the same time warm and welcoming. Lots of memorabilia and traditional ornaments such as copper and brass adornments line the walls, and the furnishings are comfortable. Licensees Sue and Paul Bayley, offer their guests genuine hospitality and excellent service and quality. All the food is home-cooked to order. There's a good range of bar snacks and a full evening menu, together with daily specials. From delicious starters through to main-course fish, lamb, mixed grill,

steak, gammon, pork, chicken and vegetarian dishes and mouth-watering desserts, there's something to tempt every palate. The Sunday lunch is also a real treat, with a choice of 4 roasts.

There's the traditional compliment of real ales, ciders, lagers, wines and spirits, soft drinks, teas and coffees, to be enjoyed indoors or, on fine days, out in the large and attractive garden.

Popular with locals and visitors alike, Sue, Paul and their helpful staff are keen to meet guests' every requirement. This fine pub combines the best in traditional home comforts with modern-day service and amenities. For a relaxing and enjoyable drink or meal, amid very pleasant surroundings, this is the place to stop off on your journeys round this particularly lovely part of the county.

- 🕐 Mon-Sat 12.00-23.00; Sun 12.00-22.30
- 🍴 Lunchtime and evening menus; daily specials
- 💷 All major credit cards
- 🅿 Car parking, beer garden
- 🎵 Quiz night every Weds, darts, occasional live entertainment
- ❓ Chew Valley Lakes, fishing, walking, Bath, Bristol, Weston-super-Mare

Somerset

THE RED TILE INN

MIDDLE ROAD, COSSINGTON, BRIDGWATER SOMERSET TA7 8LN
TEL: 01278 722333

Directions: From junction 23 on the M5 take the A39 a mile or so east to Cossington.

The Red Tile Inn in Cossington dates back to the early 18th century, when it was known as The Cossington Inn. Then thatched, it was renamed in the 1900s when the roof was added. It is an extensive and gracious inn where guests can relax and savour some great food, drink and company.

Licensees Richard and Sylvia have been here since December 2002 and they have brought with them to this venture several years' previous experience in the licensed trade.

Sylvia is the cook, offering guests a range of choices from the menus and specials board. Tempting dishes to choose from include goujons of plaice,

homemade steak and ale pie, beef lasagne and mushroom stroganoff. Booking is required for Friday and Saturday evenings and Sunday lunchtime at this popular and highly regarded establishment. The separate non-smoking dining room is tastefully decorated and furnished, with a cosy ambience. Children are welcome.

Two local real ales – Butcombe Bitter and Butcombe Gold – head a list of drinks that also includes a good range of draught keg bitters, lagers, cider, stout, wines, spirits and soft drinks.

On fine days, meals and drinks can be enjoyed in the lush and well-tended garden, where there's also a safe children's play area. Inside or out, the atmosphere at this excellent inn is convivial and welcoming.

- 🕐 Mon-Sat 11.30-14.30, 18.00-23.00; Sun 12.00-15.00, 19.00-22.30
- 🍴 Mon-Sun 12.00-14.00, 18.00-21.15
- 💷 All major credit cards accepted
- 🅿 Car parking, beer garden, children's play area
- ❓ Bridgwater (4 miles), Glastonbury (7 miles), Burnham-on-Sea (4 miles), Quantock Hills (8 miles), walking, cycling, horse riding, fishing, bird watching

THE RING O' BELLS

PIT HILL LANE, MOORLINCH, BRIDGWATER, SOMERSET TA7 9BT
TEL: 01458 210358

Somerset

> **Directions:** From junction 23 on the M5 take the A39 towards Glastonbury. Moorlinch lies about 1 mile south off the A39, midway between Glastonbury and Bridgwater.

Set in the picturesque Somerset village of Moorlinch, **The Ring O' Bells** is a handsome and comfortable inn with a relaxed and welcoming atmosphere, renowned for its food and well-kept ales.

Clive and Patricia have owned this superior pub since December 2002. Clive used to run a snooker club in East Sussex. In a short time they have created an inn that is a draw for locals and visitors alike, by virtue of great word-of-mouth about the excellent food, drink, hospitality and service on hand here.

🕐 Mon 17.00-23.00; Tues-Sat and Bank Holidays 12.00-23.00; Sun 12.00-22.30

🍴 Tues-Sat 12.00-14.00; Mon-Sat 18.00-21.30; Sundays 12.00-14.30 and 18.00-21.00

£ Visa, Mastercard, Access, Switch, Delta

🅿 Parking, beer garden

♫ Food themed evenings, quiz nights (once a month), skittle alley

@ clivecornish@btopenworld.com, www.pubexplorer.com

? Glastonbury (5 miles), Bridgwater (5 miles), The Shoe Museum at Street (4 miles), Wells (9 miles), Cheddar Gorge (11 miles), walking, cycling, horse riding, fishing

Already well known for its food, Patricia is the chef, and she is a superb one. She has put together a fine menu and tempting range of daily specials board featuring a selection of tempting homemade dishes. Booking is required for Sunday lunch. Another treat is the 'Landlord's Special', when Clive cooks one of his favourite dishes – this has proved justly popular whenever it's on the menu. Children are always welcome to dine.

The variety of drinks available includes five real ales together with a choice of draught lagers, stout and Wilkins locally-produced real cider (well worth sampling for those who have never had this pleasure). There's also a good wine list, spirits, soft drinks, teas and coffees.

THE ROYAL HUNTSMAN

7 LONG STREET, WILLITON, SOMERSET TA4 4QN

TEL: 01984 632441 FAX: 01984 634869

Directions: From junction 23 on the M5 take the A38 to Bridgwater and then the A39 towards Minehead. The Royal Huntsman lies on the main street (A39) in Williton, a few miles east of Minehead and 2 miles from Watchet.

The Royal Huntsman in Williton dates back to 1645 and has been a coaching inn since 1701. The interior boasts many charming original features such as the large open fireplaces, flagstone floors and beamed ceilings. This makes for a very cosy and comfortable ambience in which to enjoy a drink or meal.

Three real ales are available – Courage Best and Bomberdier as well as a changing guest ale – together with bitters, lagers, ciders, stouts, wines, spirits, soft drinks, teas and coffees.

Booking is advised at all times, and required for Friday and Saturday evenings and Sunday lunchtime, at this popular and well-renowned inn. The menu and specials board offer a range of delicious meals. Specialities here include huge steaks at a sensational price. Children are welcome if dining. Guests can dine in the non-smoking restaurant or anywhere throughout this handsome pub.

For anyone wishing to stay and explore this scenic region of Somerset, there are six guest bedrooms, 4 of which are on the ground floor. All are en suite and include every amenity, making for an excellent base from which to visit the coast and the many sights and attractions of Williton and the surrounding area. Paul and Joanne Clark run this excellent inn with an attention to detail and friendly demeanour that ensure that every guest will have a relaxing and enjoyable time.

- 🕐 Mon-Thurs 11.00-14.30, 17.00-23.00; Fri-Sat 11.00-23.00; Sun 12.00-22.30; summer: Mon-Sat 11.00-23.00; Sun 12.00-22.30
- 🍴 Lunchtime (12.00-14.00) and evenings (18.30-21.00). No food Sunday or Monday evening in winter
- £ All major credit cards except Amex, Diners
- Ⓟ Car parking, beer garden, function room
- 🎵 Live entertainment every Saturday evening; skittle alley, pool, darts
- @ theroyal.huntsman@virgin.net
- ❓ West Somerset Railway, Williton Pottery, Orchard Mill, The Bakelite Museum, Orchard Wyndham (1 mile), Minehead (4 miles)

THE ROYAL OAK

60 WEST HILL, PORTISHEAD, BRISTOL, SOMERSET BS20 6LR
TEL: 01275 843176

Somerset

> **Directions:** Off the A369, just a short drive from junction 19 of the M5, high up overlooking the mouth of the River Severn.

Tim and Marie Davey have been at **The Royal Oak** in Portishead since late in 2002. Their enthusiasm and genuine hospitality add to the pub's friendly and relaxed atmosphere, making this the perfect place to enjoy a quiet drink or delicious meal.

With three real ales – Speckled Hen, Courage Best and Bass - on tap, as well as a good range of draught lagers, cider, stout, wines, spirits, soft drinks and tea and coffee, there's something to quench every thirst.

Food is available every evening from 7.30 until 10 p.m. and Sunday lunchtime, with a good selection from the menus and specials board providing a

choice of tempting dishes. Using local ingredients wherever possible, all meals are home-cooked and home-prepared. Whether your preference is for meat, chicken, seafood or vegetarian dishes, you'll find something to tempt your palate.

Children are welcome in the no-smoking Family Room. Throughout the pub there are cosy nooks, and the inn's attractive décor and handsome furnishings enhance the welcoming ambience. Entertainments include darts, a pool table and traditional skittle alley, and there's live music every Saturday night.

This fine inn is owned by the Fulwidge Inns chain, who manage their many pubs with an eye for good service and high-quality food, drink and hospitality. This hidden gem is well worth seeking out for anyone travelling in the region.

- 🕐 Mon-Thurs 11.00-14.30, 18.00-23.00; Fri-Sat 11.00-23.00; Sun 12.00-22.30
- 🍴 Evenings (Tues-Sun 19.30-22.00); Sunday lunch (12.00-14.00)
- Ⓟ Car parking, beer garden
- 🎵 Darts, pool, skittle alley, live entertainment Saturday night from 8.30 p.m.
- ❓ Bristol (6 miles), Clevedon (4 miles), Woodspring Priory (5 miles), Middle Hope Nature Reserve (5 miles), Severn Estuary (1 mile), walking, bird watching, horse riding, golf

THE SEXEYS ARMS INN

BLACKFORD, WEDMORE, SOMERSET BS28 4NT

TEL: 01934 712487 FAX: 01934 712447

> **Directions:** The Sexeys Arms lies on the B3139 near Wedmore, midway between Wells and Burnham-on-Sea; just 10 minutes from Cheddar and Glastonbury and a few miles east of the M5 junction 22 at Highbridge.

The Sexeys Arms Inn is a spacious and inviting pub dating back to the 16th century. Among its many original features are the stonebuilt walls, beamed ceilings and large open fireplaces, all adding to the attractive and comfortable ambience. The pub takes its unusual name from one Hugh Sexey, born in 1556. Born of poor Bruton farmers, he became an auditor to the Exchequer at the Court of Elizabeth I. In recognition of his services, she bestowed upon him the estate of Blackford. He died childless in 1619, and his will bequeathed his estate to charitable purposes. The sign

on the inn shows the coat of arms of the Sexey family: the lamb represents farming, while the ship signifies trade.

Today, Christine Frost brings a wealth of enthusiasm to this, her first venture in the licensing trade. She and her friendly, attentive staff offer a warm welcome and quality service to all their guests.

Three real ales are on tap, including a regularly changing guest ale – as well as a good selection of draught lagers, cider, stout, wines, spirits and soft drinks.

Food is a highlight and guests can choose from the menu or specials board to sample a range of delicious home-made dishes. Meals can be enjoyed throughout the pub or in the separate non-smoking restaurant. Booking is advised Thursday to Sunday at this popular and welcoming inn. Children are welcome.

- 🕐 Tues-Fri 11.00-14.30, 17.00-23.00; Sat 11.00-23.00; Sun 12.00-22.30; Bank Holidays 11.00-23.00
- 🍴 Lunchtime (12.30-13.30) and evening (19.00-21.00) menus; daily specials
- 💷 Visa, Mastercard, Access, Switch, Delta
- 🅿 Car parking, beer garden; weddings and private parties catered for
- 🎵 Long skittle alley
- @ e-mail: thesexeysarms@aol.com, website: www.sexeysarms.co.uk
- ❓ Wedmore (4 miles), Wells (6 miles), Cheddar (5 miles), Wookey Hole Caves (4 miles), Glastonbury (6 miles), walking, cycling

THE SHIP INN

UPHILL, WESTON-SUPER-MARE, SOMERSET BS23 4TN
TEL: 01934 621470

> **Directions:** From junction 21 on the M5 take the A370 towards Weston-Super-Mare. Uphill is just 1 mile south of Weston.

Guests are assured of a warm welcome at **The Ship Inn** and this handsome and spacious pub is well worth seeking out. Being so close to the sea, there's naturally a nautical feel to the furnishings, ornaments and memorabilia adorning the walls of this very pleasant and convivial inn.

The traditional features and décor enhance the cosy atmosphere, where guests can relax and enjoy a quiet drink or meal. There are four real ales

- April-September Mon-Sat 11.00-23.00; Sun 12.00-22.30. October-March Thurs-Sat 11.00-15.00, 19.00-23.00; Sun 12.00-15.00, 19.00-22.30
- Lunchtime (12.00-14.30) and evening (19.00-21.45) menus; daily specials
- All major credit cards
- Quiz nights Tuesday (from 9 p.m.); live music the last Friday of every month; numerous regular charity events
- Weston-Super-Mare (1 mile), Middle Hope Nature Reserve (5 miles), Clevedon Court (8 miles), Bristol (15 miles), walking, cycling, horse riding, fishing, bird watching

available – Bass, local Hook Norton and London Pride plus a changing guest ale – together with a good complement of keg bitters, lagers, cider, stout, wines, spirits and soft drinks.

To tempt your palate, the menu and specials board offer a host of hearty favourites served in the bar or in the restaurant, which is aptly named The Captain's Table. All the snacks and dishes are home-prepared, while the staff are attentive and offer a high standard of quality and service. Meat, fish, fowl, seafood and vegetarian dishes make up the range of excellent choices, with the superb Sunday lunches being especially popular. Booking required on Sundays. Children welcome.

THE THREE HORSESHOES

BATCOMBE, NEAR SHEPTON MALLET, SOMERSET BA4 6HE

TEL: 01749 850359 FAX: 01749 850615

Directions: From junction 18 on the M4, take the A46 to Bath and then the A367 and A37 to Shepton Mallet. Bypass Shepton Mallet and take the A371 for 1 mile before turning onto the B3081. Take the first left and follow the road through Westcombe and for a further mile to The Three Horseshoes.

The Three Horseshoes, as its name suggests, started life as a blacksmith's back in the 1500s. Located next to the impressive village church, which has one of the finest church towers in Somerset, this traditional Free House has been tastefully restored while retaining many original features including its large inglenook fireplace, exposed ceiling beams and many quiet alcoves. Once an important centre of the wool trade, Batcombe is an ancient village situated in an area of outstanding natural beauty. This fine inn maintains the age-old tradition of providing excellent hospitality to travellers and locals alike.

David and Liz Benson bring a wealth of experience to bear on providing all their guests a warm welcome and great food and drink.

Batcombe ale is local, one of two real ales on tap. There are also a good range of lagers, ciders and spirits, as well as an international wine list, soft drinks, teas and coffees.

The extensive menu offers a wide range of delicious dishes, complemented by tasty daily specials. All meals are freshly prepared and made with fresh local ingredients, and include such tempting options as grilled English lamb, roasted duck breast, marinated beef, vegetable couscous and much more. Seafood and fresh fish are among the specialities. Diners will also want to leave room for one of the mouth-watering desserts.

- Mon-Fri 12.00-14.00, 19.00-21.30; Sat 12.00-14.00, 19.00-22.00; Sun 12.00-14.30, 19.00-21.00.
- A la carte restaurant
- Delta, Switch, Visa, Access, Mastercard
- Car parking, function room
- www.threehorseshoes.tablesir.com
- Royal Bath and Wells Showground (4 miles), Longleat (8 miles), walking, riding, horse-racing

PENSFORD HILL, PENSFORD, NEAR BRISTOL SOMERSET BS39 4JF
TEL: 01761 490347

Directions: Bristol to Shepton Mallet Road; Weston-super-Mare to Bath road junction at Chelney 1 mile south

---

The Travellers Rest is a charming and welcoming pub that is well worth seeking out. The open-plan bar has a function room at one end and offers a cosy and friendly spot to relax and savour a pint or meal. The walls are adorned with brasses and prints of local themes, including mining scenes, which heighten the traditional and comfortable atmosphere. This is very much a local pub and centre of community life, with a convivial ambience.

There are plenty of snacks and light meals on offer, together with an extensive menu of dishes such as rump steaks, marinated lamb, breaded plaice and vegetable kiev.

The special OAP menu is available every Wednesday to Saturday from 12.00-14.00. There's also a children's menu, and very popular Sunday roasts. All meals are home-cooked to order, freshly prepared and expertly presented.

The rear garden area is very attractive, and secure for children, and makes a lovely place to enjoy a drink or meal on fine days.

Licensee Steve Chard switched from a career in the corporate sector for the pleasures of providing hospitality, and he and his wife run this fine establishment with enthusiasm and flair, offering all their guests a warm welcome and excellent service.

- 🕐 Mon-Thurs 11.30-14.30, 17.30-23.00; Fri-Sat 11.00-23.00; Sun 12.00-22.30
- 🍴 Lunchtime and evening menus; daily specials
- 💷 All major credit cards
- 🅿 Car parking, beer garden
- 🎵 Games, darts, pool, quiz nights
- ❓ Chew Lakes, fishing, walking, Bath, Bristol

Somerset

THE WHITE HART

THE ISLAND, MIDSOMER NORTON, BATH, SOMERSET BA3 2HQ
TEL: 01761 418270

Directions: From Bath take the A369 to Shepton Mallet

Down a quiet cul-de-sac in the town centre, **The White Hart** is an impressive former coaching inn dating back some 300 years. Considered one of the most untouched and unchanged inns around, the interior of this charming, relaxed pub is pristine and beautifully maintained. A visit here is really like stepping back in time. The original lounge and saloon bars and snug feature panelled walls, black lead fireplaces and other traditional features. The walls and ceiling are adorned with toby jugs and tankards, as well as black-and-white and colour prints and sepia photographs and framed cigarette card collections. All add to the warm and welcoming atmosphere. This large inn also has a conference room and skittle alley and function room (in the former stables).

Food is served daily from midday until 2.30 p.m. The menu features a range of expertly prepared home-cooked favourites such as steak and kidney pie, gammon steak and chicken, along with a selection of vegetarian dishes, fish and seafood meals, salads, sandwiches, burgers and 'fast bites'. The delicious Sunday roast is particularly popular.

And to drink? A selection of real ales, ciders, lagers, wines, spirits, teas and coffees.

This inn has been in the same family for over 50 years. The present tenant, Malcolm David Curtis, carries on the grand family tradition of quality, service and hospitality.

- Mon-Sat 11.00-23.00; Sun 12.00-22.30
- Lunchtime and evening menus; daily specials
- All major credit cards
- Car parking
- Darts, skittle alley
- Bath

THE YORK INN

HONITON ROAD, CHURCHINFORD, TAUNTON, SOMERSET TA3 7RF
TEL: 01823 601333

Somerset

> **Directions:** From junction 26 of the M5, take the road to Wellington for half a mile, then first left at the roundabout. After 1 mile, turn left – Ford Street. Proceed 2 miles to the top of the hill, then turn left. Drive on for 4 miles to the crossroads at the phone box, then turn right. After 2½ miles you come to The York Inn.

The York Inn is a traditional hostelry set in the small farming village of Churchinford, designated an area of outstanding natural beauty. The inn dates back in parts to the 1700s, and combines beautiful original features such as oak beams and open fireplaces with the best in modern-day comforts and amenities. The inn enjoys a deserved reputation for good food. The menu boasts many hearty and delicious favourites such as pork escallopes, lamb chops, calves' liver, prime steaks,

chicken and duck dishes and a good selection of vegetarian choices. Local game and fish are specialities. All dishes use the freshest local ingredients. Traditional roast joints are on offer every Sunday – booking advised.

The good range of tempting bar snacks can be enjoyed in the locals' bar, which has a comfortable, relaxed and friendly ambience. To accompany a meal, or enjoy on their own, there are real ales, lagers, ciders, spirits, soft drinks, teas and coffees, together with a carefully chosen wine list.

A delightful base from which to explore the county, being equidistant from both the north and south coasts, this fine inn offers six spacious and welcoming guest bedrooms, all en suite and tastefully furnished and decorated with guests' every comfort in mind.

- 🕐 Mon-Sat 11.00-23.00; Sun 12.00-22.30
- 🍽 Lunchtime and evening menus; daily specials
- 💷 All major credit cards
- 🛏 6 rooms en suite B&B
- 🅿 Car parking, beer garden
- 🎵 Games, darts, pool table, live music at weekends, quiz nights in winter
- @ e-mail: enquiries@www.the-york-inn.freeserve.co.uk website: www.the-york-inn.freeserve.co.uk
- ❓ Honiton (10 miles), Taunton (10 miles), Chard (10 miles), golf, trout and course fishing, horse riding, walking, birdwatching

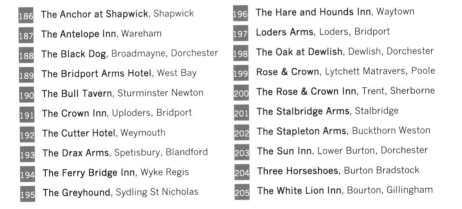

186	The Anchor at Shapwick, Shapwick	196	The Hare and Hounds Inn, Waytown
187	The Antelope Inn, Wareham	197	Loders Arms, Loders, Bridport
188	The Black Dog, Broadmayne, Dorchester	198	The Oak at Dewlish, Dewlish, Dorchester
189	The Bridport Arms Hotel, West Bay	199	Rose & Crown, Lytchett Matravers, Poole
190	The Bull Tavern, Sturminster Newton	200	The Rose & Crown Inn, Trent, Sherborne
191	The Crown Inn, Uploders, Bridport	201	The Stalbridge Arms, Stalbridge
192	The Cutter Hotel, Weymouth	202	The Stapleton Arms, Buckthorn Weston
193	The Drax Arms, Spetisbury, Blandford	203	The Sun Inn, Lower Burton, Dorchester
194	The Ferry Bridge Inn, Wyke Regis	204	Three Horseshoes, Burton Bradstock
195	The Greyhound, Sydling St Nicholas	205	The White Lion Inn, Bourton, Gillingham

Please note all cross references refer to page numbers

DORSET

Although Dorset is by no means a large county it does, in a comparatively small area, provide an extraordinary variety of attractions for the visitor. There are the dramatic cliffs of the western coastline and the more gentle harbours and bays to the east, while, inland, there is chalk upland and heathland that support a wide range of bird, animal and plant life. Ancient monuments litter the landscape, many of the towns and villages date from Saxon and Roman times and, throughout, there are connections with the life and works of the county's best-known son – Thomas Hardy.

To the west lies the charming seaside resort of Lyme Regis best known for its Cobb, the sea wall that featured so dramatically in the film *The French Lieutenant's Woman*. In the early 19th century a young girl discovered the fossilised remains of a dinosaur here and, from then onwards, the Dorset coastline has been associated with both professional and amateur fossil hunters. To the east the wonderful natural harbour of Poole continues to be a commercial port while also supporting a thriving tourist industry. In the shelter of the harbour lies Brownsea Island, an important place for both sea and land birds but, more famously, home to one of England's few remaining colonies of red squirrels. Now almost amalgamating with Poole, Bournemouth, one of the south coasts more exotic seaside resorts, was a relatively late developer. As late as the early 19th century, this was just a small fishing village. However, perhaps the most charming of the county's seaside towns is Weymouth, where George III came to sea-bathe as a sug-

Corfe Castle

gested cure for his nervous disorder. It has grown into a delightful town that has not fallen for the more populist tourist attractions.

Inland, as with the coastal towns and villages, there are ancient settlements founded either in Roman times or by the Saxons. Many of the towns suffered devastating fires in the 16th and 17th centuries when all the timber buildings were razed to the ground, but the elegant Georgian rebuilding makes these especially attractive places to visit today. Shaftesbury is best known for its steep cobbled street that featured in the Hovis bread advertisements. Dorchester, the county town, founded by the Romans, is undoubtedly, one of the country's most appealing market towns, but there is a darker side to Dorchester's history. Here, in the 17th century, Judge Jeffreys presided over the trials of many of the followers of the Duke of Monmouth and so harsh were the judge's sentences that he was dubbed the Hanging Judge. Just 150 years later, the town saw another famous trial, that of the Tolpuddle Martyrs and, again, justice was swift and harsh and the six men were transported to Australia for seven years. It was close to

Bournemouth Beach and Pier

Dorchester that Thomas Hardy was born and, though he spent much time in London as his novels became more successful, he never lost his love for his native county. The writer maintained a house in Dorset throughout his life, as well as featuring many of the towns and villages in his works. Another Hardy is also remembered in Dorset: the Hardy Monument; on Black Downs near Martinstown, the Hardy Monument is a memorial to Vice-Admiral Sir Thomas Masterson Hardy, Flag-Captain of HMS *Victory* at the Battle of Trafalgar.

Along with its many ancient monuments, including some superb Iron Age hill forts, the countryside of Dorset is littered with magnificent country houses such as Kingston Lacy, Athelhampton and Parnham House, although it is perhaps Sherborne Castle, built by Sir Walter Raleigh in the 16th century that interests most people. Dorset's churches provide prime examples of several architectural

Dorchester

periods: Norman at Christchurch, Decorated at Milton Abbey, Perpendicular at Sherborne. And in St Peter's and St Stephen's Bournemouth the Gothic interiors are among the finest of their type. The mild south coast climate and the rich fertile soil of this rural county provide the perfect environment for gardeners. Over the centuries, many have surrounded their country mansions with glorious estates and beautiful formal gardens that, today, make Dorset a horticulturists' delight. But Dorset offers something for every visitor with its combination of glorious countryside and equally glorious coast, of thousands of years of history and a wide range to up-to-date amenities - but not a single racecourse! Above all, Dorset is Thomas Hardy's county, and the Tourist Information Centres and the Thomas Hardy Society produce a wealth of leaflets concerning the great man. Many of the towns and villages were well known to Hardy, and today's visitors will recognise many of the towns and buildings and geographical features that appear in his novels: Dorchester becomes Casterbridge, Weymouth is Budmouth Regis, Bridport is Port Bredy, Portland appears as the Isle of Slingers.

Abbotsbury

Almost nothing remains of the Benedictine Abbey, founded here in the mid 11th century by Orc, a follower of

The Swannery

Canute, except its tithe barn built in the 14th century to store the abbey's tithes of wool, grain and other produce. With its thatched roof and stonewalls, the barn is a glorious sight and one of the largest and best preserved barns in the country. The village has three other main attractions that draw holidaymakers here in their thousands each year – **The Swannery**, the **Sub Tropical Gardens** and the **Tithe Barn Children's Farm**. While each is very different, the combination, in close proximity, makes a visit to Abbotsbury ideal for a family day out.

Beaminster

This attractive and ancient market town was destroyed by fire by the occupying Royalist forces during the English Civil War. After being rebuilt, Beaminster then suffered again, twice, from fire, in 1684 and in 1781, and as a result the centre of the town is a handsome collection of 18th and 19th century buildings. However, some older buildings did survive the flames, including the 16th century Pickwick's Inn and the 15th century Church of St Mary with its splendid 100 foot tower from which, it is said, a number of citizens were hanged during the Bloody Assizes. Another religious house, the former Congregational chapel of 1749, is now the home of the **Beaminster Museum**. A short distance south of the town lies **Parnham House**, a beautiful Elizabethan mansion enlarged and refurbished by John Nash in the 19th century and surrounded by glorious gardens. The house is also a showcase for

Parham House

Georgian buildings that grace the town today were mostly designed by two talented architect-builders, the brothers John and William Bastard, who were charged with rebuilding much of the town after a devastating fire in 1731. However, three important buildings escaped the flames: the Ryves Almshouses of 1682, the Corn Exchange and the splendid 15th century Old House in the Close built to house Protestant refugees from Bohemia.

the very best in modern furniture, much of which is created by owner John Makepeace and his students. John's wife Jennie has undertaken the restoration of the gardens, creating a magical environment with unusual plants, a lake rich in wildlife and a play area for children. To the southeast of Beaminster, **Mapperton Gardens** surround a fine Jacobean manor house with stable blocks, a dovecote and its own church. This western region of Dorset is, indeed, a gardener's delight as, just to the north of Beaminster is yet another lovely garden, **Horn Park Gardens,** laid out around an Edwardian country house.

To mark the completion of the town's rebuilding in 1760, the **Fire Monument,** disconcertingly known locally as the Bastard's Pump, was erected in front of the church. This had a dual purpose – to provide water for fire-fighting and as a public drinking fountain. Inside the church, there is a memorial tablet listing all the buildings created by the Bastard brothers. To the northeast of the town lies **Blandford Camp** and the **Royal Signals Museum,** where there is a wealth of interactive displays on communication, science and technology and, in particular, on codes and code breakers, animals at war and the SAS.

Blandford Forum

Beautifully situated in the wooded valley of the River Stour, this attractive town is the administrative centre for North Dorset. After being granted a market charter in 1605, it prospered as the market centre for the Stour valley and was also known for its production of lace and buttons. The handsome and elegant

Bournemouth

Already established as a resort by the 1830s, Bournemouth continued to expand during the Victorian age and the town blossomed into a place of wide boulevards, grand parks and handsome public buildings. The splendid pier built in 1855 was later rebuilt and extended in 1880 when a theatre was erected at the sea end. Above the Cliff Gardens is **Shelley Park** named after Sir Percy Florence Shelley, son of the poet, and sometime lord of the manor of Bournemouth. Shelley House, where Sir Percy Florence lived for over 40 years, is now the home of the **Casa Magni Shelley Museum** and is the only one in the world devoted to the life and works of the poet, Percy Bysshe Shelley. The poet's heart is said to have been saved from his funeral pyre in Italy and is buried, along with the body of his wife Mary, in a tomb in the marvellous **Church of St Peter**, where, in 1898, the ailing Prime Minster William Gladstone took his last communion.

The town is home to several other museums, including the **Rothesay Museum**, which maintains a mainly nautical theme, the **Teddy Bear Museum** and the **Russell-Cotes Art Gallery and Museum**. As elsewhere in Dorset, Bournemouth has a strong connection with Thomas Hardy. It is mentioned in *Tess of the d'Urbervilles* and *Jude the Obscure* as Sandbourne.

Bridport

Hemp has been grown in the area around Bridport for over 2,000 years and this crop has provided the town, and neighbouring Loders, with its industry, ropemaking. Throughout the centuries the town's rope works have produced cables and hawsers for the Royal Navy, nets for fishermen and hangman's nooses known as Bridport Daggers. Rope production in the town declined severely when the Royal Navy built its own rope works but the industry is still in existence today, though on a much smaller scale; the nets for the tennis courts of Wimbledon are made here. The legacy of Bridport's most profitable industry can be seen in the town's unusually wide pavements and alleys as this is where the ropes were laid out for twisting and drying. **Bridport Museum** tells the history of the town and the surrounding area.

Broadwindsor

Just to the south of this pretty terraced village is a trio of hill forts, the **West Dorset Hill Forts**, for which the county is renowned. Each dates back to the Iron Age and, as they were built on hilltops, **Pilsdon Pen**, **Lambert's Castle** and **Coney's Castle** all provide magnificent views out across the Marshwood Vale to the sea. The poet William Wordsworth took a house on Pilsdon Pen for a short while and declared that there was no finer view in England.

Brownsea Island

Out in Poole Harbour are several islands, the largest of which is the National Trust's Brownsea Island. With its mixed habitat of heath and woodland it is home to a wide variety of wildlife and, in particular, it has one of the few remaining colonies of red squirrels in England.

certainly large, but the Wilmington Long Man in Sussex is taller.

Brownsea Island

In 1907, General Robert Baden-Powell carried out an experiment, to test his idea of teaching boys of all social classes the scouting skills he himself had refined during the Boer Wars, when he brought a party of 20 boys to the island. The venture was a great success and, a year later, Baden-Powell set about creating the Boy Scout movement.

Cerne Abbas

This pretty village beside the River Cerne grew up around a Benedictine **Abbey** founded here in the 9th century. All that remains of the buildings are the imposing 15th century gatehouse and a 14th century tithe barn converted into a house. Once dominated by its monastic house, the village today is famous for the **Cerne Abbas Giant**, a colossal figure cut into the chalk hillside just to the north of the village. Brandishing a club, the giant is naked, uncensored and full frontal and is, undoubtedly, a powerful pagan symbol of virility. First mentioned in 1742, the giant has always been well looked after. At 182 feet tall he is

Charminster

Situated on the River Cerne, on the northern outskirts of Dorchester, is the attractive village of Charminster, where **Wolfeton House**, a splendid medieval and Elizabethan building surrounded by water meadows, lies close to the confluence of the Rivers Cerne and Frome. The house contains some magnificent original features including a great stone staircase, superb carved oak panelling and glorious plaster ceilings.

Charmouth

This peaceful coastal village, whose steep streets are lined with fine Regency properties, was a favourite with the novelist Jane Austen, who called it "sweet and retired." It remains a quiet and attractive little place with a wide main street and a stretch of sandy beach that gradually merges into the shingle. In 1925 a section of the river mouth was exposed to reveal various fossils, including the vertebrae, skull and antlers of a red deer, which are now all housed in the British Museum, London.

To the west of the mouth of the River Char is the **Charmouth Heritage Coast Centre** established in 1985 in an old cement works. Designed to be an education and information centre, its aim is to further the public's understanding and appreciation of this area's scientific wealth, its natural beauty and the potential dangers posed by the unstable cliffs.

Christchurch

In 1094, Ranulf Flambard began the construction of the magnificent **Christchurch Priory**, which has been in continuous use as a place of worship. Said to be the longest parish church in England, it houses many treasures, including a memorial to the poet Shelley and the **St Michael's Loft Museum**, above the Lady Chapel, which contains a fascinating exhibition on the history of the priory. Christchurch has two other museums that are well worth visiting. The **Red House Museum**, housed in a charming Georgian building, follows a local history and natural history theme, and the fascinating **Museum of Electricity**. According to the Guinness Book of Records, Christchurch boasts the most modern of all the country's Scheduled Ancient Monuments, a World War II pillbox and anti-tank obstacles.

On nearby Hengistbury Head are the ancient ditches called the **Double Dykes**. This area is also well known for its superb walking and wonderful views. Britain's first air show took place here in 1910 and the historic event was attended by all the great names of early aviation, among them Wilbur Wright, Louis Blériot and the Hon Charles Rolls, who

was killed when he crashed his plane during the show.

Corfe Castle

This greystone village is dominated by the majestic ruins of Corfe Castle high on a hill. An important stronghold that protected the gateway through the Purbeck Hills, the castle was constructed in the years immediately following the Norman Conquest. Additions were made to the fortification during the reigns of King John and Edward I and, on one

Corfe Castle

occasion, King John is said to have thrown 22 French knights into the dungeons from a hole in the ceiling and left them to starve. Now owned by the National Trust, the castle is part of an extensive estate, with a network of footpaths taking in both the coastline and the inland heath, and encompassing important habitats for many rare species.

Cranborne

This pretty village has a glorious setting, beside the banks of the River Crane, and, with its fine church and manor house, it creates a charming picture of a traditional English village. The imposing Church of St Mary is noted for its fine Norman doorway and exquisite 14th century wall paintings. **Cranborne Manor**, the home of the Cecil family, stands on the site of a royal hunting lodge built by King John for use during his excursions into **Cranborne Chase**.

In the neighbouring village of **Wimborne St Giles**, the church contains a marvellous monument to the 7th Earl of Shaftesbury, who is more memorably honoured by the statue of Eros in London's Piccadilly Circus.

Dorchester

After capturing the Iron Age hill fort of **Maiden Castle** in around AD 50, the Romans went on to found a settlement here called Durnovaia. The hill fort, just to the southwest of Dorchester, is one of the biggest in England and the steep ramparts and ditches of this complex defensive structure are still visible today. As with so many towns in Dorset, Dorchester played host to the infamous Judge Jeffreys, who presided over the trials of the followers of the Duke of

Monmouth in 1685 sentencing over 70 men to death. Later, in the 1830s, the town was once again the scene of a famous trial, as it was here, in the **Old Crown Court**, that the Tolpuddle Martyrs were sentenced to seven years transportation to Australia for swearing an oath of allegiance to their newly-formed union. The Old Crown Court and its cells are now open to the public and provide an ideal opportunity for

Dorchester

visitors to gain an insight into over four centuries of trials and gruesome punishments. The excellent **Dorset County Museum** contains a wealth of exhibits spanning the centuries, from fossil trees, Iron Age warrior skeletons and Roman weaponry to a 19th century cheese press and a stuffed great bustard, a bird often seen in Dorset before it became extinct in Britain in 1810. However, it is the museum's Writers Gallery that draws most visitors as this honours the town's two most famous adopted sons, Thomas Hardy and his friend, the dialect poet William Barnes. To the northeast of the town, lies **Max Gate**, the house that Hardy designed and lived in from 1885 until his death in 1928.

East Lulworth

This charming little village stands on a minor road leading down to one of the country's best loved beauty spots, **Lulworth Cove**, an almost perfectly circular bay surrounded by towering cliffs. Over the centuries, the sea has eaten away at the weak points in the limestone creating a breathtakingly beautiful scene. East Lulworth is home to **Lulworth Castle**, built as a hunting lodge in the first few years of the 17th

Durdle Door

century. Down the ages, no fewer than seven monarchs have been entertained here but a devastating fire in 1929 reduced the castle to a virtual ruin. With the help of English Heritage, the castle has been restored to something resembling its former glory. In the grounds is a curious circular building, dating from 1786, that was the first Roman Catholic church to be established in the country following Henry VIII's defiance of Rome

in 1534.

About a mile west of Lulworth Cove stands a remarkable natural feature, **Durdle Door**, a magnificent archway carved out from the coastal limestone by wind and sea erosion.

Lyme Regis

The first record of the town is in 1294, when Edward I granted Lyme a charter to allow it to add 'Regis' to its name, but it is known that there was a saltworks here at least 500 years earlier. In 1588 Sir Francis Drake's fleet fought a small battle with the Spanish Armada in Lyme Bay. During the English Civil War, surprisingly, the town was staunchly anti-Royalist and the forces of Prince Maurice suffered a heavy defeat here when over 2,000 of the king's followers were killed. Just a few decades later, in 1685, the Duke of Monmouth landed at Lyme Regis and began his unsuccessful rebellion that would lead to the Bloody Assizes of Judge Jeffreys. Held throughout the West Country, the trials started at Winchester before moving to Salisbury and then to Dorchester. By the time the trials had finished, more than 300 men had been hanged, 800 transported to Barbados and hundreds of others had been fined, flogged or imprisoned. Lyme Regis developed during the 18th century into a fashionable seaside resort famed for its clean sea air. The town's most famous landmark is **The Cobb**, built in medieval times to

The eight mile stretch of coast to the east of Lyme Regis includes the highest cliff on the south coast, **Golden Cap**, so called because golden sandstone can be seen on the cliff face.

The Cobb

protect the harbour and sandy beach from the southwesterly storms, but finally joined to the mainland in 1756. This was the location for one of cinema's most enduring images, of a lone woman standing on the wave-lashed Cobb. The film, *The French Lieutenant's Woman*, was based on the novel of the same name by Lyme resident John Fowles. Jane Austen and her family visited here in 1803 and part of her novel, *Persuasion*, is set in Lyme Regis. The **Jane Austen Garden** on Marine Parade commemorates her holiday here. Along with its historical and literary connections, Lyme Regis is also famous for its fossils, first discovered by Mary Anning in the early 19th century. Many of the fine specimens discovered by her and other collectors are on display at the award winning **Philpot Museum**. At **Dinosaurland**, there are, naturally, dinosaurs but also a fossil clinic where visitors can bring their own fossil finds for expert analysis, a Time Gallery that chronicles the history of the Earth, a fossil shop and a natural history room with a collection of live animals.

Martinstown

In a county that is so dominated by the life and works of Thomas Hardy, it is easy to suppose that **Hardy's Monument**, on Black Downs to the southwest of this village, must commemorate the writer. However this is a memorial to Sir Thomas Masterson Hardy, the flag captain of HMS *Victory* at Trafalgar and the man to whom the fatally wounded Nelson famously said, "Kiss me, Hardy." Born in Portesham, a village just below the monument, Hardy the sailor was, like Hardy the writer, descended from the Hardys of Jersey.

Milton Abbas

In 935, King Athelstan founded an abbey here for 40 monks and gradually a settlement grew up around the monastic house. After the Dissolution of the Monasteries, **Milton Abbey** fell into private hands and, in the late 18th century, it was the home of Joseph Damer, the Earl of Dorchester, who lived in the converted abbey buildings. In 1771, Damer decided he needed a large house, so he demolished the monastic buildings, built a new mansion and surrounded it with grounds landscaped by Capability Brown. Unfortunately, the village, which by now was a considerable size, spoilt the views from the earl's new home and gardens so he demolished the village and moved it and its people, a mile or so away. Today, Milton Abbas is an attractive model village of simple thatched cottages in a beautiful setting. The one part of the original abbey that has managed to survive is the Abbey Church, which contains some superb Pugin glass and also the tomb of Joseph Damer. To the north of the village lies **Bulbarrow Hill**, one of the highest points in Dorset, taking its name from the prehistoric burial mound that can be found not far from its summit.

Moreton

Thought to have been inhabited since prehistoric days, this charming village of old cottages beside the River Frome is home to the 18th century Church of St Magnus and St Nicholas built on the site of an older church by the local Frampton family. Close by the church are **Moreton Gardens** a tranquil place of woodland, lawns, streams and ponds, which were originally the kitchen gardens to Moreton House, the Frampton family home. A family of illustrious members, it was Tregonwell who founded Newmarket racecourse, James who built the grand house and founded the Dorset Yeomanry and another James who led the prosecution against the Tolpuddle martyrs. However, the village is best remembered as the last resting place of

TE Lawrence (Lawrence of Arabia), whose funeral was held at the village church in 1935 following his fatal motorcycle accident on the nearby country lanes. The distinguished list of mourners at his funeral included Winston Churchill and the King of Iraq and his headstone was made by his great friend Eric Kennington. Close to the village is **Cloud's Hill**, a tiny redbrick cottage where Lawrence lived after retiring from the RAF in 1935. The life of Lawrence was memorably told in the epic film *Lawrence of Arabia*, which starred a young and dashing Peter O'Toole, of whom one wag said that if he had been any prettier the film would have been called *Florence of Arabia*.

To the east of Moreton lies **Bovington Camp**, which has been used as a training area by the army since World War I and where TE Lawrence served as a private in

Tank Museum

the Royal Tank Corps. Tanks are still a common sight on the surrounding heathland and this is therefore the obvious place for the **Tank Museum**, an impressive collection of over 150 tanks and armoured vehicles from over 26 countries. From Britain's first tank of 1915, Little Willie, to modern day battle tanks that saw action in the Gulf conflict of the 1990s, there is plenty of interest here, including the TE Lawrence exhibition and the fascinating 'The Trench – Tanks on the Somme 1916' attraction. Southeast of the army camp and tank workshops is an altogether different family attraction – the award-winning **Monkey World** established in 1987 to provide a permanent home for abused Spanish beach chimpanzees. Along with rescuing chimps from all over the world and rehabilitating them into social groups, Monkey World is home to numerous other primates while its conservation and rehabilitation work is described at the visitor centre.

The land to the southwest of Bovington Camp is **Winfrith Heath,** which supports a wide range of plants, animals and birds, including sand lizards, smooth snakes and Dartford warblers.

Portland

The Isle of Portland is not, strictly speaking, an island but a peninsula joined to the mainland by the amazing **Chesil Beach**, a vast bank of pebbles worn smooth by the sea, stretching for 18 miles from the island westwards to Abbotsbury. The effect of the tides here is such that the pebbles along the bank are graded in size from west to east and fishermen and smugglers reckoned that they could tell exactly where they were along the bank by the size of the pebbles.

The beach has long been the bane of sailors and many ships have come aground on the pebbles. This island is also famous for its Portland stone, a building material that has been quarried here for centuries and has gone into the construction of some of the country's most famous buildings including St Paul's Cathedral and Buckingham Palace. The island's most famous building is undoubt-edly, **Portland Castle**, constructed by Henry VIII as part of his south coast defence. It remains one of the best examples of his coastal fortresses. From then, until the 20th century, when the castle was used as a D-Day embarkation point for British and American soldiers, the castle has been in constant use. It acted as a prison under Cromwell. Visitors to the castle, today, can see Henry VIII in his Great Hall and climb up to the battlements from where there are superb views out over Portland harbour. The breakwaters here were constructed by convict labour to create the second largest man-made harbour in the world. Close to the castle, and housed in a charming pair of thatched cottages, is the **Portland Museum** founded by the birth control pioneer, Marie Stopes, in 1930. The tip of the island, **Portland Bill**, is now a base for birdwatchers, who congregate around the now decommissioned lighthouse. Also of interest here is the tall, upright Pulpit rock, which can be scaled.

Puddletown

Formerly known as Piddletown ('piddle'

is a Saxon word meaning 'clear water') this village's name was changed to its present form by the sensitive Victorians. This was the birthplace of Hardy's grandfather and great grandfather. Just to the southwest, in the woods above the village of **High Bockhampton**, lies the small thatched cottage where Hardy himself was born in 1840. Built by his grandfather in 1801 and little altered today, it was at **Hardy's Cottage** that the novelist grew up and he continued to live here, on and off, until his marriage to Emma Gifford in 1874. Now in the hands of the National Trust, Hardy featured his birthplace in his novel *Under the Greenwood Tree*. Visitors can see the very room in which his mother gave birth, only to hear her child proclaimed stillborn, before an observant nurse noticed that the infant was, in fact, breathing.

To the east of Puddletown lies one of the country's finest examples of a 15th century house, **Athelhampton**, which features magnificently furnished rooms including its Great Hall, Great Chamber and a State Bedroom with a Charles I tester bed. The wonderful grounds feature world-famous topiary pyramids, fountains and the Octagonal Garden designed by Sir Robert Cooke in 1971.

Poole

Poole has a huge, natural harbour that is actually a drowned river valley. Its history goes back to the time of the Romans. The silting up of the River Frome might have been the downfall of Wareham as a port but it was the making of Poole and by the mid 13th century it was well established as a town and port. Trade has continued from here ever since and, today, the town happily combines its dual functions as a commercial port and ancient town. Still proud of its long maritime history, the **Waterfront Museum**, housed in an 18th century warehouse and the adjoining medieval town cellars, tells the 2,000-year story of the port; **Poole Aquarium and Serpentarium** is home to all manner of marine creatures, reptiles and insects, including sharks, piranhas, pythons and rattlesnakes. The town has also lent its name to **Poole Pottery** and this expanding complex, where the famous red tiles for London Underground were made, is Poole's third major attraction. Poole lies at beginning of the 630 mile long **South West Coast Path** that runs continuously from here around the coastlines of Devon and Cornwall to Minehead in Somerset.

Puncknowle

This village's name rhymes with tunnel and it is best known as being the birthplace, in 1761, of Henry Shrapnel, an English artillery officer who invented a bomb that was first used in the Crimean War. To the east of the village are two of the area's many ancient monuments: **Kingston Russell Stone Circle**, a Bronze Age circle of around 80 feet in diameter, and **Poor Lot Barrows**.

Sandbanks

This spit of land, along with Studland to the southwest, almost cuts off the harbour at Poole from the sea but it is these two headlands that provide the harbour with its shelter. Just at the top of the headland lies **Compton Acres**, a series of themed gardens separated by paths, steps, rock walls and terraces that have been delighting visitors for years.

Gold Hill

Shaftesbury

This hilltop town, which stands over 700 feet above sea level, was founded in 880 by King Alfred, who fortified the settlement here and established a Benedictine abbey for women, installing his daughter as the first prioress. Just a hundred years later, King Edward, who was murdered at Corfe Castle, was buried at **Shaftesbury Abbey** and it soon became a place of pilgrimage. Today, the abbey remains have been excavated and lie in a quiet, peaceful walled garden. The nearby **Shaftesbury Abbey Museum** houses many of the finds from the abbey's excavations and state of the art, touch screen displays bring the ancient religious house to life.

Apart from the abbey, there are some interesting buildings here, such as the Tudor style **Town Hall** dating from the 1820s and 17th century **Ox House** that receives a mention in Hardy's *Jude the Obscure*. However, the town's most famous sight is **Gold Hill**, a steep cobbled street, stepped in places and lined with delightful 18th century cottages. Many people who have never visited the town will recognise this thoroughfare as it was made famous through the classic television advertisement for Hovis bread. The cottage at the top of the hill is home to the **Shaftesbury Museum**, where each of the former dwelling's little rooms is filled with objects of local interest and outside there is a cottage-style garden. Button making was once an important cottage industry in the town and some of the products can be seen here, including the decorative Dorset knobs, which share their name with a famous, also locally-made, biscuit.

Sherborne

It was here, in 705, that St Aldhelm founded **Sherborne Abbey** as the Mother Cathedral for the whole of the southwest of England, a status it retained until 1075. There are few traces of the original Saxon church, but the present building, which dates chiefly from the mid 15th century, is notable for its wonderful fan vaulting. Among the many other treasures are two enormous stone coffins in the north aisle containing, according to legend, the remains of two Saxon kings, Ethelbald and Ethelbert, who were the elder brothers of Alfred the Great and Ethelred. Ethelbald and Ethelbert, and perhaps even Alfred himself, were among the earliest pupils at what was eventually to become, in 1550, **Sherborne School**, whose more recent old boys include Cecil Day Lewis, the poet laureate, and the writer David Cornwell, better known as John Le Carré. The school, which is housed in some of the old abbey buildings, may be familiar to cinema goers as the setting for three major films: *The Guinea Pig* (1948), *Goodbye, Mr Chips* (1969) and *The Browning Version* (1994). Sherborne's best-known resident was Sir Walter Raleigh, who, while enjoying the favouritism of Elizabeth I, asked for and was granted the house and estate of **Sherborne Old Castle** in 1592. It was a stark and comfortless residence, especially for someone of Raleigh's sophistication and ambition, and he chose to build a new castle rather than refurbish the old. The result is the splendid **Sherborne Castle**, which Raleigh dubbed Sherborne Lodge to distinguish it from its predecessor.

Sturminster Newton

An unspoilt market town on the River Stour at the heart of the rich agricultural area of Blackmore Vale, Sturminster and Newton were separate communities on opposite riverbanks until Elizabethan times. Shortly after the graceful Town Bridge was constructed to link the two communities, a mill was built a little way upstream. Now fully restored and powered by a 1904 turbine, **Newton Mill** is once again producing flour and it is an ideal place to find out more about the milling process. It was in Sturminster Newton that Thomas Hardy and his wife Emma had their first home, and he often referred to this period of his life as "our happiest time."

Swanage

This seaside town, complete with its fully restored Victorian pier, built its early fortune on Purbeck stone and the gentleman who really put Swanage on the map was John Mowlem, a quarryman, who built the town's first roads. With the aid of his nephew and partner, George Burt, they built several civic buildings and even gave the town piped water. However, the Town Hall's magnificent front façade was not their work but that of Christopher Wren, who had originally designed the front for Mercers Hall in the City of London. When the building was demolished, the facade was taken down, piece by piece, and reconstructed here. Several other buildings in the town made use of architectural salvage from London and even George Burt's home, Purbeck House, included additions from the metropolis. One monument in the town is purely Swanage: the **King Alfred Column**, on the seafront, records that this was where the king fought and saw off the Danish fleet in 877. Housed in the late 19th century market hall is the **Swanage Heritage Centre** that tells the story of the town and, in particular, features the Jurassic coast, Purbeck stone and the two men, Mowlem and Burt, who transformed the town.

To the north of Swanage lies **Studland**, whose fine sandy beach stretches from Handfast Point to South Haven Point and the entrance to Poole Harbour. The heathland behind the beach is a haven for rare birds and is a National Nature Reserve. This glorious area of National Trust owned land incorporates bird hides, several public footpaths and two nature trails.

Tolpuddle

It was here in the 1830s that the first trades union was formed, when six villagers, in an attempt to escape from both grinding poverty and their harsh employers, banded together and took an oath of mutual support. Their leader was a Wesleyan Methodist preacher, George Loveless, and the others were his brother, James Loveless, James Brine, James Hammett, John Standfield and his father, Thomas Standfield, in whose cottage the union, the Friendly Society of Agricultural Labourers, was formed. Fearing a spreading uprising, the landowners acted quickly and invoked the Mutiny Act of 1797. The six men were found guilty in court, of swearing

the oath, not for the formation of the union. That had been made legal in 1824. The six were transported to Botany Bay, Australia for seven years. However the harsh sentence caused such a public outcry, led by Dorchester's member of Parliament, that they were granted a free pardon and allowed to return home. Only one of the six, James Hammett, returned to Tolpuddle; the others went first to Essex, before seeking new lives in Canada. The story of the martyrs is told in the **Tolpuddle Martyrs Museum** housed in some memorial cottages built in 1934 by the TUC. James Hammett is buried in the village churchyard.

Wareham

Situated between the Rivers Frome and Piddle (or Puddle), Wareham lies within the earthworks of a 10th century encircling wall and was an important port until the River Frome silted up the harbour approaches. However, Wareham's history goes back much further, to the days of the Romans, and it was these invaders who laid out its street plan – a grid of streets that faithfully follow the points of the compass. Having lost its direct links with the sea, the town was then hit, in 1726, by a devastating fire that destroyed all but a few of its buildings. Fortunately, for today's visitors, the town was rebuilt and it is now dominated by elegant Georgian stone houses. The town's **Museum** has a special section devoted to TE Lawrence, who lived for the last few months of his life at nearby Clouds Hill and who was trained at Bovington Camp close by. The **Rex Cinema** here is a fine period building now restored. This Victorian building has a gaslit auditorium and the original carbon arc projectors are still in use.

Weymouth

Originally two ports dating back to Roman times, Weymouth and Melcombe Regis, on either side of the mouth of the River Wey, owed their early prosperity to the woollen trade. As elsewhere, the woollen trade suffered a rapid, if temporary, decline during the Black Death. The years following the plague saw further expansion but Weymouth received a great boost when Henry VIII built **Sandsfoot Castle** here as part of the south coast's defences. Like many coastal towns and villages in the late 18th century, Weymouth began to develop as a resort for those looking for fresh sea air and sea-water bathing and, in 1789, George III came here to try out the newly invented bathing machine. Fashionable society followed in his wake, and the grateful town thanked the king for his patronage by erecting an unusual painted statue of their frequent visitor in 1810. Close by, the colourful Jubilee Clock was put up in 1887 to celebrate the golden jubilee of the king's granddaughter,

Queen Victoria.

One of the town's most popular tourist attractions is **Brewers Quay**, an imaginatively converted Victorian brewery close to the harbour that is home to a shopping village of over 20 specialist shops and superb attractions. Nearby **Weymouth Museum** holds a fascinating collection on local and social history as well as the important Bussell Collection.

Not far from Brewers Quay is **Nothe Fort**, built between 1860 and 1872 as part of the defences of the new naval base that was being established at nearby Portland and from where 10 huge guns faced out to sea while two smaller ones were trained inland. The fort remained in active service until 1956 and is now the home of the **Museum of Coastal Defence**. One of the harbour's imposing Victorian grain warehouses is now the home of **Deep Sea Adventure**, a wonderful family attraction that tells the story of deep-sea exploration and marine

Weymouth Harbour

exploits down the centuries. Another tribute to George III can be found carved into the chalk hills above the village of **Osmington**, just a short distance north-east of Weymouth. One of many **White Horses** caved into hillsides around the country this particular one is different as, besides being the largest, it is the only one that carries a rider, although it is unrecognisable as a likeness of the king.

Kingston Lacy House

Whitchurch Canonicorum

Delightfully situated on the edge of Marshwood Vale and in the steep valley of the River Char, this charming village of thatched cottages is home to the Church of St Candida and the Holy Cross, which is often referred to as the Cathedral of the Vale. A handsome building dating from Norman times, with an imposing 13th century tower, the church is one of only two in the country that still has a shrine to a saint. The other is Westminster Abbey with its shrine to Edward the Confessor.

Wimborne Minster

A wonderful old market town set among meadows beside the Rivers Stour and Allen, Wimborne Minster is dominated by its **Minster**, a glorious Norman building of multi-coloured stone. Close by the Minster is the **Priest's House**, a 16th century town house now home to the **Museum of East Dorset Life**. To the east, at **Hampreston**, is **Knoll's Garden and Nursery**, a delightful, informal and typically English garden planted over 30 years ago with a collection of rhododendron and Australasian plants while, further east again, is **Stapehill**, a 19th century Cistercian nunnery that is now a craft centre and countryside museum. By far the finest example of the country house in the area lies to the west of Wimborne. **Kingston Lacy House**, set in wooded parkland with attractive way marked walks, contains an outstanding collection of paintings and other works of art. Elsewhere on the estate is the Iron Age hill fort of **Badbury Rings**, three concentric rings of banks and ditches were cut and raised by the Celtic tribe of Durotriges.

THE ANCHOR AT SHAPWICK

WEST STREET, SHAPWICK, BLANDFORD, DORSET DT11 9LB
TEL: 01258 857269 FAX: 01258 858840

Directions: Blandford-to-Wimborne Road

A warm and friendly atmosphere, home-cooked food and real ales await visitors to **The Anchor at Shapwick**. This spacious and attractive inn has a spacious open-plan bar area warmed by log fires on chilly days.

Rob and Karen Reynolds have been here since 2000; together with chef Rupert they have built up a fine reputation for quality and service.

The food alone is worth the journey. Booking is advised because the menu of delights such as steak, mushroom and ale pie, honey and mustard chicken, curry of the day, steak grills, delicious fish and vegetarian dishes and daily specials are justly popular. From Baguettes and snacks to a la carte, there's something for every appetite and palate here. Birthday parties and other special occasions for up to 15 people are happily catered for.

In addition to the selection of real ales on tap there's a good range of lagers, ciders, wines, spirits, soft drinks and speciality coffees and teas. All can be enjoyed indoor or, when the weather is fine, outside in the attractive beer garden.

An ideal stop on the way to or from exploring the many sights and attractions of the area, this fine inn has everything required for a relaxed and very pleasant few hours.

- 🕐 Mon-Sat 11.00-15.00, 18.00-23.00; Sun 12.00-15.30, 19.00-22.30
- 🍴 Lunchtime and evening menus, daily specials Tues-Sun 12.00-14.00, 19.00-21.00
- £ All major credit cards
- Ⓟ Car parking, beer garden
- 🎵 Darts, boulet court, quiz nights, music at weekends, functions catered for
- @ info@anchoratshapwick.com, www.anchoratshapwick.com
- ❓ Blandford, Badbury Rings, Wimborne, Kingston Lacy House, Stour River, golfing, fishing

THE ANTELOPE INN

13 WEST STREET, WAREHAM, DORSET BH20 4JS
TEL: 01929 552827   FAX: 01929 553660

Dorset

> **Directions:** Go into Wareham from Poole, right at main traffic lights. Situated 30 yards down road on left.

Set along a bustling street in Wareham, **The Antelope Inn** might be easy to walk by – but that would be to miss out on a real treat. Owner Paul Mitchener was once a gamekeeper, then manager of a Whitbread Public House. Here at the inn he marries his two trades and brings a wealth of experience to bear on providing great food and drink and a welcoming ambience.

The interior is traditional and cosy, with exposed beams, lots of exposed brickwork and a large open fire. Comfortable and inviting, it's just the place to enjoy a delicious meal and satisfying drink. There's a full range of beers, including two real ales in winter, three in summer, as well as spirits, soft drinks, teas and speciality coffees, together with an excellent wine list chosen to complement the food on offer. And this food deserves special mention: guests can sample fresh fish caught by Paul from his own boat, together with an impressive range of truly exceptional dishes including venison, game pie, chicken, king prawns, chilli con carne, sirloin steaks and more. All of the food is hearty and exceptionally tasty, expertly prepared and presented.

Plans are also afoot to offer bed and breakfast accommodation in the converted barns to the rear of this fine inn.

- 🕐 Summer: Mon-Sat 11.00-23.00; Sun 12.00-22.30; Winter: 11.00-15.00, 16.00-23.00; Sun 12.00-22.30
- 🍴 Lunchtime and evening menus; daily specials. Limited family Dining area in Summer
- 💷 All except Amex, Diners
- 🅿 Beer garden, skittle alley
- 🎵 Occasional live music

THE BLACK DOG

50 MAIN STREET, BROADMAYNE, DORCHESTER,
DORSET DT2 8ES
TEL: 01305 852360   FAX: 01305 853714

Directions: On the A352 to Wareham. Approximately 3 miles from Dorchester.

The Black Dog in Broadmayne is a large and impressive inn with a warm and cosy ambience. Traditional features of this fine pub include beamed ceiling, log fire, exposed timers and a wealth of lovely pictures adorning the walls. Comfortable and relaxed, this inn offers great food and drink and excellent accommodation.

There's a full range of drinks on offer, including a minimum of three real ales at any time, wine by the glass or bottle, and a full compliment of lagers, ciders, spirits, soft drinks, teas and coffees.

Home-cooked food on the menu makes use of the freshest locally produced ingredients to create delicious dishes such as steaks, chicken, duck, pies, ham, pork, lamb, grills and vegetarian options. There's also an extensive lunchtime menu, daily specials, and Sunday lunch offering a choice of three different roasts.

The accommodation comprises three ensuite guest bedrooms, attractively and comfortably furnished.

Owned by Allan and Yvonne Warnes, who together with their friendly, helpful staff offer the best in service and hospitality, this superior pub is well worth seeking out. Allan has many years' experience in the trade, in London and here in Dorset. He and Yvonne offer every guest personal attention and a warm welcome.

- 🕐 Mon-Fri 11.00-15.00, 18.00-23.00; Sat 11.00-23.00; Sun 12.00-16.00, 19.00-22.30
- 🍴 Lunchtime and evening menus; daily specials
- 💷 Visa, Access, Delta, Switch, Mastercard
- 🛏 3 rooms en suite B&B
- 🅿 Car parking, beer garden
- 🎵 Games, darts, pool table, children's play area; occasional live music

THE BRIDPORT ARMS HOTEL

WEST BAY, BRIDPORT, DORSET DT6 4EN
TEL: 01308 422994 FAX: 01308 425141

Dorset

> **Directions:** West Bay is one mile south of Bridport off the A35. The Bridport Arms Hotel is beside the harbour.

Famed as the location of the TV series Harbour Lights, West Bay is a charming seaside village and home to the excellent **Bridport Arms Hotel**, which offers great food and drink and comfortable and attractive accommodation. Set beside the harbour, on the beach, this relaxed and convivial hotel is handsome inside and out. Its long, low, cream-washed and thatched exterior, with a dark green, also thatched hotel extension, presents a welcoming face to the world. Inside the décor is traditional, with two bars and restaurant furnished and decorated in keeping with the village's long history of fishing. There's a

good range of ales, lagers, cider, stout, spirits and soft drinks, and a full complement of wines from around the world. The restaurant is proud to boast a menu that includes fish straight from the fishing boats, together with a range of delicious favourites to tempt every palate. Seasonal, and always with an accent on the freshest local ingredients, the dishes mix traditional and more innovative choices. Landlords Adrian and Sarah Collis are amiable and friendly hosts, with a wealth of local knowledge. They and their helpful, cheerful staff offer all their guests a high standard of quality and service.

There are 15 lovely guest bedrooms, some with views over the beach. Relaxed and cosy, each room makes a very pleasant base from which to explore the region or just enjoy a peaceful and memorable break.

🕐 Mon-Sat 11.00-23.00; Sun 12.00-22.30

🍴 Bar and restaurant meals available all day

💷 All major credit cards

🛏 15 guest bedrooms

🅿 Car parking, beer garden

@ e-mail: adriancollis@westdorsetinns.co.uk
website: www.bridportarmshotel.co.uk

❓ Beach, walking, golf, bird-watching, fishing, diving, pleasure trips, Bridport (1 mile)

THE BULL TAVERN

TOWN BRIDGE, STURMINSTER NEWTON, DORSET DT10 2BS
TEL: 01258 472435

Directions: A303 to Sturminster Newton, Blandford.

The charming Hugh Edward-Jones is the landlord of **The Bull Tavern,** ably assisted by his wife Patricia and their longtime friend Mrs Elaine Parsons. The women lead the way in producing excellent meals in this intimate establishment. A true tavern in the very best sense of the word, exposed beams, rough plaster and open fireplaces add to the cosy and welcoming ambience. There's a L-shaped bar with rough-hewn timber uprights supporting the ceiling. A large piano sits along one wall, while gentle classical music fills the background.

Patricia and Elaine create all the dishes on the menu from fresh local produce. Steaks, chicken, lamb, pork, crab, fish and vegetarian meals are fresh daily. During the winter months, game dishes are the order of the day, with venison casserole being something quite special. People from all walks of life within a 40 mile radius frequently lunch here.

Hugh has been awarded three Cask Marque for his cask ales, which are supplemented by a full range of local and imported beers and spirits. There is also an excellent range of wines to complement the food on offer, which can be purchased by the bottle or glass.

The character and warmth of this fine pub make it somewhere guests want to return again and again.

- Mon-Sat 11.30-14.30, 18.45-23.00; Sun 12.00-15.00, 19.00-22.30
- Lunchtime and evening menus; daily specials
- Delta, Switch, Visa, Mastercard
- Car parking
- Skittle alley

THE CROWN INN

UPLODERS, BRIDPORT, DORSET DT6 4NU
TEL: 01308 485356

Directions: A35 Bridport to Dorchester, 2½ miles out of Bridport, signed to Loders and Uploders on the right. Proceed for half a mile to The Crown Inn.

Set against a backdrop of rolling hills, **The Crown Inn** in Uploders is a welcome sight. The traditional features inside this distinguished old inn include beamed ceilings, a wealth of warm wood panelling and a plethora of brass and pewter adornments.

Close to the beach and some wonderful walks, this cosy and comfortable inn is run by Walker John Davies, who has been landlord here since October of 2002. Brought up in Somerset, he returned to this part of the world after spending much of his life in Africa. He is a fount of information about sights and attractions in the area.

Locals and visitors alike are attracted to the friendly ambience and great food and drink on hand at this fine pub. Family groups are made welcome, with good facilities for children and a separate restaurant area.

Locally-caught fish is just one feature of the great menu, which includes a wide range of home-cooked dishes, all expertly prepared and presented. Meat, fowl, fish and seafood, and vegetarian dishes all find a place on the menus and specials board. There's also a children's menu to tempt even the choosiest palate.

There's a good selection of real ales, lagers, spirits and a wide range of wines, together with cider, stout, soft drinks, teas and coffees.

For a taste of genuine Dorset hospitality, look no further.

- winter: Mon-Sat 11.00-15.00, 18.00-23.00; Sun 12.00-15.00, 19.00-22.30; summer: Mon-Fri 11.00-15.00, 18.00-23.00; Sat 11.00-23.00; Sun 12.00-22.30
- Lunchtime (12.00-14.00) and evening (17.30-21.30) menus; daily specials
- All major credit cards
- Car parking, beer garden, children's play area
- Beach (less than 1 mile), walking, golf, West Bay (2 miles)

THE CUTTER HOTEL

4 EAST STREET, WEYMOUTH, DORSET DT4 8BP
TEL: 01305 771286

Directions: In the centre of Weymouth, near Alexander Gardens.

David and Sarah Allan are well on their way to being the perfect hosts after buying the long-established **Cutter Hotel** in Weymouth in March 2002. There are two bar areas: a public bar and a small and cosy lounge. Both are comfortably furnished and popular with locals and visitors alike. Both serve up a full range of beers, lagers, ciders, wines, spirits and soft drinks, including the ever-popular Bass real ale.

Here at this homely and welcoming hotel, bar food and snacks are available all day. All are home-made and delicious. David and Sarah have decided to keep the food on offer to a range of perfectly cooked meals utilising local seafood, meats and vegetables to create a selection of tempting favourites. They are also happy to point guests in the direction of one of the many excellent

restaurants in the area and, with their local knowledge, can provide guests with information about local amenities, sights and attractions.

Accommodation is provided in six very comfortable and attractive guest bedrooms. Guests' comfort and relaxation is always paramount at this inviting and lovely hotel. An ideal base for touring in the area, set back from the seafront, this charming and quiet retreat is a place most guests will want to revisit again and again.

- ⊙ Summer: Mon-Sun 10.30-23.00; Winter: Mon-Sun 11.30-23.00
- ⬤ Bar meals and snacks all day
- ⬤ 6 rooms (twins, doubles and family rooms) en suite B&B
- ⓟ Car parking
- @ www.thecutterhotel.co.uk
- ❓ Weymouth (9 miles)

THE DRAX ARMS

HIGH STREET, SPETISBURY, BLANDFORD, DORSET DT11 9DJ

TEL: 01258 452658

> **Directions:** On the A350 towards Poole, 3 miles from Blandford.

The Drax Arms in Spetisbury is well worth seeking out. Debbie Arnold has been a hotelier for many years who has taken up with enthusiasm the opportunity to run this charming village inn. With manager James Brixen, she brings a wealth of experience and guests are certain to find a warm welcome, good food and drink, and friendly service.

Debbie believes that all food should be cooked to order from only the finest and freshest local ingredients. The result is home-cooked food at its very best. Cooked by Debbie herself, the food on offer is a complete range from simple lunches and light snacks to more robust and hearty meals covering the full gambit of fish, meat, poultry and vegetarian options. Bar snacks are also available. The delicious Sunday lunch is extremely, and justly, popular, so booking is advised.

The pub has two adjoining areas – the public bar with open fireplace and very comfortable seating, and the large dining room. Both are decorated with horse brasses and tankards and other traditional features, and have walls adorned with old prints and photographs. The ambience throughout is cosy and welcoming.

There are two separate beer gardens on either side of the pub. Both offer a relaxing and pleasant place to enjoy a quiet drink or meal.

The range of lagers, ciders and fine conditioned cask ales is very good, along with the selection of wines, spirits and soft drinks. The warm welcome and good food and drink make this fine inn an excellent place to call in at on your journeys or to make a special journey for. You will not be disappointed.

- 🕐 Mon-Thurs 12.00-15.00, 19.00-23.00; Fri 12.00-15.00, 17.00-23.00; Sat 11.00-23.00; Sun 12.00-22.30
- 🍴 Lunchtime and evening menus; daily specials
- 🎵 Occasional live music at weekends
- ❓ Hall and Woodhouse Brewery Vistors Centre 3 miles, Dorchester 15 miles, extensive walks

THE FERRY BRIDGE INN

262 PORTLAND ROAD, WYKE REGIS, WEYMOUTH, DORSET DT4 9AF
TEL: 01305 760689

Directions: Weymouth to Portland Road

Weymouth's most southerly pub, **The Ferry Bridge Inn** is run by Geoff Bingham, who has been at the helm of this charming inn since 1995 after having spent 10 years at various inns throughout the country. He and his partner Ruth are excellent hosts and offer superb food that is expertly prepared and presented. There's a fine range of beers on offer including two cask ales all year round, with additional guest ales in summer, and a selection of wines chosen to complement the excellent menu, as well as a good choice of lagers, ciders,

- 🕐 Summer: Mon-Sat 12.00-23.00; Sun 12.00-22.30 Winter: Mon-Fri 12.00-15.00, 18.00-23.00; Sat 12.00-23.00; Sun 12.00-22.30
- 🍴 Lunchtime and evening menus; daily specials
- 💷 All major credit cards
- 🛏 4 rooms B&B
- 🅿 Car parking, sea views
- 🎵 Live music Saturday night
- ❓ Jurassic coast, coastal walking, Rodwell track, Chesil Beach

spirits and soft drinks.

The seafood could not be fresher, nor the steaks juicier. All dishes, meat or vegetarian, use the finest local ingredients. The all-day breakfasts are another feature, supplementing the fine menus and blackboard daily specials. Pleasant, relaxed surroundings add to guests' enjoyment of the good food, and there's also superb accommodation in one of four guest bedrooms, all commanding wonderful sea views. With the sea on all sides, the hotel stands on the site of the old ferry crossing, used before the bridge was built, and is the ideal place to get away from it all. Geoff, Ruth and their friendly staff go out of their way to please all their guests, and they succeed!

THE GREYHOUND

SYDLING ST NICHOLAS, DORCHESTER, DORSET DT2 9PD
TEL: 01300 341303 FAX: 01300 342045

Directions: From the A37 Yeovil to Dorchester, turn left to Cerne Abbas, then take the first right to Sydling St Nicholas. Follow this road for one mile into the village; The Greyhound is on the right-hand side.

Taking its name from the crest of the Wylderbore Smith family, **The Greyhound** in Sydling St Nicholas is an excellent traditional pub which was once the meeting place of the court lees and the scene of tenants' lunches during the 'progresse' of the officials of Winchester College. Owner Esme Mitchell has created something truly special here, offering cask ales, fine food and superb accommodation.

The small and cosy restaurant has a fascinating central feature: a well. Freshness and expert preparation

combine to make each dish a delicious and pleasing experience. The resident chef creates a wide selection of dishes for guests' enjoyment. The full menu is also available in the bar and delightful conservatory area, where guests can also enjoy light snacks. On fine days there is also the lovely beer garden complete with children's play area.

Drinks available at this Free House include cask ales and a full range of local and international beers and spirits, as well as an excellent selection of wines by the bottle or glass, including a good choice of half-bottles of dessert wines.

The accommodation is located in the converted barn, refurbished to a high standard of comfort and quality. The rooms are spacious and handsomely decorated and furnished; one has a four-poster bed.

- 🕐 Mon-Sat 11.00-15.30, 18.00-23.00; Sun 12.00-15.00, 19.00-23.00
- 🍴 Lunchtime (12.00-14.00) and evening (18.00-22.00) menus; daily specials
- 💷 Delta, Switch, Mastercard, Visa
- 🛏 6 rooms (twins and doubles) en suite B&B
- Ⓟ Car parking, beer garden, function suite
- 🎵 Occasional live music
- @ esmemitchell@onetel, www.thegreyhound-dorset.co.uk
- ❓ Yeovil (7 miles), Dorchester (5 miles), Cerne Abbas (3 miles), walking, horse riding, clay pigeon shooting, go-carting

THE HARE AND HOUNDS INN

WAYTOWN, BRIDPORT, DORSET DT6 5LQ

TEL: 01308 488203

Directions: From Bridport take the A3066 towards Beaminster. Turn left to Waytown (signed) or left at Oxbridge turning and proceed about 2 miles to reach The Hare and Hounds.

The Hare and Hounds in Waytown is well worth seeking out. This unspoilt village local is friendly and welcoming, and boasts a large garden where al fresco meals can be taken on fine days. The interior is cosy and attractive, with exposed beamwork and stonebuilt fireplaces adding to the traditional ambience.

The menu and daily specials boast an extensive selection of home-cooked country fare using local produce whenever possible. Traditional hearty English favourites share the menu with vegetarian dishes, salads and innovative specials. Meals are served in the separate non-smoking dining room. Bar snacks and a children's menu are also available.

🕐 Mon-Sat 11.30-14.30, 19.00-23.00 (18.30-23.00 in summer); Sun 12.00-15.00, 19.00-22.30

🍴 Bar meals, a la carte 12.00-14.00 and 19.00-21.00 Mon-Sat; traditional Sunday lunch served 12.00-14.30

💷 All major credit cards except Amex

🅿 Car parking, beer garden, children's room and play area

🎵 Occasional live entertainment, quiz nights Sundays in winter

@ e-mail: ron@hare-and-hounds.freeserve.co.uk, website: www.palmersbrewery.com

❓ Netherbury (½ mile), riverside walks, Heritage Coast, Golden Cap (3 miles), bird-watching, sailing

To drink there's a choice of Palmers real ales served direct from the cask and a broad selection of lagers, ciders, stouts, wines, spirits and soft drinks.

Ron Hobson and Cherry Ball have run this fine pub for about three years, developing a strong local following along the way. They and their attentive, amiable staff offer all their guests a warm welcome, genuine hospitality and excellent service.

As well as being very popular with visitors attracted by the spectacular views over the Brit valley from the pub garden, there is the unique satisfaction of a great meal and the pub's well-kept ales.

LODERS ARMS

LODERS, NEAR BRIDPORT, DOSET DT6 3SA
TEL: 01308 422431

Directions: Signposted off the A35 Bridport—Dorchester Road

The **Loders Arms** is one of those classic village inns that could best be described as special, a true jewel in the heart of Dorset. Awarded numerous accolades over the years for its fine food, when the former owners retired in 2002, chef Jane Legg and her husband Clive bought the inn – this charming couple truly have the customers in mind in everything they offer. Their staff have been chosen for their warmth, attentiveness and hospitality, while the pub itself offers its own charms in its cosiness and comfort. Decorated with hops, there are two distinct areas – the bar, complete with open fireplace and resident parrot, Basil, who seems to have an eye for the ladies,

and the intimate dining area.

The food is excellent, with the menu changing according to the availability of the freshest local produce. From elegant starters through main courses of fish, fowl, meat and game to mouthwatering desserts such as traditional sticky puddings, guests are spoilt for choice and dining here is an unhurried pleasure. Whether you are a meat-eater or vegetarian, Jane creates just the right blend of seasonings and sauces to enhance each dish. The bar offers a full range of locally produced ales and ciders along with a good selection of lagers, spirits and soft drinks, as well as wines chosen specially to complement the dishes served. Guests return again and again to this fine inn for the great food, drink and relaxed, welcoming ambience.

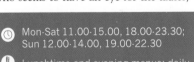

🕐 Mon-Sat 11.00-15.00, 18.00-23.30; Sun 12.00-14.00, 19.00-22.30

🍴 Lunchtime and evening menus; daily specials

£ Delta, Switch, Visa, Mastercard

🛏 2 rooms en suite B&B

Ⓟ Beer garden

@ janelegg@iol.com

❓ Dorchester

THE OAK AT DEWLISH

Dorset

DEWLISH, DORCHESTER, DORSET DT2 7ND
TEL: 01258 837352

Directions: Off A354 signposted for Dewlish. In centre of village.

The Oak at Dewlish looks more like a small country manor than a pub. This gabled inn has a brickwork exterior covered with a profusion of ivy. Warm and welcoming inside, the public bar has a traditional log-burning stove, while the lounge area has a large open fireplace and settle seating. There's also an intimate dining room. The handsome bar is made of oak, the floor is laid with traditional tiles. This cosy inn provides the perfect relaxing atmosphere in which to enjoy a fine drink or excellent home-cooked meal. There are always two or three real ales on tap at this Free House, together

with a good range of lagers, ciders, wines, spirits, soft drinks, teas and coffees. Local produce forms the basis for the excellent dishes on offer, which include traditional favourites and more modern dishes. In fine weather meals can be enjoyed in the large and attractive beer garden.

This family-run establishment is owned by Diane and John Trebilcock, who together with their children Roy and Jane provide the best in service and genuine hospitality. The heart of the community, this fine inn is justly popular with locals and visitors alike.

Plans are also afoot, at the time of publication, to add superior bed and breakfast accommodation to the many delights this pub has to offer.

- 🕐 Mon-Sat 11.30-14.00, 18.00-23.00; Sun 12.00-14.00, 19.00-22.30
- 🍴 Lunchtime and evening menus; daily specials
- Ⓟ Car parking, beer garden
- 🎵 Games, darts, pool table; occasional live entertainment
- ❓ Bovington camp, Tolpuddle, Dorchester, Thomas Hardy's cottage, walking

ROSE & CROWN

178 WAREHAM ROAD, LYTCHETT MATRAVERS, POOLE,
DORSET BH16 6DT
TEL: 01202 625325

Directions: Signed for both A35 and A350 near Poole

Alan Gregory is the owner of the warm and friendly **Rose & Crown**. His daughter Anna is the licensee, a successful landlady and holder of the Cask Marque award for real ales. There are always a number of real ales in stock along with a full range of local and

imported wines, beers, spirits and soft drinks to cater for every taste. This charming pub has all the comfort and atmosphere of a traditional village local. There are two bars and food is served daily. The inn was built in 1902. Originally the village was once down by the Church of St Mary, but after devastation by the Black Death in the mid-14th century villagers moved to the top of the hill and settled here. The name 'Lychett' is Celtic for 'grey wool', while the Mantravers family were local lords at the time of the Norman Conquest.

Anna prepares and serves hearty traditional meals, including favourites such as scampi and pies, while the menu also offers vegetarian options. All are made with fresh local produce, home-cooked and delicious. The excellent desserts are well worth leaving room for.

For a taste of genuine hospitality, and great food and drink amid warm and welcoming surroundings, look no further.

- Mon-Sat 11.00-23.00; Sun 12.00-22.30
- Lunchtime and evening menus (except Fri & Sun evenings); daily specials
- Car parking, beer garden
- Live music Fridays; karaoke Weds and Sun

THE ROSE & CROWN INN

TRENT, NEAR SHERBORNE, DORSET DT9 4SL
TEL: 01935 850776

Directions: Between the A30 and A359 signposted Trent

Ian and Christine Phillips bought **The Rose & Crown Inn** because their daughter Claire Yates lived in the village and they visited her so often it seemed logical to settle here. They bought this charming Inn and have restored it to its former glory. The pub has a true rustic feel, with many nooks and crannies and open fireplaces adding to the cosy and comfortable ambience. Originally two cottages dating back to the 14th and 15th centuries respectively, it became an inn to house the craftsmen at work on the local church.

Ian and Christine also tracked down Graham Williams, who was the chef in days gone by when the inn's food was renowned throughout the county, winning many awards. Graham is now safely reinstated in the kitchen and fast

🕐 Tues-Sat 12.00-15.00, 19.00-23.00; Sun 12.00-15.00

🍽 Lunchtime and evening menus; daily specials

£ Delta, Switch, Visa, Mastercard

🛏 2 rooms en suite B&B

Ⓟ Car parking, beer garden with childrens area

❓ Fleet Air Arm Museum; Haynes Motor Museum at Sparkford

re-creating the reputation of the food on offer, including vegetarian, fish, fowl, meat and game dishes, all the product of fresh local and seasonal ingredients. The Bar menu at lunchtime offers all the traditional favourites such as gammon and steaks, scampi, cod, steak and kidney pie, together with a good range of salads. There's also a children's menu. Local ales and ciders, perfectly cask conditioned, are changed on a continual basis; the wine list is extensive and there are also lagers, spirits and soft drinks.

Here at this family-run establishment guests are offered a warm and genuine welcome. Whether they call in for a relaxed drink or meal or for the excellent Sunday lunch, or to stay in one of the period guest bedrooms with four-poster beds, the hospitality is second to none.

THE STALBRIDGE ARMS

RING STREET, STALBRIDGE, DORSET DT10 2NF
TEL: 01963 362447

> **Directions:** A357 Blandford-Wimborne Road, turn right at the Q8 garage, then right again

An impressive and very handsome whitewashed exterior hints at the delights to come at **The Stalbridge Arms**. The superb interior is warm and welcoming, where guests feel immediately at home. The open-plan bar serves two distinct areas, both of which are comfortably furnished and attractively decorated. There's also a separate non-smoking restaurant and a function room. Outside there's a lovely garden in which to enjoy a relaxing drink or meal on fine days.

The menu also impresses, with a range of tempting traditional and more innovative dishes such as stuffed plaice, steaks, lamb, gammon, duck, pork and vegetarian dishes. For those who only want a light meal, there's a good selection of baguettes and freshly cut sandwiches and other snacks. The fine menu is supplemented by great daily specials. All meals are home-cooked and expertly prepared and presented.

To drink, there's a good compliment of lagers, ciders, spirits and soft drinks, together with an international wine list.

The friendly, helpful staff are on hand to provide the very best in service and quality. This fine inn has everything to offer and is well worth a visit while travelling through this particularly lovely part of the county.

- Mon-Fri 12.00-14.30, 18.00-23.00; Sat 11.00-23.00; Sun 11.00-22.30
- Lunchtime and evening menus; daily specials
- All major credit cards
- Car parking, beer garden
- Skittles, darts, pool, quiz nights, themed food evenings
- www.stalbridge.net
- Yeovil, golf, fishing

THE STAPLETON ARMS

BUCKHORN WESTON, GILLINGHAM, DORSET SP8 5HS
TEL: 01963 370396 FAX: 01963 371524

Directions: Exit the A303 at Wincanton, or exit the A30 on the right one mile after West Stour, or exit left at Dry Lane on B3081 Gillingham to Wincanton road.

Here in the picturesque Dorset village of Buckhorn Weston, **The Stapleton Arms** resembles a stately home, inside and out. This relaxed and friendly inn is owned and run by Chris and Andrea Wyle, born and bred locally and offering all their customers the best in service and hospitality. Renowned for its food, Andrea and her team mastermind the fine dishes on the menu and specials available. Booking required at weekends; children are most welcome. Specialities include locally-reared meats and fresh fish. Guests can also choose from such delicacies as homemade steak and kidney pie, wild boar sausages, sea bass, caesar salad etc. and should always leave room for one of the tempting traditional desserts such as

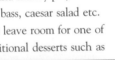

- 🕐 Mon-Sat 11.00-15.00, 18.00-23.00; Sun 12.00-15.00, 18.00-22.30;
- 🍴 Lunchtime (11.00-15.00; evening (18.00-21.30) menus; daily specials
- 💷 All major credit cards (incl Amex)
- 🛏 Three guest bedrooms
- 🅿 Car parking, beer garden
- 🎵 Occasional food nights, quiz nights and live entertainment
- @ www.thestapletonarms.co.uk
- ❓ Wincanton (4 miles), Gillingham (4 miles), Stourhead Gardens (6 miles).

Stapleton Pavlova, homemade apple pie and sherry trifle. Delicious bar snacks - sandwiches, baguettes, burgers, salads and more - are also available between 11 a.m. and 3 p.m. All snacks and meals are expertly prepared and presented. And to drink? There are five real ales, one direct from the barrel. A local real cider complements the range, including an excellent wine list. Guests can enjoy their drinks amid the comfortable and cosy surroundings of the inn or outside in the outstanding beer garden, which backs onto the village green.

The accommodation here provides a high standard of quality and comfort and is very attractive, with three guest bedrooms located on the first floor. These rooms are available all year round.

The Stapleton Arms is a free house and has recently received the "CAMRA 2002 Wessex Branch" award

THE SUN INN

LOWER BURTON, DORCHESTER, DORSET DT2 7RZ
TEL: 01305 250445 FAX: 01305 266231

Directions: ½ mile from Dorchester on the old Sherbourne Road, past Loders
Toyota, turn right and go over 2 small old bridges.

Built on land owned at one time by
Henry VIII and later by the Earl of
Ilchester, **The Sun Inn** is a 17th-
century hostelry which, from 1885
until 1923, did double duty as the
blacksmith's forge. The inn is set in
prime Dorset countryside less than a
mile from Dorchester on the old
Sherborne Road at Lower Burton
(Burton is one of the ten Saxon land
units in the area, and means 'near
fortification' – in this case most probably
Poundsbury Camp.) Once owned by the
Devenish brewery, it is now a Free House
run by Robin Maddex. He and his
friendly, helpful staff offer genuine
hospitality, great food and drink and a
warm and welcoming atmosphere. The
interior of the bar is cosy and
comfortable, with many traditional

features such as exposed oak beams,
leaded lights and log fires, and where
decorative touches include lots of china
and pottery ornaments.

The food here is a special treat, with a
fine menu supplemented by tempting
daily specials. The carvery is also a
popular choice, together with an
excellent range of fresh and seasonal
lamb, pork, chicken and fish dishes.
There are always several vegetarian
options as well, along with children's
meals, and snacks such as ploughmans,
salads, filled baguettes and jacket
potatoes. The Sunday roast is a justly
popular favourite; there are also special
menu evenings held regularly throughout
the year. The very good wine list
includes vintages from France, Spain,
Italy and North America, and here
guests will find a good selection of at
least three to five different cask ales.

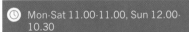

- 🕐 Mon-Sat 11.00-11.00, Sun 12.00-10.30
- 🍽 Lunchtime and evening menus; daily specials Food served 12.00-2.30pm and 6.30pm-10.00pm
- £ All major credit cards
- Ⓟ Car parking, beer garden, children's play area
- @ robin@suninn-dorchester.co.uk
- ❓ Dorchester

THREE HORSESHOES

MILL STREET, BURTON BRADSTOCK, BRIDPORT, DORSET DT6 4QZ
TEL: 01308 897259

Directions: From Bridport follow the B3157 towards Weymouth for 2 miles, or the A35 from Bridport east. The Three Horseshoes is in the centre of the village of Burton Bradstock.

It's well worth seeking out the tiny village of Burton Bradstock just to visit the **Three Horseshoes**, a lovely pub crafted of traditional Dorset stone and thatching, which has been offering great food, drink and hospitality for some 300 years. Inside, the pub boasts a large and pleasant bar, and separate restaurant.

All parts of the inn are tasteful and up to date without being brash, instead remaining very much in keeping with its quiet village setting.

Fish and seafood are very much house specialities, with the freshest ingredients used to create delicious dishes such as red snapper, fillets of plaice, baked sea bass, sirloin steaks, guinea fowl, roasted Mediterranean vegetables, shoulder of venison and much more, to be chosen from the menu or blackboard specials.

To drink, there's a large range of local real ales, together with lager, cider, stout, spirits, soft drinks and an international selection of fine wines.

Landlords Adrian and Sarah Collis are mines of information about local events and sights; they also run the excellent Bridport Arms Hotel in West Bay, and their wealth of experience shows in the excellent service and conscientious attention they offer to all their guests.

Live music is very much a feature at this fine inn, with jazz, blues, folk and dixieland evenings from locally and nationally acclaimed musicians.

- ⊕ Mon-Sat 11.00-23.00; Sun 12.00-22.30
- ⊕ Bar and restaurant meals available all day
- £ All major credit cards
- ℗ Car parking, beer garden
- ♫ Wide range of music regularly
- @ e-mail: adriancollis@westdorsetinns.co.uk website: www.3-horseshoes.co.uk
- ❓ Beach (less than a mile), walking, golf, Bridport (2 miles), West Bay (famous for the TV series *Harbour Lights*; 2 miles)

THE WHITE LION INN

BOURTON, NEAR GILLINGHAM, DORSET SP8 5AT
TEL: 01747 840866 FAX: 01747 841529

Dorset

> **Directions:** Bourton is located 1 mile off the main A303 between Zeals and Wincanton. The White Lion Inn is in High Street, opposite the junction with the B3092.

The most northerly inn in Dorset, near the Wiltshire and Somerset borders, **The White Lion Inn** was built in 1723. It is charming inside and out. The cosy and attractive bars have original flagstone floors, beamed ceilings and large stonebuilt fireplaces. In winter the log fires add to the authentic feel of this comfortable Dorset inn.

Mike and Scarlett Senior, after 11 years of success at the Anchor Inn on the River Avon, have brought their experience here to help The White Lion

Inn develop a reputation for great value and outstanding cooking. Long popular for its excellent food, this delightful inn has received praise from both Egon Ronay and The Good Food Guide. Mike is the chef, using only the finest ingredients, sourced locally whenever possible, to create a modern British menu which sets this inn apart from many of its rivals. Together with Scarlett and their cheerful staff, he creates an amiable and relaxed atmosphere for all their guests. To quench guests' thirst there's a wide range of bottled and cask beers, spirits and a carefully selected wine list, as well as ciders, soft drinks and hot beverages.

The accommodation is through a separate entrance, and one room has a four-poster bed. Both rooms are comfortably furnished and tastefully decorated.

- 🕐 Mon-Sun 12noon-3pm, Sun evening 7pm-10.30pm, Mon-Sat 6pm-11pm
- 🍴 Menu includes starters/main courses/lunchtime snacks/specials board/puddings/Sunday roast
- 💷 Visa, Mastercard, Switch, Eurocard, Solo
- 🛏 Two rooms ensuite
- 🅿 Car parking, beer garden, children and well-behaved dogs welcome, catering for up to 50 for special occasions
- @ whitelioninn@bourtondorset.fsnet.co.uk
- ❓ Wincanton Race Course, Stourhead Gardens, Duncliff Wood, Stonehenge, Old Sarum, Wilton House, Salisbury Cathedral, Shaftesbury, Poole Harbour, coast, Longleat House, walking, cycling, bird watching, horse riding

ALPHABETICAL LIST
OF PUBS AND INNS

L

M

N

O

P

Q

R

Alphabetical List of Pubs and Inns

SPECIAL INTEREST LISTS

Accommodation

CORNWALL

The Badger Inn	Lelant, St Ives	29
Carbeile Inn	Torpoint	32
The Coachmakers Arms	Callington	34
The Commercial Inn	St Dennis, St Austell	36
The Devon & Cornwall	Millbrook, Torpoint	37
The Fishermans Arms	Golant, Nr Fowey	38
Halfway House	Polbathic, Torpoint	39
The Kings Arms	Paul, Penzance	41
The Merrymoor Inn	Mawgan Porth, Newquay	44
The North Inn	Pendeen, Penzance	45
The Old Quay House	Hayle	47
The Queens Arms	Botallack, Penzance	49
The Rising Sun Inn	Portmellion Cove, Mevagissey	52
The Royal Inn	Par	53
The Royal Standard	Gwinear, Hayle	54
The Ship Inn	Par	55
Smugglers Inn	Seaton	56
Three Tuns	St Keverne	58
Trewarmett Inn	Trewarmett, Tintagel	59

DEVON

The Anchor Inn	Ugborough	81
Bullers Arms	Chagford, Newton Abbot	83
The Cricket Inn	Beesands, Kingsbridge	89
Dog & Donkey	Budleigh Salterton	90
The George Inn	Blackawton, Totnes	93
The George Inn	Chardstock, Axminster	94
Halfway Inn	Aylesbeare, Exeter	96
Kings Arms	Otterton	98
Kings Arms Inn	Stockland, Honiton	99
The Kings Arms Hotel	Kingsbridge	100
The Old Union Inn	Stibbs Cross, Torrington	104
Pickwick Inn	St Ann's Chapel, Bigbury-on-Sea	105
The Plume of Feathers	Princetown, Yelverton	106
The Rockford Inn	Brendon, Lynton	109
The Seven Stars Inn	South Tawton, Okehampton	111
The Stag Hunters Hotel	Brendon, Lynton	112

Accommodation

SPECIAL INTEREST LISTS

All Day Opening

CORNWALL

Admiral Benbow	Penzance	27
The Badger Inn	Lelant, St Ives	29
The Bird in Hand	Hayle	30
Bridge on Wool	Wadebridge	31
Carbeile Inn	Torpoint	32
The Devon & Cornwall	Millbrook, Torpoint	37
The Merrymoor Inn	Mawgan Porth, Newquay	44
The North Inn	Pendeen, Penzance	45
The Old Inn	Churchtown, St Breward	46
The Old Quay House	Hayle	47
The Pheonix	Watergate Bay, Newquay	48
The Queens Arms	Botallack, Penzance	49
The Royal Inn	Par	53
The Ship Inn	Par	55
Smugglers Inn	Seaton	56
The Tavern	Treninnick	57

DEVON

The George Inn	Plympton, Plymouth	95
Halfway Inn	Aylesbeare, Exeter	96
Johnny's Bar	Bideford	97
Kingsley Inn	Northam, Bideford	101
The Old Union Inn	Stibbs Cross, Torrington	104
The Plume of Feathers	Princetown, Yelverton	106
Ring O' Bells	Bishopsteignton, Teignmouth	108
The Tavern in the Port	Bideford	113
The Whitchurch Inn	Whitchurch, Tavistock	115

SOMERSET

The Anchor Inn	Bleadon, Weston-Super-Mare	137
The Bell Inn	Evercreech	141
The City Arms	Wells	142
Englishcombe Inn	Bath	143
The Gardener's Arms	Cheddar	144
King William IV	Combe Down, Bath	147

SOMERSET (Cont.)

DORSET

SPECIAL INTEREST LISTS

Childrens Facilities

CORNWALL

Carbeile Inn	Torpoint	32
The Ship Inn	Par	55
Three Tuns	St Keverne	58

DEVON

The Avon Inn	Avonwick, South Brent	82
Ebrington Arms	Knowle, Braunton	91
The New Inn	Sampford Courtenay, Okehampton	102
The Old Union Inn	Stibbs Cross, Torrington	104
The Plume of Feathers	Princetown, Yelverton	106

SOMERSET

Alhampton Inn	Alhampton, Ditcheat	136
The Anchor Inn	Bleadon, Weston-Super-Mare	137
The Gardener's Arms	Cheddar	144
The Greyhound Inn	Stogursey, Bridgwater	145
The Merry Monk	Monkton Heathfield, Taunton	150
The Red Tile Inn	Cossington, Bridgwater	156

DORSET

The Black Dog	Broadmayne, Dorchester	188
The Crown Inn	Uploders, Bridport	191
The Hare and Hounds Inn	Waytown, Bridport	196
The Rose & Crown Inn	Trent, Sherborne	200
The Sun Inn	Lower Burton, Dorchester	203

Credit Cards Accepted

CORNWALL

Admiral Benbow	Penzance	27
The Angarrack Inn	Angarrack, Hayle	28
The Badger Inn	Lelant, St Ives	29
The Bird in Hand	Hayle	30
Bridge on Wool	Wadebridge	31
Carbeile Inn	Torpoint	32
The Carpenters Arms	Lower Metherell, Callington	33
The Coachmakers Arms	Callington	34
The Coldstreamer Inn	Gulval, Penzance	35
The Devon & Cornwall	Millbrook, Torpoint	37
The Fishermans Arms	Golant, Nr Fowey	38
Halfway House	Polbathic, Torpoint	39
The Halfway House Inn	Twowatersfoot, Liskeard	40
The Kings Arms	Paul, Penzance	41
King William IV	Madron, Penzance	42
Lanivet Inn	Lanivet, Bodmin	43
The Merrymoor Inn	Mawgan Porth, Newquay	44
The North Inn	Pendeen, Penzance	45
The Old Inn	Churchtown, St Breward	46
The Old Quay House	Hayle	47
The Pheonix	Watergate Bay, Newquay	48
The Queens Arms	Botallack, Penzance	49
Ring O' Bells	Antony, Torpoint	50
Ring O' Bells	St Columb Major	51
The Rising Sun Inn	Portmellion Cove, Mevagissey	52
The Royal Inn	Par	53
The Royal Standard	Gwinear, Hayle	54
The Ship Inn	Par	55
Smugglers Inn	Seaton	56
Three Tuns	St Keverne	58
Trewarmett Inn	Trewarmett, Tintagel	59

DEVON

The George Inn	Plympton, Plymouth	95
The Anchor Inn	Ugborough	81
The Avon Inn	Avonwick, South Brent	82
Bullers Arms	Chagford, Newton Abbot	83

Credit Cards Accepted

DEVON (cont.)

The Bullers Arms	Brixham	84
The Butterleigh Inn	Butterleigh, Collumpton	85
The Chichester Arms	Barnstaple	87
The Church House Inn	Rattery, Totnes	88
The Cricket Inn	Beesands, Kingsbridge	89
Ebrington Arms	Knowle, Braunton	91
The Foxhound Inn	Brixton	92
The George Inn	Blackawton, Totnes	93
The George Inn	Chardstock, Axminster	94
Halfway Inn	Aylesbeare, Exeter	96
Johnny's Bar	Bideford	97
Kings Arms	Otterton	98
Kings Arms Inn	Stockland, Honiton	99
The Kings Arms Hotel	Kingsbridge	100
Kingsley Inn	Northam, Bideford	101
The New Inn	Sampford Courtenay, Okehampton	102
The Olde Plough Inn	Bere Ferrers	103
The Old Union Inn	Stibbs Cross, Torrington	104
Pickwick Inn	St Ann's Chapel, Bigbury-on-Sea	105
The Plume of Feathers	Princetown, Yelverton	106
Ring O' Bells	Landkey, Barnstaple	107
Ring O' Bells	Bishopsteignton, Teignmouth	108
The Rockford Inn	Brendon, Lynton	109
The Sandy Park Inn	Chagford, Newton Abbot	110
The Seven Stars Inn	South Tawton, Okehampton	111
The Stag Hunters Hotel	Brendon, Lynton	112
The Tavern in the Port	Bideford	113
The Toby Jug Inn	Bickington, Newton Abbot	114
The Whitchurch Inn	Whitchurch, Tavistock	115

SOMERSET

Alhampton Inn	Alhampton, Ditcheat	136
The Anchor Inn	Bleadon, Weston-Super-Mare	137
The Anchor Inn	Combwich, Bridgwater	138
The Bell Inn	Evercreech	141
The City Arms	Wells	142
Englishcombe Inn	Bath	143

SOMERSET (cont.)

The Gardener's Arms	Cheddar	144
The Halfway House Inn	Chilthorne Domer, Yeovil	146
The Masons Arms	Frome	149
The Merry Monk	Monkton Heathfield, Taunton	150
The Mitre Inn	Glastonbury	151
The Nog Inn	Wincanton	152
The Old Inn	Bishops Hull, Taunton	153
The Pelican Inn	Chew Magna	154
The Red Lion	Bishop Sutton, Bristol	155
The Red Tile Inn	Cossington, Bridgwater	156
The Ring O' Bells	Moorlinch, Bridgwater	157
The Royal Huntsman	Williton	158
The Sexeys Arms Inn	Blackford, Wedmore	160
The Ship Inn	Uphill, Weston-Super-Mare	161
The Three Horseshoes	Batcombe, Shepton Mallet	162
The Travellers Rest	Pensford, Bristol	163
The White Hart	Midsomer Norton, Bath	164
The York Inn	Churchinford, Taunton	165

DORSET

The Anchor at Shapwick	Shapwick, Blandford	186
The Antelope Inn	Wareham	187
The Black Dog	Broadmayne, Dorchester	188
The Bridport Arms Hotel	West Bay, Bridport	189
The Bull Tavern	Sturminster Newton	190
The Crown Inn	Uploders, Bridport	191
The Ferry Bridge Inn	Wyke Regis, Weymouth	194
The Greyhound	Sydling St Nicholas, Dorchester	195
The Hare and Hounds Inn	Waytown, Bridport	196
Loders Arms	Loders, Bridport	197
The Rose & Crown Inn	Trent, Sherborne	200
The Stalbridge Arms	Stalbridge	201
The Stapleton Arms	Buckthorn Weston, Gillingham	202
The Sun Inn	Lower Burton, Dorchester	203
Three Horseshoes	Burton Bradstock, Bridport	204
The White Lion Inn	Bourton, Gillingham	205

SPECIAL INTEREST LISTS

Garden, Patio or Terrace

CORNWALL

The Angarrack Inn	Angarrack, Hayle	28
The Badger Inn	Lelant, St Ives	29
The Bird in Hand	Hayle	30
Bridge on Wool	Wadebridge	31
Carbeile Inn	Torpoint	32
The Carpenters Arms	Lower Metherell, Callington	33
The Commercial Inn	St Dennis, St Austell	36
The Devon & Cornwall	Millbrook, Torpoint	37
The Fishermans Arms	Golant, Nr Fowey	38
Halfway House	Polbathic, Torpoint	39
The Halfway House Inn	Twowatersfoot, Liskeard	40
The Kings Arms	Paul, Penzance	41
King William IV	Madron, Penzance	42
Lanivet Inn	Lanivet, Bodmin	43
The Merrymoor Inn	Mawgan Porth, Newquay	44
The North Inn	Pendeen, Penzance	45
The Old Inn	Churchtown, St Breward	46
The Old Quay House	Hayle	47
The Pheonix	Watergate Bay, Newquay	48
Ring O' Bells	Antony, Torpoint	50
The Rising Sun Inn	Portmellion Cove, Mevagissey	52
The Ship Inn	Par	55
Smugglers Inn	Seaton	56
The Tavern	Treninnick	57
Three Tuns	St Keverne	58

DEVON

The Avon Inn	Avonwick, South Brent	82
Bullers Arms	Chagford, Newton Abbot	83
The Butterleigh Inn	Butterleigh, Collumpton	85
Carpenters Arms	Islington, Newton Abbot	86
The Chichester Arms	Barnstaple	87
The Church House Inn	Rattery, Totnes	88
The Cricket Inn	Beesands, Kingsbridge	89
Dog & Donkey	Budleigh Salterton	90
Ebrington Arms	Knowle, Braunton	91
The George Inn	Blackawton, Totnes	93

DEVON (Cont.)

The George Inn	Chardstock, Axminster	94
Halfway Inn	Aylesbeare, Exeter	96
Kings Arms Inn	Stockland, Honiton	99
The Kings Arms Hotel	Kingsbridge	100
Kingsley Inn	Northam, Bideford	101
The New Inn	Sampford Courtenay, Okehampton	102
The Olde Plough Inn	Bere Ferrers	103
The Old Union Inn	Stibbs Cross, Torrington	104
Pickwick Inn	St Ann's Chapel, Bigbury-on-Sea	105
The Plume of Feathers	Princetown, Yelverton	106
The Sandy Park Inn	Chagford, Newton Abbot	110
The Stag Hunters Hotel	Brendon, Lynton	112
The Tavern in the Port	Bideford	113
The Toby Jug Inn	Bickington, Newton Abbot	114
The Whitchurch Inn	Whitchurch, Tavistock	115

SOMERSET

Alhampton Inn	Alhampton, Ditcheat	136
The Anchor Inn	Bleadon, Weston-Super-Mare	137
The Anchor Inn	Combwich, Bridgwater	138
The Ancient Mariner	Nether Stowey	139
The Bell Inn	Banwell, Weston-Super-Mare	140
The Bell Inn	Evercreech	141
The City Arms	Wells	142
Englishcombe Inn	Bath	143
The Gardener's Arms	Cheddar	144
The Greyhound Inn	Stogursey, Bridgwater	145
King William IV	Combe Down, Bath	147
The Lamb Inn	Spaxton, Brigwater	148
The Masons Arms	Frome	149
The Merry Monk	Monkton Heathfield, Taunton	150
The Mitre Inn	Glastonbury	151
The Nog Inn	Wincanton	152
The Old Inn	Bishops Hull, Taunton	153
The Pelican Inn	Chew Magna	154
The Red Lion	Bishop Sutton, Bristol	155
The Red Tile Inn	Cossington, Bridgwater	156

SOMERSET (Cont.)

The Ring O' Bells	Moorlinch, Bridgwater	157
The Royal Huntsman	Williton	158
The Royal Oak	Portishead, Bristol	159
The Sexeys Arms Inn	Blackford, Wedmore	160
The Travellers Rest	Pensford, Bristol	163
The York Inn	Churchinford, Taunton	165

DORSET

The Anchor at Shapwick	Shapwick, Blandford	186
The Antelope Inn	Wareham	187
The Black Dog	Broadmayne, Dorchester	188
The Bridport Arms Hotel	West Bay, Bridport	189
The Crown Inn	Uploders, Bridport	191
The Drax Arms	Spetisbury, Blandford	193
The Greyhound	Sydling St Nicholas, Dorchester	195
The Hare and Hounds Inn	Waytown, Bridport	196
Loders Arms	Loders, Bridport	197
The Oak at Dewlish	Dewlish, Dorchester	198
Rose & Crown	Lytchett Matravers, Poole	199
The Rose & Crown Inn	Trent, Sherborne	200
The Stalbridge Arms	Stalbridge	201
The Stapleton Arms	Buckthorn Weston, Gillingham	202
The Sun Inn	Lower Burton, Dorchester	203
Three Horseshoes	Burton Bradstock, Bridport	204
The White Lion Inn	Bourton, Gillingham	205

Live Entertainment

CORNWALL

Admiral Benbow	Penzance	27
The Badger Inn	Lelant, St Ives	29
The Bird in Hand	Hayle	30
Bridge on Wool	Wadebridge	31
Carbeile Inn	Torpoint	32
The Carpenters Arms	Lower Metherell, Callington	33
The Devon & Cornwall	Millbrook, Torpoint	37
The Fishermans Arms	Golant, Nr Fowey	38
The Kings Arms	Paul, Penzance	41
Lanivet Inn	Lanivet, Bodmin	43
The Old Inn	Churchtown, St Breward	46
Ring O' Bells	Antony, Torpoint	50
The Royal Standard	Gwinear, Hayle	54
The Ship Inn	Par	55
The Tavern	Treninnick	57
Trewarmett Inn	Trewarmett, Tintagel	59

DEVON

The George Inn	Plympton, Plymouth	95
The Anchor Inn	Ugborough	81
The Bullers Arms	Brixham	84
The Foxhound Inn	Brixton	92
Kings Arms	Otterton	98
Kings Arms Inn	Stockland, Honiton	99
Kingsley Inn	Northam, Bideford	101
Ring O' Bells	Bishopsteignton, Teignmouth	108
The Tavern in the Port	Bideford	113

SOMERSET

The Anchor Inn	Bleadon, Weston-Super-Mare	137
The Anchor Inn	Combwich, Bridgwater	138
The Bell Inn	Banwell, Weston-Super-Mare	140
The Bell Inn	Evercreech	141
The Greyhound Inn	Stogursey, Bridgwater	145
The Masons Arms	Frome	149
The Pelican Inn	Chew Magna	154

Live Entertainment

Restaurant or Dining Area

CORNWALL

Admiral Benbow	Penzance	27
The Angarrack Inn	Angarrack, Hayle	28
The Carpenters Arms	Lower Metherell, Callington	33
The Coldstreamer Inn	Gulval, Penzance	35
The Commercial Inn	St Dennis, St Austell	36
Halfway House	Polbathic, Torpoint	39
The Old Inn	Churchtown, St Breward	46
Ring O' Bells	Antony, Torpoint	50
Ring O' Bells	St Columb Major	51
The Royal Inn	Par	53
The Royal Standard	Gwinear, Hayle	54
Smugglers Inn	Seaton	56
Three Tuns	St Keverne	58

DEVON

The Anchor Inn	Ugborough	81
The Avon Inn	Avonwick, South Brent	82
The Cricket Inn	Beesands, Kingsbridge	89
Dog & Donkey	Budleigh Salterton	90
Ebrington Arms	Knowle, Braunton	91
The Foxhound Inn	Brixton	92
Johnny's Bar	Bideford	97
Kings Arms Inn	Stockland, Honiton	99
Pickwick Inn	St Ann's Chapel, Bigbury-on-Sea	105
Ring O' Bells	Landkey, Barnstaple	107
The Sandy Park Inn	Chagford, Newton Abbot	110
The Seven Stars Inn	South Tawton, Okehampton	111
The Stag Hunters Hotel	Brendon, Lynton	112
The Toby Jug Inn	Bickington, Newton Abbot	114
The Whitchurch Inn	Whitchurch, Tavistock	115

SOMERSET

The Anchor Inn	Bleadon, Weston-Super-Mare	137
The Bell Inn	Evercreech	141
The City Arms	Wells	142
Englishcombe Inn	Bath	143

PLACES OF INTEREST

Places of Interest

Travel Publishing

The Hidden Places

Regional and National guides to the less well-known places of interest and places to eat, stay and drink

Hidden Inns

Regional guides to traditional pubs and inns throughout the United Kingdom

GOLFERS GUIDES

Regional and National guides to 18 hole golf courses and local places to stay, eat and drink

 **RURAL GUIDES**

Regional and National guides to the traditional countryside of Britain and Ireland with easy to read facts on places to visit, stay, eat, drink and shop

For more information:

Phone: 0118 981 7777
e-mail: adam@travelpublishing.co.uk

Fax: 0118 982 0077
website: www.travelpublishing.co.uk

Easy-to-use, Informative
Travel Guides on the British Isles

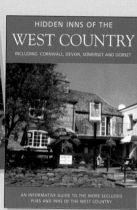

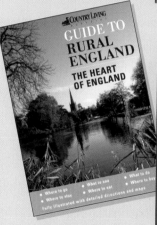

Travel Publishing Limited

7a Apollo House • Calleva Park • Aldermaston • Berkshire RG7 8TN

Order Form

ORDER FORM

To order any of our publications just fill in the payment details below and complete the order form. For orders of less than 4 copies please add £1 per book for postage and packing. Orders over 4 copies are P & P free.

Please Complete Either:

I enclose a cheque for £ _____ made payable to Travel Publishing Ltd

Or:

Card No: _____ Expiry Date: _____

Signature: _____

Name: _____

Address: _____

Tel no: _____

Please either send, telephone, fax or e-mail your order to:

Travel Publishing Ltd, 7a Apollo House, Calleva Park, Aldermaston, Berkshire RG7 8TN   Tel: 0118 981 7777   Fax: 0118 982 0077
e-mail: karen@travelpublishing.co.uk

Hidden Places Regional Titles	Price	Quantity
Cambs & Lincolnshire	£7.99	....
Chilterns	£7.99	....
Cornwall	£8.99	....
Derbyshire	£8.99	....
Devon	£8.99	....
Dorset, Hants & Isle of Wight	£8.99	....
East Anglia	£8.99	....
Gloucs, Wiltshire & Somerset	£8.99	....
Heart of England	£7.99	....
Hereford, Worcs & Shropshire	£7.99	....
Highlands & Islands	£7.99	....
Kent	£8.99	
Lake District & Cumbria	£8.99	....
Lancashire & Cheshire	£8.99	
Lincolnshire & Notts	£8.99	....
Northumberland & Durham	£8.99	....
Sussex	£8.99	....
Yorkshire	£8.99	....

Hidden Places National Titles	Price	Quantity
England	£10.99	....
Ireland	£10.99	
Scotland	£10.99	....
Wales	£9.99	....

Hidden Inns Titles	Price	Quantity
East Anglia	£5.99	....
Heart of England	£5.99	....
Lancashire & Cheshire	£5.99	....
North of England	£5.99	....
South	£5.99	....
South East	£5.99	....
South and Central Scotland	£5.99	....
Wales	£5.99	....
Welsh Borders	£5.99	....
West Country	£5.99	....
Yorkshire	£5.99	....

Country Living Rural Guides	Price	Quantity
East Anglia	£9.99	
Heart of England	£9.99	....
Ireland	£10.99	....
Scotland	£10.99	....
South of England	£9.99	....
South East of England	£9.99	....
Wales	£10.99	....
West Country	£9.99	....

Total Quantity _____

Post & Packing _____

Total Value _____

The *Travel Publishing* research team would like to receive reader's comments on any visitor attractions or places reviewed in the book and also recommendations for suitable entries to be included in the next edition. This will help ensure that the *Country Living series of Rural Guides* continues to provide its readers with useful information on the more interesting, unusual or unique features of each attraction or place ensuring that their visit to the local area is an enjoyable and stimulating experience. To provide your comments or recommendations would you please complete the forms below and overleaf as indicated and send to:

**The Research Department, Travel Publishing Ltd,
7a Apollo House, Calleva Park, Aldermaston, Reading, RG7 8TN.**

Your Name:

Your Address:

Your Telephone Number:

Please tick as appropriate:

Comments ☐   Recommendation ☐

Name of Establishment:

Address:

Telephone Number:

Name of Contact:

READER REACTION FORM

Comment or Reason for Recommendation:

READER REACTION FORM

The *Travel Publishing* research team would like to receive reader's comments on any visitor attractions or places reviewed in the book and also recommendations for suitable entries to be included in the next edition. This will help ensure that the *Country Living series of Rural Guides* continues to provide its readers with useful information on the more interesting, unusual or unique features of each attraction or place ensuring that their visit to the local area is an enjoyable and stimulating experience. To provide your comments or recommendations would you please complete the forms below and overleaf as indicated and send to:

**The Research Department, Travel Publishing Ltd,
7a Apollo House, Calleva Park, Aldermaston, Reading, RG7 8TN.**

Your Name:

Your Address:

Your Telephone Number:

Please tick as appropriate:

Comments ☐   Recommendation ☐

Name of Establishment:

Address:

Telephone Number:

Name of Contact:

READER REACTION FORM

Comment or Reason for Recommendation:

READER REACTION FORM

The *Travel Publishing* research team would like to receive reader's comments on any visitor attractions or places reviewed in the book and also recommendations for suitable entries to be included in the next edition. This will help ensure that the *Country Living series of Rural Guides* continues to provide its readers with useful information on the more interesting, unusual or unique features of each attraction or place ensuring that their visit to the local area is an enjoyable and stimulating experience. To provide your comments or recommendations would you please complete the forms below and overleaf as indicated and send to:

The Research Department, Travel Publishing Ltd,
7a Apollo House, Calleva Park, Aldermaston, Reading, RG7 8TN.

Your Name:

Your Address:

Your Telephone Number:

Please tick as appropriate:

Comments ☐   Recommendation ☐

Name of Establishment:

Address:

Telephone Number:

Name of Contact:

READER REACTION FORM

Comment or Reason for Recommendation: